Step by Step

Step by Step

Everyday Walks
in a French Urban Housing Project

JEAN-FRANÇOIS AUGOYARD

Foreword by Françoise Choay

Translated and with an Afterword by
David Ames Curtis

 University of Minnesota Press
Minneapolis
London

The University of Minnesota Press gratefully acknowledges the generosity of the French Ministry of Culture, which contributed financial assistance to the publication of this book. Ouvrage publié avec l'aide du Ministère français chargé de la Culture— Centre national du livre.

The University of Minnesota Press acknowledges the work of Edward Dimendberg, editorial consultant, on this project.

Photographs of the Arlequin neighborhood in Grenoble, France, were taken by Yves Bardin and Babette Mathieu. The map in Appendix B was created by Holger Sauer.

Lines from "Walking and Falling" and "Big Science," from the album *Big Science* by Laurie Anderson, quoted as an epigraph to the Afterword and in a note, are reprinted here courtesy of Laurie Anderson.

Originally published in French as *Pas à pas. Essai sur le cheminement quotidien en milieu urbain* by Éditions du Seuil in 1979 as part of the Espacements series edited by Françoise Choay. Copyright 1979 Éditions du Seuil.

Published by the University of Minnesota Press
111 Third Avenue South, Suite 290
Minneapolis, MN 55401-2520
http://www.upress.umn.edu

LIBRARY OF CONGRESS CATALOGING-IN-PUBLICATION DATA
Augoyard, Jean-François, 1941–
  [Pas à pas. English]
  Step by step : everyday walks in a French urban housing project / Jean-François Augoyard ; foreword by Françoise Choay ; translated and with an afterword by David Ames Curtis.
    p. cm.
Translation of: Pas à pas.
Includes bibliographical references and index.
ISBN: 978-0-8166-4590-9 (hc: alk. paper)   978-0-8166-4591-6 (pb: alk. paper)
ISBN-10: 0-8166-4590-6 (hc : alk. paper)   0-8166-4591-4 (pb : alk. paper)
  1. City and town life—France. 2. Sociology, Urban—France. 3. Urbanization—France. 4. City planning—France. I. Title.
  HT135.A8813 2007
  307.760944--dc22   2007026439

Printed in the United States of America on acid-free paper

The University of Minnesota is an equal-opportunity educator and employer.

12 11 10 09 08 07   10 9 8 7 6 5 4 3 2 1

Contents

Step by Step

Itinerary

THIS WORK takes the *step* as its point of departure under a variety of headings.

It is dedicated, first of all, to a small number of inhabitants in a town that looks like many others. Their daily strolls, which we have "joined in mid-march," have taken us, little by little, along many detours and into the flurry of particular details of *ordinary life*. To the point of rambling. We wanted to learn how these inhabitants live their relationship to the spaces of their habitat. But their approaches have come to take over our own and have obliterated the abstract itinerary we had projected to follow. We wanted to *make them say* something, likening their spatial practices to one or another of the major routes that structure present-day familiarity with the city. Yet *step by step,* confidence in our own scientific knowledge has slackened. At the rhythm with which time itself is lived, our reductionist techniques have fallen by the wayside.

We shall simply attempt to state in the pages of the present volume, and with the hope of not betraying them too much, what the inhabitants are *expressing* by themselves, every day, in their most unremarkable forms of conduct. We thank them for this salutary change of scenery [*dépaysement*] which invites us to make three somewhat unusual steps in the field of scientific knowledge about the city: a side step, a step forward, perchance to take a plunge [*un pas à sauter*].

First, a side step in urban studies.

The "quality of life" theme is "in" today. After several decades of urban planning that were characterized by an increasing mastery of space in quantitative terms, the inhabitants have suddenly become an object of concern. It is asked how the "user" can come to live within

3

these new urban arrangements. One seeks to improve the living conditions of the "consumer" or the "constituent" [*l'"administré"*]. New techniques have been invented to soften the edges of planned spaces—for example, by promoting sociocultural activities and entertainments.

Yet the everyday problems intensive urban development generates are still being dealt with in one of two ways. Either such treatment is considered *after* the development and construction have been completed, and then one searches for remedies, or it is contemplated *before* the urbanization program is carried out, and then hypothetical data are taken into account via preconceived ways of using the urban space.

For both these approaches, it seems, the instantiated principle [*instance*] of the inhabitant or "user" can be dealt with only in the form of a content that "fills in," *after the fact,* an already laid-out and developed space. In its operational mode, urban planning in reality merely manipulates representations of use. Everyday time—which cannot enter into a construction parameter—becomes secondary, accidental, incidental.

But is not this omission itself of significance? Is there not a qualitative gap between lived practices and representations of these practices? Is everyday life to be reduced to a reproduction? Is its fate to go on repeating, blindly, the urgent imperatives dictated by the economic order and the ideological order? Or does it really have a productive and expressive capacity of its own?

The question could at least be posed for once. And, were it only for the time of the present volume, it might merit a side step, or an attempt to follow lived time as closely as possible, to look into what its own powers and abilities are, and to cast, from this point of view, a different glance upon the urban world.

Such an approach is in no way an easy one. It necessitates a *step forward* in the methods of qualitative sociology.

For a few years now, there has been a marked interest in qualitative analyses of urban life. What one now considers classical sociology—which was based on statistical data that allow one to offer an overall diagnosis before it is too late and to reveal the most general causes of a growing urban malaise—has perhaps even been criticized too rashly. Today, people talk a lot about a new sociology that would free itself from the *quantum*. A qualitative methodology is nevertheless still taking its first steps, taking pains to distance itself from a search for necessary causes or from ethnological methods that abandon the exotic in order to return to the "endotic." Others, inspired by a more poetic model, attempt to describe, in first-person terms, the quality of lived space.

A step would be taken, were it granted that, on the one hand, everyday life is a fabric of ways of being (before being a set of second-order effects) and that, on the other, the modalities of lived experience belonging to each inhabitant do indeed participate in a community of meaning. Beyond the *I,* there is undoubtedly a *we,* which expresses itself in everydayness. Is a method of *modal analysis* possible in the case of urban sociology?

The present volume presents the concrete experiment we have undertaken. Because of this, however, the writing is inflected in two unusual ways. For, grasped in its lived quality, everyday life does not yield states of affairs, behaviors whose typological structure could be fixed in place. It gives us movements, *conducts.* The account we shall offer respects its evolutive or "fleeting" character. Following the *approach* we have taken over several years, each moment—and here each chapter—outstrips the previous one, correcting its errancies and adjusting its extrapolations. True, this makes the reading of the book all the more difficult. But this option, it has seemed to us, considerably reduces the gap [*l'écart*] between everyday life and our observational experience of it.

Moreover, does not every statement about everyday life that would fail to enter into its concrete particularities and singularities risk setting it too quickly and rigidly in the realm of the *represented* and, in this sense, also risk reduplicating the reductions currently imposed upon it via the production of planned space? Also, our study will hardly ever depart from a quite specific urban neighborhood that serves as an example. *Step by step,* it weaves together what we hope will be close ties between ambulatory practices unfolding in a concrete space-time and our analytic approach. May the reader therefore excuse us for our slow goings, procrastinations, and repetitions. The primary task of a modal analysis undoubtedly is to take into account such constant to-and-fro movements between the scattered pluralities of lived experience and the minimum unity required by speech.

The itinerary we are proposing will no doubt appear off-track and puzzling [*déroutant*]. What interest could there possibly be in accounting for practices so unremarkable and familiar that they would seem to us to border on the innocuous, the insignificant? What contribution can such a sidelong approach—one that, from the outset, fails to take into account the certainties of today's scientific knowledge—make that would deepen our familiarity with urban life?

Such an invitation to vagabondage might be able to alter our mental attitude about urban phenomena. It prods us to *take a plunge,* to think everyday life through its own logic, to settle ourselves straightaway into the insignificant, the plural, the patchy. Ought not a philosophy of everyday life begin by making this deliberate leap [*écart*]?

A philosophy of the *remainder* is unlikely to be possible except through a break in the hierarchy of epistemological values. Such a philosophy implies that modality would not be merely an instrument of causality—that is to say, that the way in which one does things might appear as significant as the result of the action taken—and that one's style of expressing oneself might carry as much weight as what is signified (what is called "the signified") or what is expressed (what will be called "the expressed"). The urban world has reduced everyday life to a series of functional operations; that world conditions its needs and gives the code of its usages. In this world, everyday life retains possession only of its expressive or rhetorical dimension. And so as not to reduce this last power and ability of the urban dweller even further, must not our investigation summon up all its patience and must not our scientific knowledge give proof of a great flexibility, perhaps even accepting the overthrow of a few of its certainties?

Arteries, Impasses, Side Streets

The paths, the cuts that run invisibly along the route
Are our only route, for we who speak in order to live, who
Sleep, without growing drowsy, by the wayside.

—René Char

ARTERIES

Who has not, one day or another, had the distinct impression that he has been pretty much banished from, dispossessed of, the city he inhabits? And who has not, upon the accidental irruption of such an impression, glimpsed that everyday habits get lost in the details and, indeed, that these habits seem to repeat this banishment and this dispossession, which thereby become embedded, digging in their heels?

The city is a furtive object, it seems, one that conceals itself. Far from dominating their city, the inhabitants seem to lose themselves further and further within it. The production of urban space today hardly offers the inhabitant any respite, now that it even goes so far as to reduplicate this loss of self and of "home" in the city by closing off all prospects through the shrinking of cityscapes, economic pressure, social division, overpricing of "small" property lots, and the concentration of slum areas.[1] Whence the following simple question: *In the collective space that is the city, what part is frequented, appropriated, and effectively inhabited (in the active sense) by each inhabitant?* Probably a quite small part: a few neighborhoods or broken sections of neighborhoods scattered at the will of the fragmented activities that are our lot (work, domicile, leisure, consumption), sometimes one's lodging all by itself, sometimes even less than one's full lodging. Again, quantitative evaluation is hardly of any significance. Qualitatively speaking, we have no foothold upon the city as a totality.

But what is this urban totality? Experienced daily through functional constraints and operational imperatives, it may be the "city" unit, the "neighborhood" unit, or the "high-density housing complex" unit. These "units" establish a descending series of interlocking memberships. And they take on a life of their own as *given, preexisting totalities* to which one must necessarily refer qua citizen, worker, social insurance contributor, consumer, or inhabitant.

Older urban zones or "aging" mixed neighborhoods exhibit a unity that has been built up little by little. Historical and symbolic communal memory still maintains the illusion that the city dweller has taken part in this development. But the new forms of urban living, such as the "high-density housing complex," are created straightaway as simultaneous totalities.

Whether it be in the overall organization of usages or the mode of production of urban space itself, an increasingly necessitarian rationality seems now to reign over the city. With schematic diagrams, plans, long-term and medium-term forecasts, and timing of urban programs, the urban habitat as given appears as a *conceptual space* laid out and developed according to the rules of the whole and its parts. And sometimes the parts are so well integrated into the whole, and in such an interdependent way, that

> all that is needed is a breakdown of a few power stations or strikes by public transport employees or by garbage collectors for one of the world's most extraordinary powers, such as its great metropolitan areas, to be rendered, in a few hours' time, literally helpless.[2]

The production and organization of the built and developed world have privileged a kind of manipulation of space that is based on a logic of repetition as well as on the following fundamental principle: *produce first the urban habitat so as to hand it over then for use.* Everything takes place according to a relation of container to contained. In its form, the container implies all the signs of the system that has modeled it (real-estate market, economic "imperatives," organizational logic, political conditions, strategies for domination, etc.). The inhabitant who comes

someone who can make himself heard, and these "representatives" manipulate the prevailing representations and the ruling code in the sphere of urban production. Now, "operational" constraints are different from the inhabitants' requirements; the former are posited in terms of strategy, geometric and economic quantification, as well as overall "objectives." Between the inhabitant speaking for others and the designer, a twofold distortion therefore slips in, and this renders any hope of effective intervention quite hypothetical. The cause of the malaise of which we have spoken would thus come under the heading of a communication problem. To an urban practitioner, the words uttered by an inhabitant just "do not sound right." Despite the best intentions in the world, the antagonists cannot communicate in a constructive manner. At the crucial moment (generally, when decisions are to be made), the production code blots out the user code.

4. Critique of urban political economy
The fourth type of explanation for inhabitant malaise has been formulated many times over since the mid-sixties. Well-argued analyses develop a critique of urban political economy.[6] The primary cause relates to the ruling economic power, which has transformed the old craftsman-based organization of the construction process,[7] subjugated building production to the system of commerce, and given birth to a technology-based rationality of urban development. Under cover of a second-order effect that is ideological in nature, the same cause turns housing into one *consumer* object among others. The inhabitant thus finds himself "conditioned," handed over to a de facto situation, and besieged by an ideology he cannot help but reproduce.

5. The inhabitant never totally succeeds in adjusting his desire to reality
This type of response to the question of inhabitant malaise takes as essential, if not sufficient, an explanation that would start from the individual histories of residential "subjects." Briefly put, the study of one's lived relationship to inhabited space is insignificant unless it is centered on an *analytic* deciphering of a phantasmatic space (psychoanalytic interpretation of interviews, of tests, and of daydreams). Reference must therefore be made to the initial childhood experience of space, which is

11

always tied to the parental imago. The structuration of one's own body depends on this, and it is on this basis that everyday space will later be lived. The "pregnancy" of archaic space would thus be an essential or formal cause of people's inability to appropriate the space of their habitat or of the ever possible conflicts between the spatial archetype and the lived experience of the various lodgings a user occupies in the course of his existence.

Starting from this explanatory core, psychosociology has attempted to shed some light on the problem of the inhabitant's relationship to his habitat. In the most nuanced studies,[8] economic and historical factors are also taken into account. It is granted, moreover, that such factors have had a significant impact on the initial childhood experience of space in a specific home setting, within this or that family, at such and such a time. These factors condition the "subjects" that are observed today. Also, psychosociological interpretation wavers between two systems of causality. For psychosociology, the concrete observational object is the individual; the inferences it advances concern a "social practice" or a "social change" to which, in other respects, the individual is referred. In all, inhabitant malaise would be explained by a deep-seated cause that is psychological in nature and that is incorporated into an efficient or circumstantial cause tied to economic and social status.

IMPASSES

Theoretical or Methodological Impasses

This chart of the main lanes of explanation of inhabitant malaise is obviously quite cursory. It places on the same level a quite diverse set of discourses, mixing form and content. Each of the arguments is of extremely unequal consistency. Indeed, it will not be lost on the reader that the stated causes of this inhabitant malaise seem to be highly varied. The nature of the causality in question is sometimes instrumental (the functions of the system of production), sometimes psychological, sometimes sociological, sometimes economic.

In the field of scientific knowledge that investigates the urban world, two theoretical routes have been particularly well developed. The first, which takes note of the prevailing mechanisms of economic production and social reproduction, offers an essential key to understanding that the socioeconomic setting defines our "conditioning." The second intimates that individual factors enter into the equation. Should not one be interested as much in the overall situation as in the singularities belonging to each individual?

Now, it turns out that these two paths are not complementary. They do not happen to intersect. The first, which argues along the lines of economic and social determinants, necessarily privileges a macroscopic reading of urban life. Figures at the ready, it seeks overall coherencies. It will pick up, for example, similarly occurring housing practices within a given class. The investigation will bear on statistical sets of data and on questions posed to residents in questionnaires and interviews. But this will be a "directed" reading. And the grid of analysis will not be able to take into account the microcosmic level of everyday practices, which are often complex and contradictory. For, well-argued explanatory formulations—whose goal is to obtain a restricted number of deep-seated causes—cannot linger over mere singularities. Scattering out the causes in that way would remove all coherency from one's approach to the problem. One would no longer know "why . . . ?" One would overlook the causal nature of the question. And the investigator would find no unity in the system of explanation, whose existence he had nevertheless assumed at the outset of his undertaking.

For its part, psychosociological thought finds its coherency in a set of psychological categories. In other words, the reality around which the interpretation turns is the instantiated principle of the individual. In a first stage, what is interpreted holds only for each subject taken separately. Subsequent comparisons and classifications are based on a listing of common factors (factor analysis). Inferences from the individual to the collective remain hypothetical.[9] In such a reading of urban life, the best guarantee of coherency and universality (what would hold for a collection of "subjects" would hold for the collectivity) is the system of causal interpretation. Among inhabitants, the mediations are not concrete but, rather, theoretical.

Thus, while the most well-argued applied research papers endeavor-

ing to explain urban malaise offer valuable systems of causal explanation, they fail to provide an account of either the concrete aspect of
people's everyday existence or the lived mediations by means of which
the inhabitants of an urban space form a collectivity. In order to satisfy
a scientific method that often confuses "rigor" and "exactitude," *they
neglect the intermediate and the singular.*

There is always a "remainder" in analytic operations that involve division. Indeed, daily life examined in this way must verify or invalidate
hypotheses that emanate from an already constituted field of scientific
knowledge. From what it expresses, one extracts a signified that will be
subjected to "content analysis." The containers or the signifiers (words,
drawings, and gestures of the inhabitants under questioning) have a
purely instrumental and, under this heading, negligible value.

It would seem that the expression of inhabitant malaise would always have to confirm either the state of the system of economic production and social reproduction or the theories that are considered authori-
tative in the human and social sciences. *Might not inhabitant expression
have anything to say on its own?*

Through these *theoretical and methodological impasses,* the lived
practices of the inhabitant are not apparent. This is for the simple reason that the modalities of questioning involved do not allow them to
appear.

Yet what is this "remainder," this surplus that cannot be retrieved
by the machinery of production and that is situated outside the scientific
categories currently in force? And how can it take on meaning, if not via
an investigation that takes form outside the universe of totalizing representation, outside the sphere of necessary causes and "why" questions?

An Exemplary Impasse

Beside or between the arteries of knowledge about the city, we must
find some side roads or connecting streets. Before doing that, we want
to offer, as an example, a type of approach to everyday life that we have
attempted under the heading of a counterdemonstration.

Let us consider the everyday practice of walking around and through a neighborhood. The problem is to find the signification of this practice, to evaluate how a laid-out and developed space can be frequented, and to be able to appreciate its value as a social indicator. Let us question a bunch of inhabitants. They recount to us their routes, which we can thus trace on a background map. Topographical space offers the following apparent advantage, that it provides a common frame of reference for individual practices.

Now, in this attempt to grasp their paths, their walks, several difficulties became apparent to us. First, what graphic code are we to choose? Dotted lines will indicate an occasional trip; an unbroken line, frequent trips. But all that remains quite approximative. How are we to trace one and the same trip that, for one day, merited ten minutes of detailed narrative and, for the next day, only a few seconds?

One can superimpose maps of the trips sketched on transparent tracing paper in a such way as to assess the rate at which various pedestrian pathways are frequented. Yet, when faced with the liveliness of the oral narrative and with its thousand qualitative details, such a topographical summary no longer made a great deal of sense. Either one treated the narrated lived experience with disdain, thereby sacrificing time to topographical spatiality, or one really recognized how limited graphic representation is when it comes to everyday expression.

A topographical translation, like any interpretation based on continuities and contiguities, thus seemed to us an improper way of accounting for spatial practices as they are lived day to day. We were in an impasse. Let us mention several forms of this aporia.[10]

1. Limits

Unexpectedly, limits display other forms than boundary markings. There certainly are some represented limits that do not vary at all and divide up the space in question. There are other ones that owe nothing to geometric representation of the space but exist, rather, within a mobile spatial practice; they have meaning only to the extent that the inhabitant makes reference to the *possibility of transgression*. These limits can be perceived very well in all movements of avoidance recounted by the inhabitant. In its graphic representation, the trip appears as a continuous trace that, at a certain moment, crosses some boundaries; everything is continuous and contiguous; at the same time, it clears a path through the space and is homogeneous in its extension. Nevertheless, the trace of the steps manifests a movement that varies depending on whether the space is empty or full, with curious "limits" liable to appear and disappear, to emerge alongside and parallel to the direction of one's walk, and to exist at one hour of the day but not at another. The supposed flatness of inhabited space dissolves into a heterogeneity that is connected, momentarily and fragmentarily, only by the succession of steps. The intactness [*La totalité pleine*] developers of the laid-out space had proposed now disappears. Some inhabitants who, spatially speaking, travel throughout the neighborhood nevertheless feel everywhere that they are outsiders. What has become of the totality? How has it faded away?

2. Beyond the appropriated and the unappropriated: something appropriable

The demarcation between the appropriated space and the unappropriated space pertains to a synchronic representation of limits. In narrative accounts of everyday walks, the initial consistency of these two antagonistic designations of a laid-out and developed space collapses. In lived time, one finds no appropriation or counterappropriation that would have a definitive meaning or that would be established once and for all. They are but marks momentarily affixed upon a space that has been the field of favorable or unfavorable movements of appropriation. However long lasting they might be—and there are always a certain number of inappropriate or unappropriable spaces—these marks do not account for the "how" of appropriation. How is it that one inhabitant, who strides through and knows perfectly well the zone into which he is venturing, remains an outsider; how is it that another, who takes infrequent walks but avoids nothing, also is an outsider, if it is not by the absence of something *appropriable*? The first person walks through the space in saturation mode; the second in the mode of emptiness, vacancy. There is no more place for the appropriable, or nothing glimpsed that could be appropriated. Inhabited space then becomes homogeneous; it offers one no foothold. For the inhabitant, it has no more of an everyday meaning than some geometric diagram.

In fact, the qualification of appropriation depends neither on the quantity of the space traveled through nor on the constancy of terri-torial limits but, rather, on the degree of possibilities it includes. The "trace" of a route signals an action and the way in which it unfolds in everyday time. Another totality then seems to sketch itself out on the horizon of what is to come. In what way can such a totality, which moves from the absent to the projected, and from the projected to the imaginary, be equivalent to the one planning produces for us?

3. For a daily stroll, what is more metaphorical than a map [*un plan*]? To the extent that one seeks not to evaluate the way in which a space conceived as a container can be filled in by some inhabitant content but, rather, how the act of progressively inhabiting a built-up space is constituted through the patient rhythm of one's walks, a logic of serial articulation comes to substitute itself for that of distinction and terri-torial boundaries. The totality—which is the necessary referent of the planned parts—gives way to the "globality" of the world of everyday activity, which is always present in each step, but which is also always in the course of development, in the course of an enacted process that renders things explicit.

Thus, none of the narratives of the inhabitants' trips ever omits the presence of the collective dimension. This presence is not necessarily personalized. Very often imagined or the object of a presentiment on the basis of spatial markers, it insists and persists in a silent and diffuse way. Let us cite another example. One's trip to work is not equivalent to the use of pedestrian spaces that mark out little by little the abandonment of one's domicile and the appearance of the public sphere. On the contrary, the sense of preoccupation and the feelings of constraint that are quite characteristic of this kind of activity accompany from the start, like an atmosphere, one's first morning steps. The referent for one's walks is not the simultaneity of a planned spatial whole but, rather, at each moment of the stroll, the coexistence of the different instantiated principles in-volved in everyday life. The explication, the development in movement of this coexistence, resembles a sort of creation, and through this cre-ation the space into which one has gone takes on this or that quality, de-pending on the occasion, but no longer has any permanency of its own (except in representation and on maps).

In summary, whether one sketches it on a map or sets it within the framework of a causal system, the practice of inhabiting as it is lived always escapes. Does one want to *make it say* something? It loses all consistency and fades away. It is apparent only in the extreme complexity of its *ways of being,* and it disappears in the face of all the "why" questions that are all too prompt to find causes for it.

Perhaps what is then needed is to settle into the immediacy of the plurality of *modes* of inhabiting and to stay [*séjourner*] there for a sufficiently long time without knowing in advance if these modes are causes, effects, or something else. And one must choose the paths that would be likely to make inhabitant expression appear, that would grant it the time to recite its singularities, its minuscule day-to-day variations, its detours, and its delays. It would be necessary, in short, *to postpone for some time the repetition of our "why" questions and to give free rein to the "how"*—that is to say, to substitute a modal type of interpretation for a causal type of explanation.

Side Streets

Intermediate Practices

The side street or connecting route leads "to a place to which the main road does not lead."[11] In the main lanes of analysis of urban life, one's interest lies in clearly locatable objects. The study inclines toward some portion of the space—the housing stock, the neighborhood—or one aspect of city operations—traffic, businesses, public services, etc.—or some definite practice—work, domestic life, consumption, leisure, and so on. The judicious circumscribing of the field of investigation seems to be an essential condition for the rigor of one's argument (not to mention the ease with which one then uses statistical data that have cohesion only to the extent that they concern *a single* object).

Now, there are other practices that elude such approaches, and "the main road does not lead" to them. Highly polymorphic, mixing together, in the course of lived experience, what the scientific outlook distinguishes, these are what we may call *intermediate practices.* Daily strolls, it seems to us, belong to that class of overlooked practices that apparently cannot be co-opted by the commercial economy and that are, in the view of scientific knowledge, insignificant. Defying functional classifications, these walks of course link one's place of domicile to workplaces and to various leisure and consumer sites. The important thing, however, is that these spatial mediations are ordered according to the properties of lived time. The time of walking is the time of the promenade, of "going out on the town," but also that of hustle and bustle and fuss. Activities that have been classified in functional sequences now come alive and rediscover their lived unity. One and the same trip can summon up the private and the public, the individual and the collective, the necessary and the gratuitous.

Finally, because the act of walking is an intermediate practice, it seems unremarkable and hardly of any interest. The inhabitant does not, so to speak, talk about it, and no causal explanation has yet come to apply to it any reductionist filter. This practice therefore ought to be valuable to us because, barely occulted by abstract representations, it still allows one to see how the life of the inhabitant is steeped in quite immediate sensations and impromptu actions.

Indications about the Method of Approach

So as not to delay the presentation of these walking practices, we shall simply indicate our methodological options.[12]

A methodological approach that has chosen the path of *modal analysis* (one oriented by the "how" rather than by the "why") collides right away against a major difficulty. Everyday practice is necessarily forgetful. It expresses itself through walks that speech struggles to tell over again. Nevertheless, better than topographical observation, oral expression has appeared to us to mimic quite closely the act of strolling. Like the latter, it is fluid, prone to digressions, capable of forgetting what is apparently essential and of lingering over details. Is it not another expression of an identical way of being?

Yet how is one to reawaken this experience of the everyday, which is often highly immediate in character and is forgotten as soon as it is enacted? In other words, what form of question was it necessary to pose to the inhabitants?

Let us imagine that the question would be as follows: "How do you walk through your neighborhood; what trips do you take?" The interviewee will respond in the style of the question, that is to say, *in a general mode*. Collecting his memories, he will produce an abstract collage. He will respond, "In general, I go by here." All lived qualities will disappear. In *one time,* he will have summed up his walking past.

Now, in everyday life, one does not appeal only to a memory of the past. There is also a memory enacted in the present—"protentional" memory, we would say, rather than retentional—the kind by which we organize our perceptions according to what will be memorable. In other words, one would have to take memory not only when it is no longer anything but a memory but still at the moment when it is constituted, at the very instant when it organizes the expression of a way of being to which it will be able to relate later on. In the present, memory is the "tomorrow" of currently lived experience.

It becomes possible at this point to understand both how a lived experience is constituted and how it is expressible. For, nothing of everyday life is communicable if what is perceived is not memorable, that is to say, eventually narratable, and if it is not, from the very start, constituted as an expression. Several practical consequences follow therefrom:

1. The investigation of a "how" of everyday inhabiting has no meaning except apropos of a specified (here and now) lived experience. Thus, such modalities can be apprehended only through individual narratives.

2. So as not to weaken too much the fragile ties that connect an expressible lived experience to a living experience that is effectively inexpressible in itself, one must limit as much as possible both abstract representations and general value judgments that the customary way of conducting interviews tends to induce, if not to incite. *Whence the appeal to an enacted and protentional memory, which favors observation of the most unremarkable of feelings and actions.*

3. The conduct of the narrative[13] is recognized and accepted for what by nature it is: *an oral relationship with social constraints* (the memo-

rable and the narratable are always commanded by the other person's eventual question). With such recognition and acceptance comes a reintroduction of the affective level between questioner and respondent, as against the hypothetical and illusory position of the abstract observer. And perhaps this presence of the affective within the narration of lived experience guarantees (as more faithful to the originary climate surrounding the conduct of the narrative) greater rigor than that of observational neutrality. Thus, the interviewing method is completely "directive," in the sense that a duty to recount is established, yet at the same time nondirective, in that the only obligation is to recount. One allows the narrative of the inhabitant's lived experience to appear as its mood suggests and at its own pace. It seems that the categories of "directedness" and "nondirectedness" are not relevant in this case, either because they unjustifiably bracket the necessarily social and constraining relationship of the interview situation or because they promote a "content" that is already formatted by the hidden inclusion of categories within the questions.

The question posed to the inhabitants was the following: "Will you recount in a few weeks the walks you have made from today onward?" The first interview was therefore always brief, since it aimed only at clarifying in common language the duty of self-observation that was to be accomplished. During the second interview, the inhabitant recounted his trips. A third interview seemed necessary when the inhabitants had developed a taste for going back over the unremarkable particularities of their existence and wanted to add to their initial narrative.

FINAL NOTE: A LAST WORD ABOUT THE TERRAIN CHOSEN

Any contemporary urban setting could have served as a field of investigation. Was one going to take an entire city? The number of inhabitants one would have had to question for a minimum of overlap was incompatible with the bounds of this work. One cannot be satisfied with surveys or brief questionnaires when it comes to everyday life. The narrative of a single urban voyager who travels all over the city with a floating but curiosity-filled attention and who recounts the city while recounting himself brings a richer and more coherent "givenness" than any account of the responses to a hundred "questionnaires" about lived experience.

We chose a smaller grouping of residential units. Such a grouping, we felt, was more appropriate, both as a well-delimited space common to the individuals being questioned and as a site for a coherent expression of their differences.

Finally, it was important that the residential complex chosen be conceived as a totality and that it be made the object of explicit research into its qualities. Conceived as a totality, it would be the paradigm for an increasingly common type of laid-out and developed space: the high-density housing complex, the production of which is taking place before our very eyes. Indeed, such a complex cannot be taken as going without saying, for it raises many problems. And it would include a social program aimed at ameliorating the existence of the city dweller, if not at promoting a better social life.

The "Arlequin" (Harlequin) neighborhood in Grenoble, France, seemed to us to satisfy this set of conditions, and in particular the last one.[14]

2

An Inhabitant Rhetoric
FIGURES OF WALKING

O draperies of words, assemblages of the literary art, O
massifs, O plurals, flower beds of colored vowels, settings
of lines, shadows of the silent letter, lovely curls of conso-
nants, architectures, ornamentations of periods and brief
signs, to my rescue! To the rescue of the man who no longer knows how to dance, who no longer knows the secret
of gestures, and who no longer has either the courage or
the erudition of direct expression through movements.

—Francis Ponge, *La promenade dans nos serres*

TAKE AN URBAN SPACE. What happens in the trifling everyday details
of those who inhabit this complex, this lot, this neighborhood? Nothing
at all. Or almost nothing.

Nothing of weight and nothing assessable for the managers of this
space whose action bears on general operations, who take the inhabitant to be a universal and abstract subject, and who will at best form
a representation of *one* typical neighborhood practice. Nothing very
interesting for investigators, preoccupied as they are with the major
characteristics of "social life." Managers, like investigators, have ac-
customed us to such transparencies, to these reductionist alignments, to
the abstract Essence that casts its spell upon scientific knowledge. Plural
and equivocal, the details, the singularities, the quirks, and the tics of
our everyday unremarkable existences hardly have any meaning at all
within the rational coherency of an urbanistic discourse. Our gestures?
Purely instrumental. Our attitudes? They were a system of codes. And
in these ruling representations, our movements are emptied out and our
acts lose all qualities of their own.

23

So, nothing. Or almost nothing?

Lingering over the details, casting a bit of doubt upon the systems of knowledge for producing our cities, it seems that "day-to-day" commonplaces say a bit more than nothing. A tenuous difference, to be sure, for the inhabited space one travels through is the one the designers and builders have produced. Altering a partition, placing a flower pot on the window sill, or daubing some paint on a facade does not broach the geometric massiveness of the habitat-object. And yet these rare blisters and swellings, these secretive transformations, these sporadic scratches manifest, in an almost derisory way, a force that is perhaps more insistent than it might at first appear; this is a force neglected by our scientific knowledge because it is not of a stable nature, thetic, "essential," but rather a capacity for alteration, a mode, a way of doing.

Let us develop an interest in the modalities of everyday life. Let us have the patience to follow the detours on which they send us. It will be seen that, in accordance with lived time, not only do spatial incursions never cover the totality of the built architectural unit, but also that the latter exists only in the particular form of a walking that turns it into metonymy, here accentuating and there derealizing, sometimes pursuing, sometimes avoiding—that, in a word, *orients* it.

The almost-nothing, the inconsequential dross of life could very well become the opposite of a nothing-at-all. But allowing singularities to arise with their ingenuousness and enunciating these everyday ways of being without betraying their nature, *that* would sidetrack [*déroute*] you. We lack the tools. It is difficult to overturn our mental attitudes. What sort of aid are we to call to the rescue? What kind of guides are to be found?

First, may the analysis at its best preserve the lived plurality and particularity of cases. We have labored over narratives of everyday walks gathered on a specified and dated site.[1] Yet, considering the multiplicity of individual paths, could one deduce therefrom a collection of mutually divergent orientations, of which nothing more could be said, except that so-and-so inhabits in such and such a manner? Is there no community of meaning among these neighboring existences? Might these singular ways of walking perhaps be classified typologically? Thus would hybrid gradations appear—from the most copycat kind of walking to the most inventive, or from the sort most based on use-value to the sort most favoring misuse-value, or else again, from the most individualistic and differentiating mode to the mode most repetitive of identities belonging to the social group. Yet none of all that corresponds in any way to what is actually lived. Although a given space is perhaps never lived again exactly in the same way, as it depends on different moments and the diversity of inhabitants, at the same time what one sees produced therein are both perceptions and movements that are, if not identical, at least similar in kind.

Here we have, then, a relation of "spatial practices" to practiced space whose complexity sidetracks any sort of explanation that would claim to be clearly causal in nature and would proceed by exclusive disjunction. It is not "either this or that" but, rather, conjointly and according to the moment that the represented and the lived, the reproduced and the produced, the necessary and the playful, the useful and the poetic, the individual and the collective compenetrate.

Two indices come to our aid.

Nonexclusive disjunction, the mixing together of things rational order would distinguish, the flowering of words taken for themselves— these are the characteristics of the poetic. They are those that Francis Ponge calls to the rescue of our ailing practices: indeed, they are precisely those ones that disregard the knowledge for producing a profitable space.

And then there is the following noteworthy constant in these walking narratives: there always is at once a minimum degree of submission and of action, whatever may be the prevailing tenor of each particular trip. The analogy with graphic expression is unendingly striking. Just as a book is read in company with a motionless (re)writing and is written at the same time that it is read for oneself and for others, *walking resembles a reading-writing*. Sometimes rather more following an existing path, sometimes rather more hewing a new one, one moves within a space that never tolerates the absolute exclusion of the one or the other.

Do certain trips and certain stays take place in an absentminded sort of way? Yet the succession of steps effectively rewrites the space that opens before the walker, even when done in the slightest of action modes.

Through the practice of one's walks, everyday life seems to take on the look of a language. The steps taken would expound spatiotemporal actions whose overall configuration would have a *style*. This analogy is to be pursued so long as it does not betray the lived quality that is of interest to us and so long as it does not reduce the traces of pedestrian activity to a prosaic linguistic system.

Let us speak, rather, of a *walking rhetoric*. It would be the translation of both the organization of the styles proper to each inhabitant and the correlations among these styles within a shared space.

If daily walks are a form of expression—and only rhetorical analysis can confirm this—one must patiently note down the figures of this rhetoric and the kinds of combination of which they are composed.

This is the type of reading that has been attempted here. The reader will find this path again in the chapters that follow. Many other readings no doubt remain possible for these inhabitants' gripping, varied, and rich narratives. We have simply allowed ourselves to head toward the least reasonable, the least known, the most modal, the most scientifically negligible one: draperies, massifs, flower beds of steps, plurals, lovely curls, ornamentations of movements in space. Direct expression.

These figures that are liable to enumeration and illustration on the basis of the concrete case chosen—the Arlequin neighborhood—appear more or less clearly, depending on whether they are set in particular chosen spots, in the building complex under consideration, or whether they are repeated in proliferating and hybrid varieties, the propagation of which borders on infinity. As a result, the account will aim more at exemplariness than at any sort of illusory exhaustiveness. In any case, one never makes a complete tour around the everyday as it is lived.

Here is another point about the nature of these walking figures. Analyzed in the narratives related by the inhabitants, these figures are never to be reduced to mere extrapolations, to what is commonly called "stylistic devices" [*figures de style*]. They would then be only the projection of a discourse onto an illusorily metamorphosed spatial practice. Not only can the figures these walks write be observed directly, but also a number of mixed forms found in the interviews indicate the convergence of language and of walking in one and the same expressive style. Thus, it is a collection of *figures of spatiotemporal expression* that will appear straightaway in the present chapter, figures observed and recounted by the inhabitants, figures that manifest, instead, the way in which walking is articulated, or rather the way in which it varies and proceeds via substitutions and alternations.

The names for each of these figures are borrowed either from the terms of classical rhetoric or from the vocabulary of logic. Some figures have called for the creation of neologisms, for which we apologize in advance. In all these cases, it is a matter of designating, as clearly as possible, objects that are constituted by an expression developed in space and in time.[2]

For the convenience of the reader, we shall begin by presenting the most lexical expressions (the paradigmatic axis of linguistics). Following thereafter will be the most composite modes of configuration, those that lie closest to the complexity of lived experience (combinations that are analogous to those of the syntagmatic axis of linguistics). But such a methodological choice must not make one forget that the elementary and the combinatory instantiated principles operate at the same time and that it will be necessary to look for the foundation of this concomitance. Whence the following three moments: elementary figures, combinatory figures, and fundamental figures.

ELEMENTARY FIGURES

Our project of effecting a progressive change in scenery cannot rid itself, in a single stroke, of the most common modes of thinking. Instead, it attempts, little by little, to get a feel for them. Also, the sites that bolster these fragmentary forms of writing will be well circumscribed and easily identifiable (they can be illustrated by photographs).

Appearing to the inhabitant on his walks is a spatial whole that in itself, and before his steps organize it, is nothing other than a "muddle of disparate, unconnected things."[3] A selection is to be made in a set of possibilities. There is competition among a variety of sites. Each time one walks, such a selection comes into play; and, as in language, most often it occurs without the knowledge of the expressive actor.

As a whole, the interviews we have gathered present us with some noteworthy and exemplary figures. In the absence of a complete or exhaustive enumeration, which would be impossible, they allow us to comprehend how a walk is constituted at the elementary stage.

EXCLUSION

A "figure" of exclusion? Is this first term pertinent? The narratives as a whole allow us to see that entire zones of the neighborhood are abandoned. Only the trained eye of the planner can evaluate these desertions—that is, the gaze of someone who would see everything from above. Yet, ignorant of spatial totalities, the inhabitant can exclude without refusing. This is the exclusion of an unrecounted, unlived territory, which is equivalent to a pure absence.

The same does not hold for the exclusions the inhabitants mention, which are forms of absolute avoidance within their spatial practice. What, in an active way, is excluded from a walk applies to a very diverse and quite variable number of sites, depending on the inhabitant. Most often cited are the ends of the pedestrian gallery, the mezzanines, the cove of the silos, the gallery at night. Still, one talks about them, usually in the present tense: this is a masked or latent form of absence.

Thus, exclusion seems to be less than a figure and more than a figure. Indeed, either it is fictively sketched out in the representation of a static territoriality or it leads to an avoidance in the course of the lived experience of a trip, that is to say, in the course of other effectively enacted figures. Exclusion thus denotes the "degree zero" of this writing that is walking.[4] A sort of negative or repellant force never appears except through its inscription upon something else. Its overall form borders on *ellipsis,* a figure that, as one knows, always refers to a context wherein the excluded object or term is bypassed.

In short, exclusion is at once the near side of an expression and the elsewhere of a rhetoric, its margin. Nothing more is expressed at this inchoative or inceptive stage. The citation of this pseudofigure of exclusion simply marks the beginning of the elementary figures properly speaking and tells us from what unexpressed realm they arise.

Paratopisms, Peritopisms: Elementary Figures of Avoidance

Paratopism

Paratopism is the form of ambulatory movement that proceeds via *substitution* of one path for another. That which is substituted for can be the subject either of systematic exclusion or of alternation: it can be avoided on account of a momentary obstacle that is physical (repair work, other inconveniences) or social in nature. Whatever the case may be, it is always a matter of a site avoided by the person walking. The trip actually taken unfolds therefore in the place of another one, by *divergence*.

Given the highly pedestrian texture of the design plan, the most frequent cases of "paratopic" substitution relate to variations around these charted paths (some of which the developer even hoped would be obligatory). The cases of avoidance therefore bear in large part on the gallery as a whole and the laid-out and developed paths. Depending on the context, it is by a repulsive effect or by a change of direction that people more or less voluntarily avoid them.

At the elementary level, some "wild paths" [*chemins sauvages*] thus appear, to borrow one female inhabitant's expression. These pathways leave no traces. The ground does not allow it or the substitution is a singular act that does not mark the terrain. Thus, people "cut across the grass," pass "through the massifs" of plantings, or "through the parking lots," or they even, without further specification, just "go around."

By way of contrast, what these narratives contribute can be compared with the traces other substitutions have imprinted upon the loose ground in certain spots: it could be said that here we have "semi-wild paths" that are cleared little by little through collective repetition. Some exist only for the initiated, like the "tunnel" made by children in the bushes of the North Cove that escapes the notice of the adults. Others are visible, and photographs show that they can sketch out shortcuts that avoid an obstacle or connect two laid-out and developed paths. (See Figures 1 and 2.) And yet the "shortcut" in question is often highly symbolic.

Others parallel or sometimes lengthen the trip. They may not offer any apparent meaning, like the radial figure, a set of trails that seem to lead nowhere and then die out. (See Figures 3 and 4.)

Figure 1

Figure 2

The meaning of the extreme multiplication of such paths, which footprints manifest in a detailed way, is to be found even in the narratives of some of the inhabitants who refuse to take trails that have been packed down through repeated deviant usage. Thus, one person "prefers to go completely outside on the grass." Or, as another inhabitant says:

> I don't always follow the small paths. Last time, I didn't have it in mind to tell you, but I really love to walk on the grass. Even if there is the path and the grass next to each other, well, I take the grass; it's nicer.

A shortcut over a segment of terrain can subsequently lengthen the path. Thus, cutting "through a hedge" provokes, later on, an obligatory by-pass movement. Is there a gratuitous playfulness at work here?

The proliferation of wild or semi-wild paths is often the doing of children who are seen crisscrossing the space in all directions, wherever their play takes them. For this set of deviant paths, and especially for those that, when all is said and done, do not shorten one's way, is it then a matter of particular forms of appropriation? Is there only play involved in these topical pranks?

In any case, substitutions exhibiting an indifferent attitude are quite rare. The inhabitant does not qualify them thus, except through some after-the-fact statement: there is a certain way of reducing to a spatio-geometric form of behavior the obscure and unreflected aspect of one's prior conduct. The thread of such a narrative leads us to the right; there is a halt, a few hesitations, and then, "perhaps it's a driving habit."

A change in tone, a difference in expression, a leap toward a more abstract and reassuring signification. For, paratopic figures have never had a very clear gait. To state it better, some sort of cunning conduct is always inserted therein.

Let us follow three examples of a noteworthy and richly indicative variety of paratopism that heads in this direction:

> C.: I go by way of the paved path. Right away, there's the bar. I look right away to see if there are people inside. . . . Then . . . [thirty-second digression].

> INTERVIEWER: Right, getting on with the story. . . . The bar . . . We were there. . . .

Figure 3

Figure 4

> C.: So, I look in, but I never stop there! [Laughter]

Apropos of the "Bar-bu, at number 30":[5]

> One night, there was a fight. Everything was broken! I was listening! . . . [another comment about some other fracases]. Now, one no longer goes there.

A ten-year-old child:

> INTERVIEWER: Do you go beyond number 170?

> ISA.: No, not very much. . . . Except when I do a short errand on foot to the supermarket. . . . Behind, there's a vacant lot. I often look when there are caravans, or Gypsies. . . . It's amusing. . . . But I don't go there.

These three examples illustrate a sort of false avoidance, a deviation apropos of a site spoken about quickly or about which one is not quick with the details. That is what the breaks in the narrative and the suspension points reveal. In rhetoric, we would call this figure *paralipsis*. It is a matter neither of a clear substitution of one path for another nor of a genuine bypassing. Rather, it is a swerving [*un écart*], often with a change in rhythm that responds either to an event-induced break—the place might have been frequented in former times—or to a distancing from a site one has to walk alongside, and whose avoidance is hinted at, but which is fascinating at the same time. The swerving movement attempts both to place it at a distance and to see it from a distance.

These paralipses in space correspond to mixed elementary figures that are to be found again in many other sites: the entrance to the junior high school and fragments of the gallery. Mixing a slight bifurcation with a hint of avoidance, they lead us to discover another group of figures of avoidance in which the walker does not diverge from his path by turning his back but seeks to vary rather than to avoid.

Peritopism

Peritopism is how the figure of walking that proceeds by *variation* may be designated. It proceeds like an instance of periphrasis (circumlocution) used in the place of a word or like a relation of synonymy. Here, opposition hardly finds any place. Thus do peritopisms distinguish themselves from paratopisms.

A certain number of "shortcuts" do not proceed through opposition. Under this heading, they enter into a second group of figures of avoidance: *avoidances by variation*. Only contextual analysis can sort out the different forms of shortcutting: in order to go more quickly, in order to avoid congestion in or frequentation of the gallery, or else in order to vary one's repetition of the same trips—one can then take one's time and the shortcut is no more than a form of spatial play. Would the visual (and geometric) order here be replacing the instantiated principles of play and motor activity? Path segments taken prior and subsequent to the shortcut allow an evaluation of this: such an analysis pertains to the syntactic and no longer to the elementary level. In fact, rather than a walked figure, would not the shortcut be a concept whose geometric origin is beyond doubt? The inhabitants first say, "I cut through . . ."; then, they may subsequently designate the action by contracting it into the term *shortcut*. Does the geometricality really stem from one's actual spatial conduct—or from the representation one gives of it? The descriptive phrases contained in the narrative do not use the concept, even when the statement would call for the substantive. For example:

C.: When I go home, I cut through.

INTERVIEWER: You have to go under the barrier, then. . . .

C.: Yes, there is a barrier under which one can pass. Oh! . . . But there are paths[6] that cut through there, paths made by pedestrians.

The shortcut is a complex figure. It is a figure quite symptomatic of the ambiguities of everyday life. The reality it designates is split between paratopism and peritopism. As to the gap in the relation between this reality and its substantive designation, it refers us back, beyond even the apprehension of some combinatory process, to the subsequent confrontation between the lived and the represented.

The other peritopisms resemble more clearly the procedures of periphrasis and digression.

Qua elementary figure, *bypassing* occurs each time a site that is not an absolute obstacle presents a difficulty of variable (physical or social, permanent or accidental, real or imaginary) nature. It is then easier to bypass the obstacle than to go through it. But at the same time, this by-passing underscores the site bypassed, which becomes a notable point along the trip, even though the walk did not pass through there. In re-counting his trip, the inhabitant will say, "I passed in front of the ju-nior high school." But in fact, there was a bypass: "with all those kids who hang out underneath, who are coming out, who talk unbelievably badly." Another one will talk about this zone "of silos," which he fre-quents by necessity, but in which "you're suffocated . . . , you're crushed by the concrete." The mode of walking then bypasses this spatial com-plex through a symbolic absence: "it's automatic," or "in general, it's the same old thing." Several inhabitants bypass the entrance to the bar/tobacco stand by cutting across the marketplace; the café was then seen from the back (actually, the café entrance is from the market side). Yet, conversely, during the summer months, they avoid the part of the mar-ketplace occupied by the outdoor café tables, this time passing by way of the gallery.

From this last example, one can see that bypasses are closely tied to the intervention of events. The narratives offer us quite numerous cases that vary over time, with the occurrence of accidents, and in rela-tion to the unforeseen: the temporary appearance of repair work, unex-pected dropping of refuse on the floor of the gallery, social events that have marked a formerly familiar site, or more simply avoidance of sites wherein one senses a not very pleasant atmosphere at the moment the trip is being taken. On the one hand, bypassing often occurs following an event; on the other hand, it creates at the same time an event in rela-tion to one's usual trips. Here we have a quite characteristic example.

In the neighborhood, there exists a peculiar spatial form that fos-ters brief bypass sequences. We are talking about some triangular holes made in the walls that run alongside the elevator entrances, or that lighten a load-bearing wall, under the gallery. The developer planned to put in some glass panes, but only a few have been installed. The photo-graph (Figure 5) allows one to see that the level of the sill or threshold of these "holes" involves a change in the continuity of one's ambulatory movement. These are crossing areas of choice for children, but also for a good number of adults. At rush hour, we have counted at least one or two passages every minute through the holes located near the center of

Figure 5

the gallery. As for the quality of this frequency, it becomes fully clear in the liveliness of the narrative accounts:

> OK, well, to go to the garage there's no problem; instead of taking the passage-way . . . where it's flat, and well, I pass through the hole in the wall!

> Then . . . there's something there . . . [laughter], I really like to pass through the hole, the hole in the wall at the exit to the gymnasium. Other than that, it's the same. [. . .]

> [. . .] I always pass to the left when going toward number 60. Otherwise, you have to pass through the hole, toward number 60. I've passed through five or six times—for example, when there are too many people.

> The hole near the gymnasium . . . that shortens things and . . . a few times, I find myself in front of it and I pass through.

(Here, the shortcut is entirely fictive, since the real shortcut would cut the whole area surrounding number 70 in order to approach the gallery straight on, without obstacles.)

In fact, with each clearing of the hole, something other than a choice imposed by a rational geometricality occurs: an alteration of motor function is brought into play. The variation in the vertical dimension, and the leap it induces, evoke a spatiotemporal conduct from which digression is not absent.

As another elementary figure in which avoidance takes place more through variation than via radical substitution, *digression* in the previous example, as well as in the one that will follow, takes on the exact meaning given to this term in rhetoric: "what in speech strays [*s'écart*] from the subject."[7] The process of swerving away is carried out a little bit at a time, and as if without the speaker's knowledge when he forgets to come back. One can begin a variation in this way, but here it becomes the subject of the expression and is valid for itself: this is the case of the holes in the wall.

When an inhabitant takes a "mezzanine" (see Figure 6), this is also a form of bypassing. But the peculiar spatial form of these landings, which reduplicate the line and layout of the gallery below, fosters a prolongation of the direction one has taken. Bypassing is then transformed into digression and can even be metamorphosed into paratopism. Here, the site one wanted simply to bypass is forgotten. Thus, one inhabitant

Figure 6

says, "I prefer to pass by way of the mezzanine, because one is less accosted by people." Two other inhabitants take this digression in one direction only, on their way to some place:

> It's pleasant, when there's some wind in the winter. But you get the feeling of being closed in.

> Never do you meet anyone on this mezzanine . . . there's no one; it's the end of everything.

The way these expressions advance demonstrates the imperceptible passage from bypassing to paratopism or even to paralipsis. There is a false avoidance on the part of the inhabitant who is at once repelled and fascinated by the mezzanine.

The transformation from bypassing into forgotten digression is expressed in the eleventh interview:

> In class, there's a lot of noise; coming home, it's the same. So, you are always looking for something quiet. By the mezzanines, I believe that . . . it's often . . . or then in my free time, I go there. . . . I sit down and I look out.

Another example of digression, this time for the very pleasure of it:

> Once . . . one time, I say it so I don't forget it, I went by after the silos and I was on foot—other times I always pass by there in my car—and there then, . . . I had a desire to do that, I had a desire to get lost over there, and I found that it was good for hiding . . . [laughter] and in order to get familiar, too, . . . there's a garden; well, not a garden, but a space on the concrete, the school, and then after that—on the level of the mezzanines, huh?—I went up and then came back down at number 110, I think. What's more, it was evening, so it was rather special. What I was looking for, especially, was the feeling . . . like in a labyrinth, OK? The feeling rather than . . . than the view, OK?

This entire exceptional ("one time") lived digression involving the mezzanines and occurring after a return home in the car begins with an abrupt decision. For once, the trip varies and the succession of these dark landings that abruptly open up onto the silos and then start up again elsewhere under the shadowy cover of the gallery draws one imperceptibly into a labyrinthine movement. The specifications, the unforeseen breaks, and the dizzying ramblings: are not they the very essence of digression?

These variations on a conduct characterized by avoidance, which are picked up in every walking narrative, tell us more than they first would seem to. Various styles of inhabiting begin to express themselves in their similarities and their differences. Tell me what you avoid, and I shall tell you what kind of inhabitant you are. Would not one's refusals and rejections be just as indicative of the essence of the everyday as any fillings in, fillings up, or retentions? The urbanist seeks to know what spaces are willingly frequented. Would it not be necessary to observe, first, how some sites are avoided?

There is another perplexity, another surprise than that provoked by examination of this first group of figures: between the opposite poles of paratopism and peritopism we find *theoretical distinctions everyday pedestrian statements mischievously like to mix in and confuse together through a series of imperceptible shifts*. The very order of our presentation has attempted to follow this succession of nestings in which figures deliberately envelop and overlap with one another more often than they appear in their pure state.

It is through the material of an expression walked-recounted by the same inhabitant over a short lapse of time amounting to a dozen days that one can see how the same sites can be walked in different ways from one day to the next. On the scale of a group of inhabitants, the problem becomes still more complex. Here appears an equivocality in space and in time that increasingly calls into question cartographic representation and calls for a refinement of the study of elementary figures. Now, the inhabitants we have questioned have related to us certain ambulatory practices that carry some latent significations between the lines. They walk in such and such a place and in this or that manner. Yet, in doing so, they configure either some complementary sites or some other modalities of meaning, which they mention and which render architectural forms and spatial conducts ambiguous.

Polysemous Figures

The group of figures thus designated offers some varieties of a fundamental element of this reading-writing that walks seem to us to be. The term *polysemy* describes it well. One and the same object takes on several meanings. For the inhabitants questioned, a given site can be walked through in several ways at the same time or one time after another.

Ambivalence

As one knows, in everyday life the developed architectural design plan loses its monumental and functional monosemes. The variety of usages ruins its beautiful clarity as a finished product. Now, in the narratives, the terms of ambivalence are not cited at the same time and with analogous expressions. One of the "valences" is designated, the other surmised, more or less vaguely.

This is the case with the ceiling of the gallery,[8] which serves as the firmament of the universe through which, most often, the inhabitants travel. Hardly ever perceived—people always have a hard time naming the colors of this painted ceiling—it is strongly sensed, a veritable "element" that envelops and accompanies one's walk. It crops up in the narratives by its accidental irregularities [*accidents*], a break in its flatness. Thus, we have someone saying:

> I find it hideous; there's nothing about . . . nothing studied about . . . I think that there's nothing nice about it; I don't know how I feel about it. . . . First of all . . . , first of all, you go down there . . . and for me, as for me, I prefer . . . Going down, it should already be pleasant for me; there, you get the impression of going into a hole . . . a hole like . . . because there are buildings right away . . . , a hole! And then, in addition, it's somber, and the ceiling is maybe lower?

It will be noted that the essential element defining the climate of this walk arose only at the end of the narrative. In fact, the gallery does not go down; it is just that one sees only the prospect of a descent that occurs after the end of the gallery. It is the ceiling that has gone down; and this accidental irregularity in the inhabitant's path makes her suddenly feel its heaviness. The sky has darkened and becomes a basement for the buildings. Other inhabitants offer equivalent expressions, saying that under the gallery "it's somber." We have even heard the following truism, which appears to be so only when taken too quickly: "Under the gallery, it's darker than on the Market Place." The Market Place is an open-air market. In fact, not being perceived in a clear way, the gallery's ceiling is always taken as the celestial vault. Simply, the sky is lower.

Conversely, this same ceiling can be genuinely perceived, distinguished, and its function can be recognized. But then it is heavy only to the gaze that evaluates it from outside the gallery: a "feeling of being overwhelmed," someone says—which, curiously, is not felt underneath the gallery, "even if there are stacks of apartments above!"

Seen from the outside, the gallery's ceiling does indeed seem like the raised basement supporting the residential buildings. Thus, it is at once a top and a bottom, a ceiling and a floor. These two meanings for one and the same spatial element that accompanies one's walk place two instantiated principles, of different natures, into competition: recognition and vague feeling. Only one inhabitant recognized the permanent double meaning of this "ceiling." Others make indirect reference to it through connotations of quite distinct values:

> Underneath the gallery, you feel right at home; there's no longer any danger.
>
> It's nice to pass underneath.
>
> [. . .] You're underneath a gallery all the time; for my part, I really like it.

These are so many expressions that are centered on the action of walking rather than on recognition of this ceiling-roof spatial element. Other expressions, however, refer to the order of the visual. The gallery is perceived or has been perceived from the outside, and then one finds the connotations of "somberness," of "being crushed," of an absence of the "real" sky: "Oh! I practically never see the sky on my trips!"

Apropos of one and the same spatial element—either this gallery ceiling, or the "ramp" at number 150, or else the "passageways"[9]—the walking narratives reveal only one or the other of the two meanings. It is therefore a matter of a concealed ambivalence that manifests itself only by accident or by reference to the context ("outside the gallery").

Staggered Polysemy

Another spatial element, an essential commonplace both of people's walks and of everyday discussions in the Arlequin complex, offers an interesting example of *staggered polysemy*. Here, various possible meanings are set in nonexclusive disjunctive relation, the manifestation of one calling for reference to the other. This is how people experience their passages in the elevators at the beginning and end of their walks. Such passages take on the following significations:

1. Site of fear, anxiety, technological aggression—which, by necessity, people are obliged to frequent

2. Site of physical and social constraint (with the possibility of overt conflict)

3. Site where a stationary posture and minimal verbal exchanges are obligatory

4. Site of complicity among the communal victims of (possible) abuses by a machine that is much maligned, and apropos of which conversations are possible

In a paradoxical way, the elevator, of which it is said so often that it has nothing of a tool of communication about it, becomes, when pushed to the height of discomfort, a commonplace topic of conversations and, in this sense, a "lever" for verbal communication. At the same time, it encloses within its cab a maximum amount of tension that pours out first through sighs, then with words or exclamations of fear and anger. At this point, three outcomes remain possible: a return to silence upon exiting; discussions involving complaints, quibblings, or protests; the third outcome is suspected or assumed: physical aggression against the machine itself.

Of the four meanings we have cited—four ways of passing time in the elevator—each always can actually call out for the others in the course of one and the same descent or ascent. Above all, each assumes the others. Thus, the following expressions show these staggered connections in their order of appearance:

> As for me, I take it only to go up. [. . .] As far as I'm concerned, and I'm speaking from professional experience, there are some defects; they're ill conceived.

> They're no good, OK? . . . They work when they want to or there's no light. You see, these elevators, you gotta change the cables, or else. . . . As for me,

I've always been afraid of elevators; I don't know why. But I tell myself, "One of these days, I'll be in there, huh?"

I'm always scared for the kids who go in.

If there were a fire, who knows what would happen?

Finally, the elevator door opens. No one inside! While going down, I feel a sense of insecurity; after an infernal clanking noise announcing the arrival, the door opens on the ground floor [diary entry].

Oh, and then there's the missing buttons! I don't know if it's due to vandalism; I don't think so. But at the beginning that really gripped me; people were terribly frightened of the doors. They believed it was a vice that was going to crush them!

[To go up] you take it at the mezzanine level and it always goes down. [. . .] You feel like an idiot when you don't get out at the bottom.

In the elevator [while getting out], for me, I am really out, you know? Good morning, good evening. You can't start a conversation, huh? It's an intermediate kind of thing. I see people who say lots of stuff in the elevator. For me, no way! Well.

Finally, in order to provide the two extreme outcomes of the combinations among the four modes of spending time in the elevator, here are two opposite examples:

The elevator is mine, I'd say. When I see a piece of paper on the ground, I pick it up.

Listen, there's a lady who insulted me in the elevator the other day, OK? I asked her to hold the door. She said to me, "Yes, it's not like you're in your country. . . ." But I told her, "I don't attack people like you; because you're French in any case, huh?" She insulted me! You had to see it, huh, a very young woman!

Here is the first outcome: an appropriation of the space in the maintenance mode, but this mode is favored by the less deteriorated state of some elevators, that is, small elevators or co-op elevators. And a second outcome: the conflict arises specifically on the basis of a question of which code to follow (hold the door for someone/have the door held) and degenerates into social or racial conflict (sending each back to his or her typical group). This is the case with the high-capacity elevators, especially those serving renters.

At the Arlequin, the elevator easily becomes a vehicle for the imaginary, moved by staggered and vaguely nervous feelings of ambivalence. An unremarkable form of transport, it is through the significations it carries with it that it is of precious value to us. The inhabitant makes no mistake about it. The pressed button sets in motion a certain, and truly destinal, voyage that nothing will stop: toward well-oiled habits as well as catastrophic breaks. These irrepressible slippages indicate to us already the load, which will have to be weighed later on, of an imaginary that turns up where one hardly expected it.

Bifurcation

Different from staggered polysemy, bifurcation may be presented as an equivocality of meanings. Such equivocality is practiced in the instant one walks, but only in an exclusive way. By way of contrast, the previous figure had offered a simultaneity through transference of one meaning to the other within the same moment.

The exemplary case is that of the thick pillars planted in the middle of the pedestrian gallery, the Sphinx and Janus of high-density housing complexes. (See Figures 7 and 8.) People necessarily have to pass either on the right or on the left. They are the precise transcription, within space, of the ambivalence between two simple terms, and they are commutable in a rather homogeneous way. Indeed, most of the time the inhabitant chooses this or that side without noticing anything more about it. Spontaneous choice for reason of avoidance is much rarer. Here is a solitary and firmly deliberate example of this: "I pass to the right, if there's a lot of people, to the left if there's no one."

Most often, there is something like an expression of surprise in the narrative and a touch of amusement that one has in recounting these ordinary accidental irregularities in one's travels. The scenarios are as follows:

1. *Almost always on the right; symmetrical case in both directions*

   PH.: Well, through the gallery . . . , there's a pillar, there in the middle, which poses a problem [laughter]. . . . People pass on the left [laughter]. You see where this pillar is?

   INTERVIEWER: Yes, after number 100.

Figure 7. The pillar at No. 100, seen from the north.

Figure 8. The pillar at No. 100, seen from the south.

PH.: Yes, people pass preferably on the left. And as for me, well, it's always on the right [laughter]!

INTERVIEWER: When coming back . . .

PH.: Ah, well, I think that I pass on the same side. Well . . . it's a thorny point in one's travels, huh? Then, it depends on the time, whether there are people there or not. But . . . basically . . . basically, I pass maybe on the right in both directions. It's not systematic; I maybe do it like that, but it's without paying attention.

2. *Always on the same side of the pillar, local univocality, asymmetry of directions for coming and going*

Ah, I never do it on the . . . I never pass *behind*! I find that there's less of a path, OK! [Laughter.] And, . . . there's less wind, I think. It seems to me that people pass preferably on this side, I think. [The context and the pencil sketches this young inhabitant draws while talking show that she passes to the west.]

3. *Mixed figure, which clarifies the hesitations of the first example*

So, at number 100, in order to go to number 90, uh, . . . there's a pillar and there's a little thing there. . . . I pass all the time on the right—in the direction of number 90—, . . . except to go get my car. . . . My car is in the garage, there, so I pass to the left when I go out.

Recalling the purposes of one's trips helps this last inhabitant who spoke to specify the forms of bifurcation she carries out. On the other hand, the inhabitant in the first example tries to invoke, beyond any particularities, the habitual patterns likely to shed light on his return trip. But *the pillar becomes an ironic object* and creates perplexity: it is "a thorny point."

What is going on is that this figure of bifurcation can show us something of greater interest. The pillar is ironic not only for the inhabitant. For, while it allows one better to understand and to illustrate the equivocalities of figures of walking, it also marks, as a matter of fact, an important point of bifurcation in the connotation of the figures we have expounded so far. Examination of these polysemous figures clarifies only too well the cases of walked variations that become spatialized and are fixed in place. Spatially speaking, bifurcation represents the simultaneous polysemy offered by a site; one can then attribute to this figure thus localized the qualifiers of randomness and indifference as to the nature of the competing terms. A sketch would yield the last word of explanation. At the same time, the act of walking would be dissolved.

For us, bifurcation makes itself felt between the order of sight and the conduct of one's walk. Indeed, in this specific example of the pillar, only one of the directions for passing by it seems obvious from afar (in coming from number 60, on the left; in coming from number 110, on the right). Up close—that is to say, when the bypass becomes imminent—everything does change and everything can change, for the perspective itself, beyond the fact that it is completely altered, leaves room for the more immediate conduct of one's steps. When the inhabitant bifurcated most often as if "without noticing anything more about it," this unnoticed quality was not the equivalent of something "random." Depending on the walker's mood in his actual conduct, although there is still a "game," it is no longer played on the field of some overall probability but, rather, within the competition between indetermination and anticipation; it plays itself out through all that the walker's temporality can offer that is different and unforeseen within the fore-*seen* space to be traversed, through all that the conduct of the walk may have anticipated, and it throws the order of perspective off its game.

The hesitations one finds in walking narratives are of precious value. Universal representational clarity would have led to an irreversible spatialization of the figures of walking. That this "point in one's travels" would be "thorny" is the sign of the presence of something other than a spatial logic at work in these polysemous figures, namely, *time.*

The Metathesis of Quality

This figure occurs in cases where repeated traveling through one and the same site can accidentally change in quality via nothing more than the effect of a difference in one's everyday chronological cycle. The willingness to use a comparative in one's narration expresses the *deferred polysemy* that affects one's ambulatory practice. A single element changes and the whole atmosphere of the walk finds itself metamorphosed. The pedestrian statement is then inscribed upon a background of transitivity, of a plurality of significations that vary with time.

Thus, the last word, the decisive step around the pillar-obstacles previously encountered, pertains no longer to a purely spatial game but, rather, to a particular quality of the walk. This is the difference between one's way out and one's return for one and the same trip, a difference that is prompted by the project moving the walk and its foreseen duration.

Other examples follow. The short segment of the gallery traveled by a female inhabitant:

> I really like mornings . . . the housewives who come and go; it's calm. . . . And then at noon, it's the opposite. There's more of a bustle, more noise. You can feel that people are in a hurry. . . . In the afternoon, I go out very little. . . . Otherwise, it depends on the day; for example, there are days when, despite the hours being the same, it's very different. For example, Sundays, it's very calm. . . . The passageway is calm . . . pleasant kitchen smells in the street; it's nice. The elevator comes right away; no one's in the gallery. . . . People go for walks; indeed, there are but very few people around, if the weather's good.

This sequence contains in shortened form all that we have been able to find in the narratives as a whole. It notes the day-to-day, hour-to-hour, and season-to-season variations. It only was missing day and night:

> Oh, then [nighttime], it's different; I didn't talk about that. . . . I'm scared; I'm very scared. I went out only once [. . .] the wind, which was blowing hard, carried away my scarf, and I didn't go looking for it. I felt reassured only after getting in my door. [. . .] At night, the galleries, it's like a labyrinth.

This extreme expression of the difference between night and day finds more temperate forms in other cases:

> At night . . . at night, you get the impression that it's . . . it's smaller, *narrower*.

From the standpoint of climate, this same gallery, whose connotation is often that of a site of convenience and shelter, can take on the opposite quality. One and the same female inhabitant will say:

> I sometimes happen to go on the outside, too. . . . [. . .] I go outside because, first of all, there's a lot of wind currents and then because I find that it's quicker that way.

> Everywhere in the gallery there are wind currents!

> Coming home, I always go on the inside [because of tiring quickly].

49

It may clearly be seen, when comparing the first quotation with the third, that brevity is an interchangeable assessment. It is the excesses of the climate that in fact provoke the paradoxical passage to "the outside."

Here is another metathesis of quality: when a moment is available, the entire layout of the gallery, bifurcations included, becomes part of a game for a ten-year-old child who "passes through the whole gallery." Likewise for a visit with friends, when what, from the standpoint of the design plan, is most "functional" becomes the most playful.[10]

With these examples, it appears that the metathesis of quality risks becoming the most general figure possible from the strictly spatial standpoint, yet the most specific one depending on one's mood in the act of walking, that is to say, at the moment when one includes context, time sequence, and differential memory of one's varying gaits. At the outer edges, it is no longer a matter of polysemy, for synchronism explodes into diachronism.[11]

With the extreme figure of polysemy, the elementary level can no longer be understood without summoning up [*une convocation de*] sequencing and combination. From the site walked to walking on the scale of a trip or of complexes of trips, we reach combinatory figures.

COMBINATORY FIGURES

The combinatory figures noted on the scale of whole trips and of complexes of walks seemed to be divided up into two groups, centered on two notions rhetoric holds to be of capital importance: redundancy and symmetry. What relevance do they have when it comes to expressive walking?

Figures of Redundancy

By redundancy, we intend the meaning given to this term in the Art of oral and written expression: overabundance. This notion, which in rhetoric had a connotative meaning of abuse, of excess, in the wake of the new Arts of thinking developed in the Cartesian era, has been re-employed by communication theory and has been introduced into linguistics. Redundancy henceforth appears as a fundamental mechanism in the functioning of language.[12] By contrast to ellipsis, it explains and permits identification of the term it takes up. Such overabundance is, in short, of precious value.

Now, in examining people's walks, one can see that *the essential features of walking activity unfold in the mode of redundancy*. One needs only refer back to the examples illustrating the metathesis of quality: the difference between a day trip and the same trip at night varies one's walking conduct, which can be very repetitive, if not exclusively identical to the look of a topographical map. Little by little, these differences in one and the same trip come to explain the way in which an inhabitant takes his walks. Such an operation is highly variable in degree and sometimes can be extreme (see the day/night opposition), yet most often it remains on the scale of the details involved and takes place in some sort of a chromatic way.

The examples would be innumerable. The everydayness expressed in the narratives we have gathered presents itself as essentially redundant—and this is probably the case for all forms of everydayness. The variations, the substitutions either are exceptional or else bear on fragments—which does not mean that they are insignificant.

Nothing is settled between the same and the different. Everyday lived experience takes our representations by surprise, because it persists in a slow and tenuous modification of *properties*.[13] The very same inhabitants will say at the start of their narrative, "It's always the same, huh? Always the same thing!" and will go on to recount so many different details apropos of one and the same trip, one day at a time. Redundancy is thus a phenomenon of composition or combination.

Four varieties of redundancy are worthy of note:

- redundancy of combination, with variation of details;

- repetition of one and the same set, in varied combinations;

- polarization of varied trips toward one and the same site; and

- amplified repetition of walking one and the same site.

The first of these four varieties is the most ordinary. It may be illustrated by the relationship of elementary figures to combinatory figures or in the discrepancy one will be able to pick up between ordinary trips retraced on maps and figures of variation and substitution.

The three other figures of redundancy are found less often. Yet they are no less interesting.

The rarest one, the one in which redundancy bears on the repetition of a finite set in varied combinations (ABC, BCA, CBA . . .), corresponds to the rhetorical figure of *metabole.* A bounded spatial set is walked at one's pleasure, according to combinations whose variety seems endless (that such variety should be reasonably finite is an argument of the planner or surveyor). Indeed, this combinatory model is lived in a mode that has nothing to do with rational exploration. Metabole is always carried out in one's walks with a poetic, ironic, or playful tone to it. The space walked is valued for itself. The exhaustiveness toward which this form of redundancy tends expresses precisely the gratuitous character of the act: "to have all the time to . . ." This figure of composition and recomposition of leisure space is to be found especially among children and young people, either over the whole of a single "trip" or through a tendency to vary as much as possible the path from home to some goal or from some goal back home. Sometimes, adults have the time to play with this figure, or they take it up.

The narratives illustrating metabole offer some extreme forms. They are either three or four pages in length (we have not been able to resist quoting at least one notebook page written by a ten-year-old girl, who makes one understand how, for someone of this age, metabole is possible even outside a moment of play, properly speaking; see Figure 9)[14] or the expression, in a few words, of a long moment of strolling, which seemed to go without saying and which is cited in an allusive way, yet in a knowing tone. A given Saturday of a sixteen-year-old girl will offer one example of this. It is but one inordinately long trip from morning till evening (six times she returns home, yet she hardly remains there at all), a huge festive end-of-the-week metabole, the narration of which fills no less than five handwritten pages. And yet, like a key, the whole thing can be related in a few expressions:

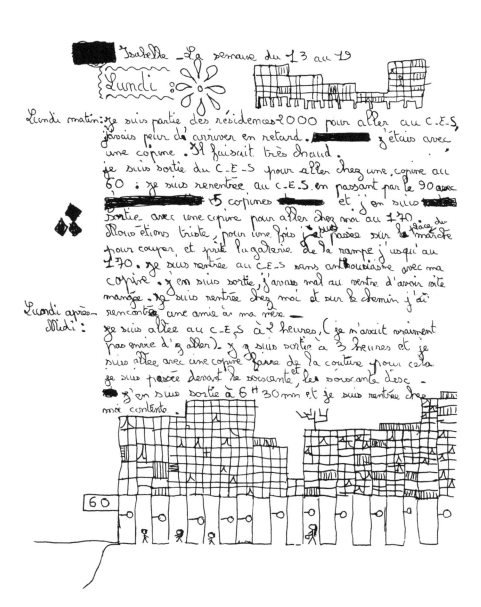

Isabelle – La semaine du 13 au 19

Lundi :

Lundi matin : je suis partie des résidences 2000 pour aller au C-E-S, j'avais peur d'arriver en retard. ████████ j'étais avec une copine. Il faisait très chaud.

je suis sortie du C-E-S pour aller chez une copine au 60 ; je suis rentrée au C-E-S en passant par le 90 avec ████████ +5 copines ████████ et j'en suis ████ sortie avec une copine pour aller chez moi au 170. Nous étions triste, pour une fois j'ai passée sur la marche du pour couper, et pris la galerie de la rampe jusqu'au 170. je suis rentrée au C-E-S sans enthousiasme avec ma copine. j'en suis sortie, j'avais mal au ventre d'avoir vite mangé. je suis rentrée chez moi et sur le chemin j'ai rencontré une amie à ma mère —

Lundi après-Midi :

je suis allée au C-E-S à 2 heures. (je n'avait vraiment pas envie d'y aller). j'y suis sortie à 3 heures et je suis allée avec une copine faire de la couture pour cela je suis passée devant le soixante, les soixante disc. ████ j'en suis sortie à 6 H 30 mn et je suis rentrée chez moi contente.

60

Saturday . . . [laughter] there were some things!

Afterward, . . . we went around the market, all the way!

When I go out, I run toward the elevator. Ten seconds . . . if the elevator isn't there, I run and go down by foot. When I get to the bottom, I say deep down within myself, "No one can catch up with me" [laughter], it's like that.

And I was at the Park [resuming her lively and gay voice]. Then the Park [. . .] went to the Mounds, ran! No shoes, ran [. . .] when you go up the hill, the sun's out there. . . .

In a few sentences, everything is said: the feverish activity, tending toward exhaustiveness ("all the way"), the play, the poetics.

For adults, metabole is more accidental and is limited to a circumscribed territory over a given time.

INTERVIEWER: You follow your dog's rhythm?

PH.: Oh yes, yes! Quite so. Same for the path. Until . . . let's say up to the lawn. I direct him a bit, and then afterward, he does what he does; he goes where he wants to go. He runs where he wants. If he sees another dog, I wait for him.

Thus begin the stray ramblings of the early-morning stroller: behind a dog. All combinations are possible.

Likewise in a discovery stroll, or some errant wandering:

[In the park] I stroll around in all directions; there is always . . . each time you scale the Mounds [. . .] there is an impression of freedom.

Once, I went all around the New Town via the passageways on the top floor, in all directions, in order to have a look from above.

Let us also recall the narrative of the female inhabitant who went out "to get lost," near the silos and the mezzanines.[15] On this scale, the "labyrinth" effect sought after was to summon up an exhaustive trip that would have overtaken her, one from which she would not have been able to exit.

Metabole functions all the times when one seeks, through varied repetition, to diversify a site that can be walked in a multitude of directions. This dispersal of means and this wasting of steps, which are inexplicable from the functional standpoint of traffic movement, refer back, specifically and directly, to a poetics of space that depends on an unmeasured time or a time the inhabitant refuses to measure. The metabolic process marks out what can be most gratuitous and irrational in the conduct of one's walks.

In contrast to metabole, which tends toward divergence, *anaphora*, the third figure of redundancy, articulates the spatiotemporal organization of one's routes in terms of convergence, centering. (Its logical model would be bcA, deA, . . . , yzA.)

Each time a mode of walking is organized in its entirety around some localized pole that may attract or repel, yet will always fascinate, there is anaphora, repetition of the same term in some series in which the rest varies. In the detail of the space traveled, substitutions or variations (paratopisms or peritopisms) therefore appear that manage to effect a delay between the departure point and the avowed or unavowed goal. These *postponements* are noteworthy elements in walkers' writing. By reason of prudence or for pleasure, one gives oneself the time to render explicit and explain one and the same object. It is in terms of temporality that anaphora is to be apprehended.

In this way, a particular inhabitant does not allow the true center of attraction of her walks to appear right away. Along the narrative of her different trips, and despite the variants she introduces, one must follow the play of meaningful effects found in her designations of landmarks. It is by comparing the semantic slippages that, little by little, come to specify the object ("Arlequin," then "gallery," then "commercial gallery," and finally "Community Center") to the walks actually carried out at various moments that the figure of centering is sketched out. In fact, the dynamic center of attraction of the main portion of these walks will be stated only later on; it is "the commercial gallery—well, the commercial gallery . . . , especially the Community Center." Now, this Community Center is not an important site of activity for the woman who is speaking. Simply, she "traverses it" and, in doing so, does "not have the impression of being ill at ease." The true attraction can hardly be discerned here. Does not fascination then take on its full force in the promising name that goes into this space? Whence the following words: "It's to see what is going on, to try to become integrated into the Arlequin." The attraction of this site is not for reasons of usage or convenience but, rather, through symbolic reproduction of the function given by the designers: activity center.

All examples of anaphora go beyond the simple quest for a site. At the heart of this figure, one discovers a centripetal dynamic that is symbolic in nature: that is why some time is needed. However diverse they may be, the variations persist in repeating one and the same attraction. Spatial diversity matters much less than the untiring search for additional postures of attack. In the narrative of one adolescent girl, the Junior High School/Community Center forms the center of almost all her walks; the places where she crosses barely vary. But going to the "junior high" as a schoolgirl, then to the "Community Center" to "see girlfriends," or else "to smoke a cigarette in the library," allows one to bring diversity to the site. There is a tendency for these gradual differences to encompass it, to exhaust its various significations. Moreover, one finds numerous occasions for pauses and stays in the areas bordering the "Junior High School/Community Center": this is a tempting site, but one likely to encourage dilatory detours.

Anaphora organizes one's walks according to a postponed movement of contraction, of systole. The central site undergoes, as an aftereffect, an opposite movement of diastole; it "monopolizes the surrounding area" and "overflows [*déborde*] its own limits," to use Pierre Sansot's expressions.[16] An excellent example in which the rivalry of "approaching" [*aborder*] and "going beyond" [*déborder*] is recounted in the following narrative:

> It's the same with the bistro, with its tables outside, but I don't have the impression of overflow for all that. Well . . . I'd compare it, maybe . . . for example, when people at the café, the people who are outside on the terrace, they are already at the café. Right, . . . the people who are with their baskets in front of the Gro, it's the same thing; they are already at the Gro. Hmm . . . ! Because, if not, without that basket of items, they are neither at home nor at Gro's, nor . . . nor at the stationery store, nor . . . uh . . . nor close by. As for me, I don't know what to say!

The more the site throws up resistance and fascinates at the same time, the more the interested inhabitant makes it into the main locale.

Hyperbole, the final figure of redundancy, occurs when one's siege of a site is finished. The inhabitant then leaves the impression that he is or passageway, sometimes gallery corner) than the exit (in this case, the apartment's front door marks the "caesura," the abrupt transition). The dissymmetric relation between one direction and another reveals the difference between one's housing and one's domicile. The domiciliation process can contract or expand according to the direction of one's walk. The signification of these everyday dissymmetries refers us back to the act of appropriation and the dynamic it brings into play.

3. Asymmetry

Qua figure of combination, *asymmetry* may be observed in all cases where a trip is affected as a whole by multiple and divergent variations. Some inhabitants thus go on walks whose exact route cannot be foreseen. The overall direction retains the same basic orientation, but numerous inopportune branches are grafted onto it. Between the trip out and the return trip, there is neither symmetry nor dissymmetry but, rather, absence of symmetry. The walking style, whether uneven and jerky or feverish, is transcribed via an abundance of verbs in the narrative. The variations, which are almost always hyperactive, bring into play the three combined dimensions of space, as well as the rhythm and posture of the inhabitants' steps. Let us listen to what one inhabitant has to say:

> Ah, if necessary, I hop, I bend, I thread my way. I find it's very badly done, because it was thought that people were going to take the gallery. They don't do that, because they're in a hurry, because there are barriers you bump your nose against, there are cars everywhere. Nothing is thought out. You're obliged to lift up your feet to pass through, and to top it all off, you get tickets.

Inhabitants who are less than twenty years old are particularly inclined to take the asymmetric approach. For two adults, their walks often display this organizational figure, but as the pages go by one discovers that it is dictated by a rational functionalism: the technical upkeep of the neighborhood. In several inhabitants' narratives, the tone, barely contained, ill conceals a decided pleasure they take in breaking up[20] the built-up space with each step. Sometimes, there is the joy of a spatial form of irony, sometimes a willful shattering of everyday isochronisms.

Thus, the last figure for organizing one's walks appears as a disorganization of the laid-out and developed space. The least coherent with regard to the functions of traffic circulation, it tells us more than the others about how walking is practiced in a global way according to specific styles of inhabiting the space.

From here, are we going to end up referring each way of organizing one's walk to the style of the inhabitant producing it, this style being a particular way of using certain elementary figures in certain elective combinations? Would the "material" of this reading-writing of space be the sole entity shared in common and never exhausted by the actual and singular usage performed by these walks? As is the case with one's tongue, for language? Or do there exist one or two invariants that would yield a community of meaning for all the walking styles we have observed?

Two Fundamental Figures: Synecdoche and Asyndeton

From the elementary to the organized, through the progressive discovery of the figures these walks write, it seems that something else has been running alongside, surfacing here, totally absent elsewhere, the oversight of which vaguely pursues us. In its good-natured willingness to trim down and to clarify, the exposition has demonstrated, but also has taxidermized as stuffed "specimens," a collection of elementary figures and model figures of organization. We have barely caught a glimpse yet of the role played by the actual way these organizations function and by the way in which the elements do or do not take their place therein. In other words, we are still in the dark as to the role of the expressive movement by which the inhabitant comes and goes.

Now, one also finds in these walks two quite singular figures. They can operate on the elementary level, but they are not elementary. They clearly manifest themselves on the scale of the overall combinations, but they do not correspond to a complete syntagmatic model. Their nature differs therefore from the figures previously expounded. Their role is to articulate among themselves the elementary figures that are present in

Third instantiated principle: when the part stands for the whole, on the one hand the phenomenon is expressed in descriptive terms, on the other hand the part *takes the place of* the totality in the form of a climate and in a relation of symbolization. As lived, the climate of the mezzanine is concretely equivalent to one's overall representation of the Arlequin. The atmospheres on the Mound or at the lake symbolize everything poetic that can found in the park and in the neighborhood.[26]

In the rhetoric of one's walks, synecdoche grounds a universal mode of organization in which the part stands for the whole. When the whole stands for the part, the walking process becomes allusive, and then Representation governs one's apprehension of space. Thus, through one of the keys to the organization of walks into a reading-writing, one can see being sketched out, along with one fundamental characteristic, the disassociation between a representation of the trip and the narrative of a lived experience of walking. The selection of one of the instantiated principles tends to reduce and to exclude the others. More likely, however, what it does is include them in a concealed way, referring each back to the overall context in which this selection is based—which is what the relation to the signified is supposed to clarify.

Asyndeton

Asyndeton—"figure by which one suppresses conjunctions," as we are told in rhetoric—is the second key to the process of organizing one's walks.

Whereas synecdoche shows the way in which selection operates, the second fundamental process should bring juxtaposition, connections, and conjunctions into play. These are the links through which every element of expression follows another one of them in the constitution of the expressive whole. That is how things proceed in language proper, such as the process of connection that is characteristic of this or that style.

Now, ambulatory expression seems to be grounded essentially on an absence of connections. Only a topographical map will give the illusion of something "linked," by transcribing the succession of steps and putting them into continuous lines. When grasped as a whole, the transcribed narrative can also make one believe in a relatively homogeneous sequence: a mere overall impression. Yet let one listen to the interviews more closely, consider in detail how oral expressions repeat walking expressions, and take account of the silences, the suspended intonations, and the punctuation breaks, and then one will perceive, behind the well-connected fragments, a background of discontinuity that is present in all these interviews. Indeed, in considering the narrative in itself, one can identify patches of description that evoke the spatiotemporal unfolding of the moment of densely narrated walking, then, between these fragments, either a digressive transition in which value judgments break through or a connection of a temporal nature ("afterward," "next," "at such and such an hour, I . . .") that leaps onward to another description and skimps [fait l'économie] on concrete spatial continuities.

There is an economy of narrative, it will be said, an economy of memory. One cannot recount everything. What can be known about what occurred during a walk? And yet narrative styles differ from one story to the next, as walking styles differ. What to us appears to be a fragment limited by the unit of description always tends to be given as a totality. The way in which synecdoche takes place, the prevalence of certain "fragments," and the mode of occurrence of asyndetons (where connections disappear) are so many characteristics of a style belonging to the inhabitant.

A ten-year-old child thus offers us an expression that is typical of this age group, with connections by subject-point. The connections proceed along the lines of contiguity, and not sequence, and exhibit a constant economy of descriptive detail (few adjectives, especially for personal subjects and words).[27] Being played out here is a point-by-point account of an overall movement, sometimes broken up by a sudden encounter with a few rare favored sites: the lake, the passageway, the Olympic Village.

A young girl uses many coordinating conjunctions ("and," "right"; the latter being a popular conjunction not recognized in grammar) and sometimes sequential ones ("finally," "however"), but they occur *within* these long, quite storied descriptions. Between these descriptions, recollection of the hour or the day takes the place of connection ("then . . . ,

Saturday afternoon . . ."). Now, these transitions by leaps mask the chief asyndeton that structures the everyday life of this inhabitant: a forgetting—indeed, the discreet rejection—of everything about her lodgings and the surrounding area. She speaks of her lodgings, in the end, only reluctantly:

INTERVIEWER: At number 50, what floor do you live on?

N.: On the first floor.

INTERVIEWER: Then you haven't told me about the end of your trips?

N.: Oh! . . . um, well, in order to arrive home, [sound indicating indifference]. . . . Right [beginning a small sketch], right . . . it's always the same thing.

In this case, asyndeton permits her to leap from one path in her public life to another path of the same type: the aspect of her existence that this young girl values as against the problems at home that are placed within brackets. Except for stylistic differences, asyndeton fulfills an analogous function in the spoken and walked expressions of the ten-year-old child. The deceptive succession of contiguities hides a discontinuous style of walking in which nothing truly sticks to the child's hurried steps, these short hops. Two forms of asyndeton are already taking shape: a state that, when taken on the scale of these trips as a whole, is diffuse and that the play of the narrative's expressive contiguities does not succeed in masking; and a state that may be deemed as condensed in relation to a qualitative leap that occurs between this first mode of walking and the few rare sites that are walked with enthusiasm.

The same parallel between what is said of these walks and the way in which it is said holds for all the interviews. Beneath the variety of styles belonging to each inhabitant, asyndeton operates insistently and with an identical function: in the narrative of a seventy-year-old inhabitant, for whom the "holes" in the narrative correspond to a kind of walking that is designed to conserve her energy and is concerned with brevity from the start; in that of the thirty-year-old worker, where the division established by the break between the narrative of his walks to work and the narrative of his leisure walks corresponds only too well to the reality of everyday life as it is modeled in a certain mode of production; and in that of the forty-year-old housewife, where the poetic mode of walking appears only through a break from the repetitive utilitarian mode. Thus also, monotony seems incapable of being altered, but only of being "broken."

A few choice, specific examples will better illustrate the general and fundamental role asyndeton plays. Indeed, following the example of synecdoche, asyndeton crops up from time to time from beneath an obvious and succinct expression that offers us a digest version thereof. Other times, this same figure clearly dominates the organization of a walk: these are precious accidents that shed undiffracted light on the way in which the absence of connections grounds one's walking expression.

Holes

Asyndeton manifests itself in the following examples not only as a lapse in memory [*trou de mémoire*] but also as a hole [*trou*] in the narrative and as the very porosity of space:

> J.: I never take, I don't know why, I would take it, besides, the . . . as there are the passageways . . .
>
> CHILD PRESENT: —the mezzanine!
>
> INTERVIEWER: Why?
>
> J.: Um, well, it's a bit complicated; I once wanted to take it with the kids, you remember? Then, there were some . . . dead ends, huh? That's what they were . . . ? We made a U-turn and took the gallery again.

There is a loss of the name of the site in which one gets lost. The mezzanine as walkway thus becomes doubly absent. It is a parenthetical site that is left up in the air, as manifested in the equivalent three dots of silence.

> INTERVIEWER: In your [written] account, you talk about a few spots, but between these spots, what is there? . . . nothing of importance? . . . or else? . . .
>
> E.: Yes, that's right. . . . What's more, there is a passage from there to there [she points this out on a small sketch she makes]. Well, there, that's the gallery and there, the little place. . . . Yes, this passage, I don't talk about it. It must be quite harmless. . . . I don't know.
>
> INTERVIEWER: Right. On the left- or right-hand side of the trip? It doesn't interest you?
>
> E.: Oh, well that, it's to be discovered! Later. . . . When I'll go everywhere . . . um, well . . . I'll be myself, huh?

Reflection on the first absence (between two poles) leads the inhabitant to discover that her walks are written on the background of an absent totality. This "everywhere" that allows for a reserve of possibilities is, for the moment, only an unwalked area that surrounds her trips. Between the gallery and the little place, there is nothing to say because nothing acted or suffered is expressed therein. The absences allow for a project of coming appropriation at the same time as a future elucidation of one's identity as an inhabitant.

The compartmentalized state of the memorable and recountable walk appears as such only upon the background of a graphic representation. From this point of view, there very well are "holes." On the other hand, over the whole of the context that envelops the lived experiences of one's walks, these "holes" distinguish, rather, the moments of the present from those that are to come later on from a long-term effort at appropriation.

Absences

The climate within which a walk is carried out is an essential agent of the frequency of asyndetons, of their quantity, and of their duration. The trip to work will easily be permeable to large absences. The narratives transcribe this through holes in the phrasing or sometimes explicit recognition of the absence, of the "hole" that can affect a large portion of the trip, indeed the totality of it.

For the inhabitant at number 60 who leaves for work in the morning, his presence in the neighborhood is remarkably short-lived. It all ends at number 50:

> Oh, practically . . . I am thinking of number 50, huh? Afterward . . . afterward, I dash off, huh?

After number 50, there is nothing more to do than to "dash off." Focused on the worry and the repetitive burden of his job, which begins at the end of this trip after twenty minutes on a moped, the inhabitant has already left, even though he has not yet mounted his vehicle. The walk loses all detail, because, right away, the landscape is already "dashing off."

Some other examples:

INTERVIEWER: Was it the same trip when it rains?

N.: Oh, I look at nothing; I don't give a damn at all! I don't know anyone here . . . [fifteen seconds of silence]. In the afternoon, I had some worries about work. I *saw nothing*.[28] Nothing to say!

The two expressions of silence, the first acted out, the second spoken, perfectly well punctuate, in this narrative, the way in which the walk was carried out: overall absence. Here we are dealing with genuine *hole-trips*. Only the "duty to remember" feature imposed by the framework of the interview has allowed these minimal expressions of walks with neither any thickness nor any density: ectoplasm-trips. The absence of connection at this point merges with the absence of memorable lived experience. The asyndeton has taken up the entire place.

In combinations of figures, round trips organized according to symmetrical alternations had already shown the phenomenon of a longitudinal hole (absence of a right or of a left). Henceforth, we can recognize in it a stylistic effect of prolonged asyndeton.

From then on, one can see how this impression of not having truly walked but, rather, of having traversed some sites in complete indifference is not some accident, an anomaly of lived experience, but, quite to the contrary, the very background for the organization of our walks. Whether it is expressed in terms of worry, preoccupation, weariness, neglect, or the wear and tear of everyday life, and whether we recognize therein the mark of a certain kind of civilization, the sign of a failure in building as it is subjected to the mode of production that directs it, this paradoxical phenomenon of articulation through absence of conjunction continues to be probably the most universal one there is among all the modes of walking through an inhabited space today.[29]

FROM FIGURES TO CODE

Walking rhetoric is a quite particular form of expression. Its identity owes as much to the elective place of two figures carrying greater weight than all others as to the typical layout of these two modes of constitution.

These walks yield a surprising idea of everyday life. Nothing is ever lived except partially, the fragments giving themselves out to be the "globality" of the situation. These discontinuities exist only upon a background of absence, of "blanks," of "holes," as the inhabitants say. *Asyndeton is the condition of possibility for synecdoche.* In the pedestrian statements in which synecdoche privileges the usage of the part for the whole, asyndeton renders possible the appropriation of the whole via the part.

The Poetic Idiom

Thus do the proposed analogies between linguistic analysis and a walking rhetoric begin to fall apart.

Here is a first difference. In our language, there is greater consistency when the task of connecting things together is performed well. But here, in the practice of one's walks, one does one's utmost to disconnect, to instaurate discontinuity. And a second difference emerges. A word is not chosen for itself all alone but, rather, in terms of the syntagmatic series. Yet daily strolls persistently confer value upon certain elements, spatial particularities that overflow the rightful functional partitions and shake up the territorial sequences.

The linguistic analogy is lame. No doubt, we rediscover in the enunciation of one's steps the two axes language theory[30] names as the "axis of combination" and the "axis of selection"—the combined play of a "metonymic process" and of a "metaphorical process" in which internal relationships (the meaningful relation) and external relationships (the contextual relation) produce, at their intersection, a certain type of expression. But this intersection takes a quite peculiar turn owing to the eminent position of synecdoche and asyndeton.

How would linguistic theory evaluate what we call "walking expression"? Probably by likening it to a specific form: poetic language, in which the measured hierarchization one finds in prose is broken up in favor of a rhythmic arrangement that lays emphasis on the terms first of all for themselves. "The poetic function projects the principle of equivalence from the axis of selection into the axis of combination."[31]

"Equivalence" does not mean "indifference." This sort of autonomy the word preserves in the poetic syntagma is the persistence of the process of selection, which is not forgotten when combinations are made—but on one condition, that is, that the process of combination would have created a vacuum, that the enunciative model privileged in prose (wherein words take only the fair share granted to them by the signifying whole that is to be stated) would be broken up. As in poetry, a part of the walk can be valid for itself and render itself autonomous in relation to a totality it shakes up and deforms while attempting to go beyond it. This process is possible because asyndeton breaks the connections that, when present, would prevent such interference of what is selective within the combinatory.

The final contribution we could ask of linguistic knowledge may be formulated in a proposition that creates the dividing line between the language of prose and the rhetoric of walking: *the organization of one's walks is constituted in the manner of a poetics*. The act of walking is not the progressive totalization of a given space to be traveled through but, rather, the uneven and jerky articulation of a movement that constructs the lived experience of space in an often diverting mode. Take, for example, that first moment of organization via exclusion, an initial figure about which we can now understand that it stems directly from the combined play of asyndeton and synecdoche. Take, also, that law of contrast at the level of overall combinations, which was permitted by the absence of conjunction and which leaves the part free to "stand for the whole" in the symbolic mode. Too vacant at times, overcharged at other times, walking styles seem excessive and chaotic only from the geometric outlook, which would like to see in a coherent—that is to say, well-connected—way how, and to what extent, the inhabitant does or does not "fill in" a traffic space. But in the practice of one's walks, one neither fills in nor fails to fill in. The rhetorical form indicates in what sense it has to be structuration, constitution of singular space-times, and not mere general usage of constructed spatialities.

The discovery of the two metafigures thus moves into a more theoretical lane of analysis, which will be taken again later on. Our rhetorical exposition still remains incomplete, and the question of signification has been left hanging.

Toward the Instantiated Principle of the Collective

The various modes of walking that belong to each inhabitant share a community of style that is henceforth recognized. There is *one* inhabitant rhetoric in the sense that the fundamental principles of articulation do not vary. This community of meaning is nevertheless entirely theoretical. The inhabitants do not play in vain at their comings and goings. The figures of walking rhetoric propose an arrangement of signifiers. But what concrete and everyday signifieds do they express?

A new reading of the narratives is required, one more attentive this time to comparison of the referents each stylistic effect calls for. Here is our first overall impression: everyday poetics rarely abandons itself to lyricism. Only episodically does one experience elation in one's approach or does an unforeseen and gratuitous event suddenly emerge and cross one's steps (daydreaming at the edge of the lake or on the mounds and fascination at the play of light and shadows under the gallery at night are two of these rare examples). More ordinarily, these walks unfold mainly in the epic mode: a poetics of narration.

The epic is characterized in modern rhetoric by the strong contribution it implies for the referential function.[32] Like all expression, one's walking conducts refer back to a context that situates them. In other words, one's ways of doing (the rhetorical modes) tell us in a mediate way one's ways of being. Pedestrian statement signifies two things: one's immediate goal (going to work, going shopping, going home, going for a walk) and one's way of living the situation. This last signified encompasses, among other things, the dimensions of spatial position, temporal situation, psychological attitude, and the presence of the other. Now, the contextual element most often mentioned by the inhabitants questioned is a social referent, which is sometimes so explicit that it serves as a "message."[33] No one walks, it seems, without at least the vague presence of the instantiated principle of the collective.[34]

The descriptive study of everyday comings and goings is therefore to be pursued in the direction of its most manifest signification: the social dimension. We are hardly talking here about a sociological study in the scientific sense of the term. Our purpose is more modest. Just as each chapter began with a simple configuration of traces, so we are attempting to do nothing more, at the perimeter of the chapter to come, than to describe the code through which he who walks and those who surround him are signified throughout the walk itself.[35]

3

An Inhabitant Rhetoric

THE CODE OF APPROPRIATION

AT ALL TIMES, knowledge of the art of rhetoric has seemed to confer upon its owner a certain power. Well-chosen, well-handled words exert a sort of magical effect. A tight and mobile interlacing of terms charms, bewitches, and finally, like a quickly cast net, ensnares the listener, who forgets all his own arguments. The goal of rhetoric is to convince, to draw one's adversary, or he who remains indifferent, into one's game. This art of persuasion minimizes or exaggerates, avoids or repeats, anamorphoses or transfigures at that very place where the flat statement would employ only the right and strict series of words deemed necessary to produce, as closely as possible, the truth that is to be spoken.[1]

Although the effort to render the truth of words equivalent to the truth of things remains an unresolved problem, there is no doubt that the essence of rhetoric is to flow beyond the object of discourse, to make it accessible and convincing, to "make it truer." Through its propensity for stylistic effect, rhetoric strays from the literal meaning. The use of figurative meaning produces this interval [*écart*] that has always rendered undecidable any evaluation of the art of speaking well.[2] Is one to appreciate rhetorical expression for its capacity to make the stated object splendidly appear or for its performance in "figuring" things so well? Does what is expressed have more or less importance than the expression, one's way of expressing?

The same questions hold for inhabitant rhetoric, which, like figurative speech, is a swerving sort of [*de l'écart*] practice. We shall not respond to these questions before having sought out what the singular, everyday fashioning of space described in the preceding chapter might signify.

Without doubt, each inhabitant always reveals, through his pedestrian practice, the peculiar traits of his personality and his choices in relation to social attitudes as well as to the available options about the usage of space. And the depth psychologist, the classical sociologist, the political scientist, and even the economist will read, each in his own way and each through his own semiology, the "content" of these ambulatory configurations. It is not our wish, however, to snap so quickly the thread of the inhabitants' narratives.

When a passerby bypasses a site, he traces a figure of avoidance. In the same stroke, however, has he not identified, opposite himself, the real or possible movement of someone else? We already had a premonition of these mutual anticipations of avoidance or encounter when expounding the figures of walking.

Even more than that, the inhabitants to whom we have listened state explicitly in their narrations how the other intervenes in the everyday landscape through which they travel. Thus are woven together relationships of collusion, of similarity, and of cohesion, but also those of oppositions, of rejections, and of differentiations. Through repetitions and variations, spatial readings and writings, and the produced and the reproduced, the inhabitants recognize one another and make themselves recognized. A sort of *code* appears. Through this code, the signifieds find at least a minimum of homogeneity. The ways of organizing space figure the similarities and differences existing among the inhabitants.

How is this code to be qualified? Every urban zone, high-density housing complex, group of single-lot homes, or island of buildings has particular ways and customs. Each has its own "good manners." Beneath the general codes revealed by sociology in its study of the oppositions between the urban and the rural, among various social classes, and among diverse ethnic groups, there exist more particular codes. Over a small unit of space, one can observe how, from day to day, the forms of sociability knit themselves together and unravel without stop. A more phenomenological approach would find that the code for the fashionings[3] of inhabited space is the fruit not of a state but, rather, of a mobile collective process that unfolds, most often, without the knowledge of the inhabitants (save in moments of extreme tension, where this or that law of the code is suddenly perceived as an obstacle).

The explicit stake involved in inhabitant practice is what may be called *qualified space*. My steps qualify the path taken. But before me opens a space already traveled by the other. My way of coming and going is sometimes going to repeat the already accepted or sought-after qualifications; sometimes it is going to disqualify, or even to deny, hostile sites. The concrete seizure of space begins via the question of *the appropriable*. Are the sites to come beneath my steps appropriated or appropriable? And how are they so?

Everyday language talks about a "feeling of being at home" that meets with success or struggles to be successful or that fails, depending on the case at hand. One also hears, "This place feels good to me," "I feel good here," "I don't feel rejected here." This syncretism among oneself, the space, and the other seems to be designated quite well by the term *appropriation*. We are dealing here with a notion that is never clearly definable, that has justifiably been criticized, but whose fuzziness seems to us to designate rather felicitously the barbarisms and "blurrinesses" of everyday life. In the pages to come, it will have a wholly instrumental, entirely provisional value. And, repeated too often, it will perhaps end up losing its meaning altogether and disappear of its own accord, as happens with words spoken over and over again that suddenly become empty sounds. When we shall employ it, it will be above all in order to indicate the concomitant presence of the instantiated principles of the individual, the social, and the spatial.

These reservations having been made, the writing of one's walks seems to signify that there is a dynamic of appropriation. We shall endeavor to bring out progressively its code. The rules that will be stated will not, however, all converge at the same time toward a closed definition of this code of appropriation. They indicate the heavy punctuations of an observational approach—which is, first of all, attentive to the most obvious forms of appropriation (and the most explicit ones in the inhabitants' narratives) and then curious about more complex phenomena expressed in a discrete and sparse sort of way.

THE NAMING OF PLACES

If we talk about the everyday circulation of pedestrian traffic, about networks of spatial frequentation that acquire consistency on a map, place-names will serve to indicate enduring landmarks, the stable boundary markers between which the lines of people's trips are stretched. Names are but one of the abstract elements in the system of cartographic location. All toponyms are then of equal value. None of them will tell more than any other in what direction the inhabitant walks with or against the others, granting value to some space or rejecting another one.

Our reading of the narratives of one's walks has driven us, however, to overturn this reductionist attitude. In the configurative movement of one's steps, toponyms do not in any way precede something else, nor do they constitute anything by themselves. They appear along the walk that instigates them, that informs them, and that annihilates them as it pleases. Signs among other signs, they reflect the qualification one's pedestrian gait inscribes therein by making them be.

In this sense, the inhabitants carry out a veritable *process* of place-naming. The narratives indicate this designation-assignment of the space within which speech expresses, within every community of style, what steps configure. Now, it should be pointed out that no naming is performed without the involvement of the instantiated principle of the collective.

The narrative of one's walks calls for a citation of sites in a form that can be identified by "the listener": he who listens and, behind him, "everyone." Through employment of the toponym, the narrative makes one recognize the space through the statements of a shared discourse. Nonetheless, the reference in question is not always clearly apparent. Some namings fail to achieve their project of shared designation. Thus do we discover a few moments in the narrative that are spent entirely on specifying an ill-understood or barely clear name. This is a metalinguistic phase of the narrative where one goes off in search of equivalent units. The first difficulty encountered is therefore *the relevance for a community of meaning of the appellations that are stated in the narrative.* The words do not always succeed in encompassing the spatial feature involved on the background of a language-imposed requirement of univocality. Between the individual and the collective, words do not express a spatial relation defined identically for everyone at all times.

While not being univocal, names do not, for all that, just sink into an irremediable state of equivocality. Indeed, as manifested in narrative, the mode of appellation contains a more or less faithful, but always insistent, reproduction of the memorable relation places maintain with names. And this occurs through the general practice of one's walks in the neighborhood. One's hesitations and the mishaps that occur in the naming of spaces do not seem to be, in this case, purely formal and linguistic phenomena. They betray a certain way of having lived these places from which the collectivity is never absent. My toponymic landscape merges to a large extent with the others' landscapes. Whence arises a second difficulty: *How is one to evaluate the collective connotation involved in the apprehension of places walked?* "Apprehension," we say here, for it really is a matter of a seizure by words as well as by one's steps.

These namings are revelatory of a lived experience of one's walks that is not exempt from difficulties, errancies, even failures in relation to the instantiated principle of the collective. They can be arranged into a progressive series with two constants. On the one hand, the most common names are those that bring the least tensions and differentiations into play. On the other hand, the more specific place-names become, the more atomized the collectivity becomes on the scale of the entire neighborhood and the more mutually distinctive social subgroups become.

Let us begin with the most common form of naming.

Numbering

So, the inhabitant says: "at number 60," "toward number 100," "from number 130."[4] Such appellations are used by all the inhabitants questioned, employed either exclusively or as synonyms for a previously stated name deemed insufficiently precise. They do not in themselves call for any particular commentary in the course of the narrative—save, on occasion, in order to criticize or praise the graphic or chromatic inscription of the numbers. Reproducing the location devices imposed by the design plan and by the management, they connote what is most common and most clear in the identification of sites. Nonetheless, self-assurance in the employment of the appellation and its frequency differ from one inhabitant to the next. The youngest inhabitants, the regulars at attending various activities in the neighborhood, and those who work around there juggle easily with the numbers. These are the same people who do not get lost and can circulate through the neighborhood "as if they were at home"—though this apparent ease does not necessarily correspond to a successful overall appropriation of the area. Others hesitate sometimes, do not know certain numbers, or are familiar only with the number of their domicile and those of their neighbors. This is the case, in particular, of an inhabitant in her seventies. It would seem that the ease with which one employs these numbers should be a function of the level of one's overall adaptation to the neighborhood. For, the places designated by the numbers, as well as their placement and the graphics used, display an unusual type of organization. Referencing by numbers selects, de facto, a certain type of inhabitant who is likely to adapt quickly.

Functional Appellation

This form of naming differs very little from the usages commonly employed in other urban neighborhoods. The shops and activity areas in the neighborhood permit unmistakable location—all the more so as these place-names also mark the environing space. "Toward the bakery" and "toward the butcher's"—these two shops being next to each other—are indications that allow for no ambiguity as to the space thus named. One sometimes uncovers more accidental names that refer to a transient operation of some sort. When one inhabitant says, "next to the children's bedroom display," he summons up in the listener the practice of a group of inhabitants who are well informed about the events that take place in the Arlequin neighborhood. More generally speaking, the perennial operations of the junior high school, the shops, the schools, and the neighborhood's activity rooms, which everyone can place, do not require that one belong to the groups who make practical use of these sites, but simply demand a knowledge of the most obvious features of the neighborhood.

Other sites, designated by less well-known functions and prompting frequentations for specific purposes, connote references to groups of initiates. They harbor activities of which other inhabitants are unaware or about which they are familiar by hearsay, without these activities being able to serve for them as spatial landmarks. Thus, appellations like "toward the photo shop," "toward the other retirement home," "next to the insurance office," which are obvious for the three inhabitants familiar with these places, would be perplexing or ambiguous for other people. Finding one's bearings [*Le repérage*] is then loaded with a clear allusion to a specific aspect of everyday life, because one's walks are articulated with precision over these sites that are prone to a definite and limited appropriation.

Singularized or Particularized Appellation

This type of naming is to be distinguished from the others in that a synecdoche is produced. This happens either through an effect of personalization or by reference to the part rather than to the whole.

When one inhabitant says, "I make *this* detour," "I cross the small place, *here*," the designation is narrowed down, with several noteworthy effects: substitution of an allusive singularity for the discursive universal; restriction of the meaning of the appellation through rejection of commonly accepted names; introduction of the motor order specific to the lived experience of one's walk into a sequence of the enunciative order. Demonstrative pronouns and adverbs of place then indicate a latent appropriation that other expressions will come to confirm more clearly: "my spot," "I arrive home," "toward my stairwell." It is not a matter here of one's own lodging but, rather, of the area bordering one's domicile: the space near the elevator entrance that overflows onto the gallery. It is then that the act of appropriation delimits a space with no physical markings and makes it change its nature. The appropriated space stands out either as not being the place that is common to everyone—and then the value is placed on the singular, which borders on itself—or as being perceptible only to initiates, who in this case are summoned [*convoqués*] onto the field of speech but who are supposed to exist for real also in similar practices that have them frequenting "this" detour or "that" little place.

The process of particularization heads in the same direction. When one inhabitant says "on the mound," she either is provoking the ostracism of those who do not know whether one is speaking of the park and which mound or is spurring the complicity of those who understand immediately that she is talking about "the big mound in the park with the stairs"—which is no higher than the others, but which is "very well known" and "where one sees so well," as some inhabitants say. In this case, a shared appropriation is possible because the synecdoche and the ellipsis used here correspond to one and the same kind of frequentation of the park and to a seizure of the space that is carried out in the same mode.

Another concrete signification of the fundamental figure of synecdoche is manifested here. To say the less for the more is to refer to a particular appropriation that is liable to bring together a group of similar spatial practices among distinct inhabitants.

Singularized appellation and particularized appellation tell us as much and more about spatial relations as about the space itself. And this relation is always formed with reference to the collective.

Unnameables

The case of unnameable places shows very well that an appropriation and a qualification of space would be impossible without appellations.

We are dealing here still with new or unusual architectural forms, ones that the authors have sometimes nicknamed by themselves but that do not correspond to any coding recognized or practiced by the inhabitants before they began to reside in the neighborhood. The angles characteristic of the facades[5] and the layout of the street beneath the buildings take the inhabitants right away out of their usual element [*dépaysent d'emblée l'habitant*]. Moreover, the names given by the developer are not always convincing:

- the "gallery" is the main street beneath the buildings;

- the "passageway" is the access corridor on three floor levels;

- the "cove" is the exterior space outlined by the building's curves; and

- the "ramp" is an incline fifty meters long that raises the gallery from zero to seven meters in height.

The inhabitants make attempts to use these words. Some of them succeed in doing so from the start. They have quickly integrated the representations of the neighborhood design plan and sometimes have reduplicated the official appellations. Thus, one female inhabitant likes to name the Arlequin "New Town" each time an innovative feature is described. Others, less knowledgeable about the Arlequin "project," confuse things in a way that the first group would find "glaring": one inhabitant, for example, mistook the "Community Center" for the "Arts Center" (situated in the Malherbe neighborhood). Whatever the case may be, the names for the walkways and crossing areas retain an uncertain character. All the inhabitants questioned misuse the "official" appellations at least once. One very often hears "gallery" for "passageway," "passageway" for "gallery," "galleries" for "the gallery," "pool" for "lake"—so many places whose names put one off track, as they are more or less alien to usage and lived practice. These confusions are of *practically* no importance. And from this point of view, such "slips" are a matter of indifference. Indeed, we are dealing here either with common names (cove, passageway) or proper names (gallery, ramp) whose suitability to the site seems arbitrary or seems to designate a space too large to fit the mood of a well-defined appropriation. In short, these place-names—still fairly alien to one's everyday practices, wherein they are often likened to nonplaces [*non lieux*]—allow of only one kind of social differentiation: that between those who know how to employ these terms perfectly well and those who make mistakes or who are unfamiliar with them. Spaces with nominal definitions hardly occasion anything but differences in one's representations of them.

Other places are genuinely unnameable because they lack any imaginable name. What is one to call the parts of the gallery adjoining the elevator entrance doors when, on the one hand, the gallery itself is not a street, as the inhabitants note, yet not a corridor either, and when, on the other hand, these doors open either directly onto the gallery or onto a half-enclosed space that is quite handy in protecting against the wind but looks quite expletive, like filler? In order to describe this spatial form that is of importance in one's walks (a place for extended, and very often collective, waiting), the periphrases used reemploy what can be designated by use or proximity: "at the bottom of the elevator," "by the mailboxes." And what is one to call those "passageway" nooks that sometimes end in a window and sometimes lead to two or three apartment doors? One tried to pass them off as "social squares" but only those really in the know were able to connect the name to the place beyond the incongruity of the relation. For others, they are "bicycle garages," "garbage disposal areas," "corridors" as opposed to the passageway, "entryways" (but where, then, are the entrances?). Clearly, these unnameable and unappropriable places are given over to accidental and erratic uses—for the children who play there a moment or two, for some adults who periodically make them into the corridor of an apartment whose rooms would be each open lodging, and for "people who put beds in the corridors, in an emergency exit area!"

This difficulty in naming unusual places does not last forever. Certain spots, like the passageways and their nooks, remain an undefined area open to anything. Others, ill defined from the start, become characterized one day by a memorable appropriation. Between the groups that first name places by appropriating them—thereby recognizing one other and being recognized by the quality of the names they have affixed thereupon—and the rest of the inhabitants, a distinction is created through which a differentiated social relation is organized. *The power to name is power over space and at the same timea distinct force within a sociospatial whole.*

Collective Neologisms

Through the use of a created name, the process of appropriation appears to us to be an effort to identify spatial forms. Figure 10 shows a few examples of collective neologisms.

As for what they denote, either these appellations impose a name where there was none before or they substitute themselves for the "official" name, of which the inhabitants are unaware. "Agora" is employed only on maps of the neighborhood and in the notices of the "Video-Gazette"[6]—with a meaning, moreover, that is different, the site for televised meetings most often being the "six-hundred-seat room."

On the other hand, connotations differ from one appellation to

Official name	Nature of the site	Common appellation
(nonexistent)	installation for the morning market in Arlequin	Market Place
(nonexistent)	main approach to the junior high school and the Community Center on the gallery side	junior high school entrance
Agora	fragment of the park paved in bricks and half-enclosed by a low wall	Red Square

Figure 10

another. Although it refers to a country-village-like feature that contradicts the urban setting of this neighborhood, the term *Market Place*
nevertheless was established spontaneously and appears, at the time of
the market's creation, in the narratives of all inhabitants, irrespective
of social group, age, or sex. The reemployment of an ever-so-common
term has therefore marked the site according to its temporary function
and with an indistinct appropriation performed on the scale of the entire neighborhood, as by general consensus.

The appellation "junior high school entrance" does not display the
same lack of differentiation. Quite to the contrary, it generally occurs in
the course of people's trip narratives at the point where an obstacle is
being mentioned. Rarer are the inhabitants who speak of this place as
they approach it "without any problem." Because of this, the denota-
tion may vary beneath one and the same designation. For those whom
it disturbs, the junior high school entrance lies outside and overflows
too far onto the gallery, thus inducing figures of paratopism. That is to
say, the part on the near side of the glass panels, "the inside," the most
outlying part is hardly visitable at all but, rather, imaginable, "with all
those kids, those hooligans hanging around." For the regulars at the
junior high school or in the activity areas, this "junior high school entrance" corresponds more to an entrance than to an exit. The part of
the gallery of concern here is only a terminal point of the "entrance"
within, the hall that penetrates deep into the buildings. Different uses
of one and the same term therefore connote, from the collective point

of view, either a differentiation via rejection or an identification with groups that are able to "enter the junior high school." As one inhabitant says, "It's open. Everyone can go there. We have the right, huh?" She enters the junior high school easily and even makes use of it from one end to the other as a crossing area; but "I . . . I don't think that just any woman would get the idea in her head to do it . . . ," she had said right beforehand.

Less polysemous, and used in a more restricted manner, is the appellation "Red Square." Some inhabitants of the neighborhood employ the term as a matter of course, marking by this common word a shared sense of belonging. Greater actors. or greater participants, to them none of the important events in the life of the neighborhood is alien. They know the history of the appellation, which recalls a stormy meeting, about work being done in the park, that took place on this small square between some inhabitants, "accompanied" by a political group, and the landscaper. The color of the material became associated with the color of the event upon the background of a well-known word-form (Moscow), in one of those syncretisms of which parallel languages hold the secret. This is also the case with languages of initiates, which other inhabitants speak only with care. Thus, twice do the interviews reveal the use of the term in a metalinguistic comment clause: "what is called the Red Square," "the little square [. . .] that is named the Red Square." The evocation of equivalencies and the discrepancy between speech proper and the appellations cited stem either from hesitations (like the one of the female inhabitant who knows the "park affair," as it is seen later on, but has not made the connection, and who says, "Yes . . . I don't know, because of the concrete, maybe. Maybe it's dangerous for the kids.") or from an effect of ironic distancing expressed by inhabitants who are quite up to speed about the "park story" and who, in a knowing tone, express astonishment that the appellation has become so matter of course.

Starting from nameless places or places of unknown name, the apposition of a term allows a noteworthy appropriation of these places at the same time that it permits the manifestation of an identification process for the social group that first played with language's relation to the space in question. While certain collective neologisms spread to a whole neighborhood and become elements for identification, others, more restrictive in character or even jealously guarded by those who employ them, have a strong connotation of belonging to this or that group or social subgroup. The definition of these social subgroups or aggregates is not given only in terms of "socioprofessional categories." It is a matter more concretely of a self-definition through which the aggregate distinguishes itself by recognizing itself in a sociospatial practice of its own. We have seen, through prior examples, how important can be an act of naming that informs a site. Such a naming makes the site known, under one and the same qualification, to all those who employ it and who thus recognize themselves in this identical usage.

It is often difficult to understand the meaning of the neologisms used by groups of inhabitants. Indeed, the more closed and typical the group is, the more hermetic is its language. One can detect in groups of children the appearance and rapid disappearance of neologisms that exist for the time of one game. When the child recounts the game to an adult (and to the sociologist who questions him), he no longer tells what quality the cement tube had for the group (house? airplane? ship?, etc.). He decodes it by saying, "stuff . . . thingamajigs to have fun in." Such mischievous concealment prevents knowledge of the concrete qualifiers lived within the game. This appropriation set aside by private appellations equally operates among adults. When one inhabitant says he has taken a walk over "this sort of place in which there are bricks" and when others, either activity organizers or "active" inhabitants, call a meeting "on Red Square," it is a matter of the same site, which is no more one person's property than that of the others. However, from the standpoint of the lived activity, it is not the same place. It has, straight off, a particular qualification, depending on whether this or that group fashions it in its own manner.

First Sketch of the Status of Appropriation on the Basis of Namings

The naming process yields an initial, approximative idea of the nature of appropriation. In naming everyday places in such and such a way, the inhabitants are concretely expressing the fact that they belong to some groups or collective aggregates. What is more, it is the social quality of every apprehension of space that hangs over the selection of this or that appellation. *Appropriation does not bear, first of all, on space but, rather, on such and such a relationship between a form of sociability and space.*

One and the same space can be designated by different codes: simple codes of naming for the moment, but ones about which we have already had a hint that they signify ways of being. Certain times, appropriation by a group may coincide with a veritable social ownership of a coded site. Such is the case with all gang hideouts. Nonetheless, over the entire public space of the neighborhood, no place has been observed, or has been described to us by any of the inhabitants questioned, as remaining exclusive property on a permanent basis. The junior high school entrance, which is avoided by certain inhabitants, is not always "occupied" by the young. The school courtyards that are impassible at recess time become a perfectly calm crossing area at other moments of the day. While certain places are strongly marked by the coding of a few subgroups and lead others to avoid them, one can nevertheless grasp that, beyond the sociospatial relation involved, *appropriation basically is a matter of time.* It is in time that a group manifests or does not manifest its existence and that it occupies a determinate public space at the same time as everyone else, but in a privileged way, or, on the contrary, at a specific moment.

It may be noted, moreover, that, in going from the sites most commonly frequented by all sorts of groups that tend to be indistinguishable to sites specified by a private, even secret, name that marks the exclusive relation of certain subgroups to these places, appropriation bears less and less on the given, reproduced space and more and more on the re-created space, in accordance with a specific time. It is the regulatory system of namings that indicates what type of social relation to space is at issue. Naming is the most obvious information the inhabitants set in opposition to the space as it is built.

A First Rule of the Code of Appropriation would thus state:

> *The collective nature of the frequentation of a space is inseparable from the process of naming that characterizes that space.*

TERRITORIAL APPEARANCE

In their narratives, the inhabitants mention spaces that, for them, do not change their social quality. These would be sites that are always well bounded. One could therefore draw up a synchronic map of the socio-spatial allotments inscribed upon the neighborhood and thus see *territories* appear. And yet, beyond the fact that the map would constantly be changing, one would not know from it in what way these territories are constituted, nor would one be able to predict the likelihood of permanent occupation by this or that group over such and such a privately set-aside space. As we know, territories are not, practically speaking, permanently occupied in the same manner; the figure of the metathesis of quality has helped to demonstrate this point.

For the inhabitant who speaks of or suggests recognition of such a "territoriality," his relation to the space is always a negative one. If the limits seem to him so precise, that is because he delineates them through his acts of avoidance. The site under consideration is doubly "ill lived": *sensed in a harmful way and, in addition, often seen, not traveled through.* The permanency of the occupation then felt by the inhabitant does not stem from his practical experience of the space but, rather, from the pure representation he makes of the spatial relations practiced by others. These territories, which are apparently so enclosed, are occupied by groups of inhabitants. Most often cited are "the young," "the children," "the North Africans" (and, within this pseudogroup, the "Tunisians" are distinguished from the "Algerians," and vice versa). Also mentioned are "those from the activity areas," "those who know how to talk," and "the Video-Gazette." Still other ways of occupying sites are manifested: "by the dogs" that have covered certain grassy areas with their messes and "by the cars" that must be walked around when they are parked. And, although they occupy space only in an episodic sort of way, bicycles and mopeds always appear as menacing features in the walking narratives.

The extension of the "occupant" category to other interveners than "people" allows one to suppose how imprecise is the definition of "occupation." In the act of sensing a counterappropriation, the delimitation and supposition of territorial permanency matter much more than the precise identification of the occupying agency [*l'instance occupante*]. Groups that are apparently well encompassed by an appellation meant to define them do not necessarily correspond to any reality. Such is the case with the group called "North African," which appears as such only for those who do not belong to it; the aggregate known as "Video-Gazette," to which a particular power is attributed;[7] or "children" and "young people." Heading in this direction, let us cite the following expressions:

> In the market, there are too many children coming out of school. And as the school is next to the market, they all come to steal something.

> I even find that there are never many children at number 130. They play in the gallery or in the park.

> You see, there are people who hang around all day in the passageways. Some of them piss in the passageway.

> The Community Center, it brings in lots of things. It brings in . . . , there are always young people.

> No, I didn't go into the Community Center, because . . . it seems to me that you especially see young people in there.

At its outer reaches, "the group" extends to all other people beside oneself. This is quite clearly apparent in several of the interviews: it is that one can inhabit one's lodgings, "despite" the whole New Town, or that the whole neighborhood finds itself incorporated into a sort of phantasm of the threatening collective, or that all the other inhabitants would be represented as mineralized, part of an overall landscape one only grazes against:

> [At number 50,] there are some people concentrated around there and garbage cans lying around. When I can, I keep clear; unless, that is, I go on the road.

> People watch us from the bistro. Their expressions are indifferent, rather hostile. Or maybe it is the shape of their faces that bothers me?

Generally speaking, the group is first of all "the others" who are distinguished and identified only through vague names, by one or two determinants. Here is a particularly evocative example in which a site's state of being-rejected reduces recognition of hostile collective forces to some simple topical assignments:

For all the good there is that the Community Center is located in the middle of the gallery, people don't find it very easy to go in there. *One hasn't been taught to speak; one has only been taught to listen.* So, it's always the same. The other day, a lady talked so well during the meeting that no one said anything afterward.

For that inhabitant, this not easily accessible site would be the property of a group that is doubly determined—namely, by the fact of being at the Community Center and by the privilege of their power of speech. Beyond the character of destinal facticity well underscored in the expression, for which we grant our respect, the state of passive fixedness is confirmed by the phrase that follows: "it's always the same." One's way of being in space passes on one's wholly negative way of being with the other. The failure of appropriation is attributed in the end to a prohibitive counterappropriation in the face of which the inhabitant identifies herself with a still imprecise "one" whose identity is but that of being situated outside the occupied site. Nothing is more vague than this community of rejects that does not recognize itself in itself but is to be inferred simply along a Manichaean dividing line. A general judgment that arises soon after the first quotation confirms this point:

> The New Town belongs to a category . . . to *one* category of inhabitants, that's all! The others feel themselves housed, that's all!

Once again, we see the partial phenomenon erected into a symbol of everything. The lack of a precise definition of the "others" considered as a group makes possible the unlimited extension of the power of appropriation that is ascribed to them. It suffices to compare such a way of apprehending this site called *Community Center* to the way a regular does so in order for us to understand how much the closure of territorial limits and the permanency of such and such a social quality are manifestly obvious only for the person who feels excluded. The inhabitant deemed to be a regular at the site and belonging to the group of the "others" will not necessarily have the same opinion, nor will he carry out the expected conduct. He can be excluded at a certain moment or not feel himself to be a member of one and the same occupying group. He will say:

> Sometimes, when passing by, I cast a glance at the half-opened door to the six-hundred-seat room to see if there is another meeting.

Or:

> I pass by the Community Center because there is always something to see.
> Even without any specific purpose, I really like to pass by there . . . to try to
> better integrate myself.

Confronted with the modalities of occupants' lived experience of a
site, definition of a permanent territory seems quite fictive. It holds but
one interest for us: it brings to light the tensions centered on impossible-
to-achieve or difficult appropriations, which point to the minimum constituent element of the code of appropriation:

Second Rule of the Code of Appropriation:

> *The characterization of the inhabited space in terms of fixed territoriality is but
> the apparent effect of the assignment to a site of the group one has difficulty
> defining.*

TERRITORIAL FLUIDITIES

Is territoriality a fiction? Do there exist only counterappropriations? No
doubt, the process of rigidification of a territory corresponds to one's
inability to identify the lived way in which a group occupies this space.
It stands in for a definition of the occupying unit. But an inhabitant's
domain of appropriation does not have the nature of a no-man's-land:[8]
a hollowed-out constitution delineated by postings of "filled-in" sites.
A positive appropriation will come to light if the space is seized not as
appropriated pieces of a puzzle but, rather, as the field that has allowed
and does allow *the appropriable*. It is not to be assessed in terms of a
locating of immutable and closed territories or of a listing of "properties" but, rather, on the basis of the nature of the movement through
which the inhabitant walks with ease or uneasiness, feeling "at home,"
in some sort of way, or "extradited," in the mode of collective complicit
arrangements or in the mode of feeling alien.

On the elementary level as much as on the level of organization,
walking figures already gave us a glimpse of some interesting indices.
Certain figures may be placed under the heading of a tendency to maintain one's appropriation. Here, we are talking about two redundant

processes (metabole and hyperbole)[9] and symmetry. Other figures signal one's search for appropriation. Included here are anaphora, which lays siege; digression, which forgets; and simple paratopisms, which create some paths in order to avoid other ones. It really was one's encounter with alien appropriations or counterappropriations that provoked peritopisms and paratopisms. Finally, synecdoche allows one to see quite well what kind of economy organizes appropriation and how the lived parts are, to an excessive degree, given therein in order to stand for the totality.

Appropriation is a dynamic process. As such, it shakes up spatial permanencies. Depending on the directions of one's walks, territories neither finish nor begin in the same spot. Thus does one see one's being domiciled dissociated from the notion of lodging; the former undergoes expansion or contraction—movements designated *diastole* and *systole* in the analysis of the figure of dissymmetry.[10] The feeling of being "at home" glides from one place to another and can extend quite far, indeed, through a series of imperceptible gradations—even when it is embodied only in those slippers one is permitted to wear under the gallery, where the "public sphere" still seems to tolerate the "domestic" one. In order to do one's shopping, a grandmother from the neighborhood says,

> You don't have to take an umbrella and you can go down in your slippers; with this gallery, you're near everything. You even see women in dressing gowns.

Conversely, where one is domiciled can be reduced to an area smaller than one's own lodging. Then, even on the interior staircases, even in one's living room,

> where there are the little ones, a twelve-year-old sister who is jealous of the other sister, the brother who does karate, the father who yells, the mother who is preparing the meal, with the television on top of that . . . you always find yourself outside.

The sole refuge, the only place where one feels at home, becomes one's bedroom.

Another breakdown in these territories (which we had thought of as frozen in place but which start to dissolve and become metamorphosed in climatic and chronometric time) is to be found once again in the figure of the metathesis of quality.[11] To the examples already cited in this regard, let us add some other, quite eloquent ones: the extended occupation of the center of the gallery during the summer months by inhabitants from the south (especially North Africans); the takeover of this same site, on Wednesday and Saturday afternoons,[12] by groups of noisy, nimble children (on roller skates and miscellaneous vehicles). Following a group of adolescents with nothing to do, one sees the territories change when night falls. From territories for hanging out that are clearly bounded during the day (junior high school entrance, two-wheel-vehicle repair shop, mezzanine at number 50), one passes, at night, to a diffuse and mobile territoriality. With this last example, we have still another dimension of appropriation, which upsets one's spatial prejudices. By day, small youth gangs *are seen,* and their uproar, if any, makes itself heard only intermittently above the clamor of daytime comings and goings. At night, most of the inhabitants sense the irruptive presence of these gangs only through their *hearing.* The territory suddenly becomes diffuse and takes on an extension incommensurable with any spatial judgment that could strictly be connected with their visual faculty. The same thing applies for unaccustomed cooking odors (grilled lamb and fish) that may waft from some unassuming balcony. These odors exhale, toward all the upper and surrounding apartments, the heightened presence of an alien group whose members are nevertheless spread out spatially.

> It's a specific odor . . . though it is summer. I think that the smell of spices comes from number 50.

> It smells like . . . how to describe it? It smells like the kind of cooking I don't do.

These territorial fluidities reveal already a first feature of the dialectical nature of appropriation processes. Anything that one would look for in terms of spatial division and permanent states would mislead us. Even the notion of a state of ease or of uneasiness merely transcribes momentarily and individually what has been, or will be, movement and a project of differentiation. When one inhabitant walks everywhere with ease and yet does not feel at all at home in the neighborhood and flees as soon as he can, whereas another inhabitant feels at ease only in a tiny territory leading up to her apartment and yet prepares a tenacious project of conquering the rest of the neighborhood (a project which, a year later, we know to have been successful), the difference in the quality of the appropriation is beyond doubt. The first person will always be an individual skirting the social as well as the spatial, without anything more. The second will not necessarily succeed in appropriating for herself the entire space, but she will live her appropriation in relation to all other appropriations, now or in the future; through this movement, she will designate the group to which she belongs.

Two phenomena that are temporal in nature shatter the bounds of territories seized in their spatial permanencies. They render the strictly spatial determinant of the code of appropriation unsuitable as an explanation of this code.[13] It is through *change* that territories appear and disappear and that two territories, which should be merged in space, do not coincide, for one's walks give them a specificity that depends on intention and orientation. It is via *anticipation* that appropriation overflows the territory's spatial forms, that it makes itself heard or felt before it is seen, and finally that, beyond space, it bears on time and on the possible.

Third Rule of the Code of Appropriation:

Movements of appropriation assume, as their condition of possibility, the surpassing of purely spatial determinants that express social relations only in the form of simple "states of affairs."

Such movements imply a dynamic that is apprehended in time.

DIFFERENTIATING APPROPRIATIONS

From the foregoing, we can retain two paradoxical remarks about territory. On the one hand, every collective movement of appropriation stands out thanks to territoriality—therefore, thanks to the identification of a space endowed with qualitative unity, if not with almost assignable limits. On the other hand, nothing can be understood about collective appropriation if one does not seek to know, via individual everyday actions (we have chosen walks under this heading), how qualitative differences are constituted.

Synchronically speaking, the state of a collective housing complex is therefore to be described as an organization of appropriations that are interconnected and opposed to one another through their specificity. Diachronically speaking, movements of appropriation enter into dialectical relation. Every identification of another appropriation produces a differentiation. And every differentiation posits the specificity of an appropriation in which the inhabitants who are operators of difference are identified.

What about the notion of territory, then? It becomes the field of assignment (from the synchronic point of view) around which move (diachronically speaking) the figures of a walking rhetoric that is productive of territorial appearances.

In following the walks taken in everyday life, one never notices this territorial "system." The representation of the whole reconstructs it, yielding for us a "state" of this system that is never lived. On the other hand, the writing of one's walks expresses quite well indifferent skirting, unpleasant encounters with oppositions and exclusions, and the search for sites that are favorable or deemed appropriable.

From this point of view and depending on the time, the counterappropriation that arises through the walk modulates, in proportion to its strength, the quality of the competing appropriation. Over a spatial whole given as a unit of habitats, the state of reciprocity in which all possible appropriations are situated displays no homogeneity. Certain sites are appropriated neither in unity nor in opposition but, rather, in dispersion. Thus, walks in the park encounter only weak counterappropriations. The park, a site for daydreaming, or a site for one's eyes, summons everyone in an undifferentiated way. Individuals or small groups always *see one another* from a distance; avoidance is easy to prearrange mutually, and one can believe oneself to be alone there.[14] Whence such expressions as the following concerning the park:

It's looking at people from behind.

It's being able to watch over the children from the mounds, because from here you have the best view.

It's the pleasure of going outside, on the grass, where you can even get a suntan without knowing you're being watched.

narratives of one's walks, a concomitance between the manifest force of an appropriation and the memory of an event. Appropriations persist all the more when the irruptive force of the event has created a greater impression.

One question posed to the inhabitants was aimed at knowing what they had felt to be events in the neighborhood since their arrival. Now here, two classes of events appear: on the one hand, more or less foreseeable changes in the collective space, the best example of which is the creation of the market, but also the openings of various sectors of activity or consumption (library, self-service restaurant); on the other hand, unforeseeable accidents that happened to individuals or groups, like the "park affair" (Red Square), the children's carnival, collective celebrations (Bastille Day, stairwell or floor meetings), fights or violent conflicts whose nature is well encapsulated in the expression of one female inhabitant: "It's not every day that there are things like that." The varieties of events are to be distinguished first of all by the duration of the event. The creation of the market was an event that lasted five or six months; the diffuse force of its impact and its nature, which was judged to be pleasant by all, authorize a collective appropriation on the scale of the entire neighborhood. Ways of inhabiting space change smoothly through the fashioning of a common usage deemed suitable to all. "The market opened Saturday," one female inhabitant recounts,

> and I find that it's good, really good. The first few days, there were some musicians. . . . Did you see them? I sensed something intimate. There are many people who know each other. Afterward, you get used to it.

By way of contrast, the carnival and the fights, though of inverse moral value, are both of short duration. And yet their strains or their din have a lastingly resounding effect upon the way one conducts oneself at such and such a moment, in this or that place, or opposite one or another subgroup. A child thus exclaims:

> There was the carnival! There was the Archi brass band. I really like brass bands. And then a big dragon; that was neat. Everyone was in disguise. [. . .] I knew that the market was going to happen, though I didn't know about the carnival.

One inhabitant living near the café says:

> For a while, it was a disaster. One night there was a fight. Everything was
> broken! I was listening; I got goose bumps because of it. Yet, I was up above,
> huh? . . . Now, you can no longer go to this bar. There's practically nothing but
> Algerians.

The marking of the appropriation or of the counterappropriation proves
in that case to be much stronger and more memorable. The recognition
of the identity of the subgroup authoring the event or the difference
tends to be heightened, and to persist longer, as one sees when relating
the tracings of one's walks to the narrative of events.[15]

Between events that include an expected change and irruptive events,
the synecdoches are reversed. Taking on a form of appropriation that
affects the neighborhood as a whole, the market in fact alters only a part
of the space and the practice of a quite particular moment of everyday
life. Having arisen in some corner of the neighborhood, fights acted out
and lived out by a small number of inhabitants tend to heighten the differentiations among groups and to mark in a lasting and memorable
way one's relation to this space or to that group; *each time* one's path
approaches the site, one recognizes the group. Morphogeneses differ in
their effect. Certain events first alter space set aside for public use; others first alter one's way of being in the space. Appropriations and counterappropriations stand out in a much stronger and more differentiating
way in the second case.

"Eventfulness" is an operator of difference that shakes up spatial appearances because it contrasts the wholly singular marking of a time of
its own with the duration of the everyday. Even more than that, events
of a similar nature (moped treks, the passing by of "gangs," altercations
as well as neighborhood celebrations) do not resound in the same way
in all cases and do not enter with equal importance into the lived experience of one's habitat. Some groups of inhabitants attempt to attenu-
ate the irruptive features of the event, to gloss over the effect of a break.
The style of their narrative abounds in incidental clauses of the following type: "that happens so often" or "it hardly surprises people any-
more." Alone, two or three events will seem inordinate, inconceivable.
Other inhabitants, by way of contrast, look for anything that shatters

the commonly held image of the living spaces in the neighborhood and anything that builds up a tension therein. All sorts of events then become for them levers for difference.

Eventfulness is creative of differentiation under several headings. Each time an event occurs, a difference is brought into play (until the point of rupture) via the tension it generates among ways of homogenizing time, ways of repeating the space in one's memory habits, and ways of shaking up spatial repetition and chronometry through the enhancement of irruptive moments, through the hyperbole of the memory of *one time*. Eventfulness differentiates, within a spatial whole, via the synecdoche of fragments that are rendered exceptionally singular and that will never again be as they were before and, for a long time, never anything other than the suddenly marked site. The third difference is the collective effect of the first two. Depending on the strength of the impression and the nature of the interpretation of the event, some groups of inhabitants differentiate themselves from other groups through an identification in their same treatment of what is memorable; they have similar ways of fashioning the event.

Fifth Rule of the Code of Appropriation:

The forces of appropriations and counterappropriations vary in direct proportion to the impact and persistence of the marking performed by the eventful memory.

Whence a twofold consequence regarding the various ways of understanding the process of differentiation in everyday life. Assuming that the code of appropriation could be classified as a system, it would not be a closed system in which the contiguities between identified elements would persist in terms of the permanency of the differences involved but, rather, a system open to change, and even to disturbances of unforeseeable effect. A second consequence follows: only if we take into account the unforeseen eventualities brought about by nonchronometric time can we clarify the nature of the dialectical movement through which appropriations and counterappropriations articulate lived collective relations—in other words, in what sense this movement, as retention of the other as other in the same, is *differance*.[16]

Appropriation via Dislocation [*Non-lieu*]

After the reversal of the hegemony of simultaneity and of purely spatial determinants that is performed through the manifestation of the force of time and of memory, there subsists an ultimate instantiated principle, one that is quite active in the appropriations recounted to us by the inhabitants. Present in the processes of heightening, of anticipation, and of synecdoche, it never is observed directly from the site [*lieu*] itself but, rather, from its negation. The "topos" in which it is willingly incorporated is the discourse that circulates among the inhabitants, and rather through snatches than in an organized manner. Beyond synecdoche, the figures it prefers are the metathesis of quality, hyperbole, staggered polysemy, anaphora, and paralipsis.

This instantiated principle, which is imaginary in nature, may be detected first of all in the *rumor*, most often disturbing in nature, that envelops this or that site. It is always connoted by a certain dose of fascination, even when one wants to treat hearsay disdainfully. Several inhabitants thus begin by saying that the rumors are not to be believed. Nevertheless, they dread trips at night, by prudence on their part or because of a lack of self-assurance in case some unfortunate and unforeseen thing might happen; it is the gallery as a whole that becomes a "fearful" place, to use the expression of one female inhabitant. Other inhabitants alter or cancel their trips solely on the basis of what they have heard others recount.

> I was haunted by this return trip. At night, the galleries, it's like a labyrinth. A lot of things have been said: the gangs, the attacks, the people you wouldn't want to associate with. Also, I refuse a bit to see people, since I fear that they would scare me with their gossip.

In the exemplary case of staggered polysemy,[17] one sees the elevator become loaded up with one signification after another. Behind or at the end of these significations, imaginary extensions borne by rumors unfailingly appear.

> People recount a lot of things about the elevators. . . . It's true that that encourages a lot of things.

One no longer knows, in the end, whether the series is ordered by the mood of the imaginary or terminates, as if accidentally, with imaginable evocations of things to come. However, the ease with which images drawn from bestiaries or science fiction are superimposed upon all the significations of restriction, tension, and worried collusions and encompass them leads one to think that these significations are quite often only the instrumental delegates for an unavowable imaginary expression. It is a matter less of a counterappropriation than of an appropriation in which social differences are easily confused and which, taking the detour into the imaginary, "derealizes" the merely spatial dimension of the site. That elevator cab suspended at the end of a cable and making its destiny-led hazardous voyage no longer encloses anything but the disturbing, the threatening, and the fatal. Thus:

> People are monstrously scared of the doors; they believe it's a vise that is going to crush them. You're trapped like wild animals there; you know: Bam!

Everyday observation shows that, inside the elevator, verbal exchanges and dramatic evocations are set into gear on the basis of *noises*. Some of the elevators do indeed emit metallic scraping sounds worthy of a Scottish castle: "an infernal noise heralds its arrival." Jokes about exorcism or exclamations verging on panic inaugurate the process of communication and explicit collective appropriation in which memory of rumors is mixed with metallic rumblings. All the passengers sink into the same sense of imminent catastrophe. But the most dramatic images arise with the *halt of the noise,* at the point where one no longer knows whether one is moving or if one is stuck: "you no longer hear anything; for me, it's the start-up of the gas chamber." The site is then completely cut off from the environment and anything becomes possible, provided that it would be the worst.

Thus, certain spaces that are lived in a mode impregnated with the imaginary tend to lose their nature as a "site" inserted into a laid-out and developed spatiogeometric context. The process stems from the effect of an excessive division owing to synecdoche and from the effect of a derealization of the representations and recollections of *visible* space. What is heard, whether collective rumor or disturbing noise, covers over and deconstructs the visual realm, which ordinarily is predominant.

One no longer sees the elevator, or the café, or the mezzanine where the development plan has situated them; imaginary instantiated principles metamorphose their reference to the situation.

Such an appropriation via dislocation is always inserted into the complex web of pedestrian movement, which follows the rhythm of singular events. A sequential attempt to take one's bearings by distinguishing spatiotemporal fragments one by one would never allow such an appropriation to be seen. In this sense, the abrupt silence of the elevator is particularly dramatic, for the preceding occurrence of the disturbing noise had already absorbed the entire lived experience of the atmosphere.

The dislocation is often of what is heard, noises or words. And yet one already has a presentiment of other varieties of atopic configuration—in the sense that the geometrically constructed space collapses—in various walking figures.

First of all, there is the metamorphosis of spatial determinants in hyperbole.[18] The dreamlike appropriation of a "site" makes it lose its "real" spatial context and tends to give it out as the totality, presented under the heading of a preeminent quality. Thus, the "mound" does not correspond to a part of the park as the latter was laid out; it recovers and symbolizes the dreamlike quality belonging to the park. Through an imaginary evocation, the staircase inside the apartment derealizes one's lodging and removes it from the context of the high-density housing complex: "With this staircase, you'd think you were going back into a small private home." These types of appropriation are hardly based on oppositions. Rather, they draw their strength within the confused cathexis of reproduced attitudes and image patterns: the solitary dreamer; one's desire for a single-unit home. Eminently singular, such a dislocation, such a nonplace is never totally dissociated from the "commonplace" or from what is named the *collective imaginary*.

In anaphora and paralipsis,[19] figures that may be compared by the presence within each of fascination and that write en route a prudent besieging of a site or its delayed avoidance, dislocation corresponds to what could happen. The increased force of attraction imaginarily projected into a site that thereby becomes fascinating comes to reinforce one's persistent imagining of possibilities, and one thereby finds one has a hard time diverting one's steps. Beyond de facto differentiation (being rejected), these figures signify delayed identification, as well. This is what one assumes about alien appropriation, about which one cannot make oneself indifferent. That is the nature of the fascination one encounters in one's walks. Frequenting the bordering areas or lingering around there is equivalent to sketching out already the projected appropriation.

Indeed, the imaginary component in the force that moves appropriation gives one last dimension to the signification of the processes of asyndeton and synecdoche. The division and the deformation of the laid-out and developed space are accompanied by a *derealization* of the relation between sites and the overall spatial context. The intention of this clearly and distinctly composed "reality," which presupposes territorial homogeneity, is to situate every everyday practice within the context of the geographic whole. Such referencing is put in check by the phenomena of rupture, delay, anticipation, and impregnation by the imaginary. The dialectic of appropriations and counterappropriations refers to the lived spatiotemporal situation and not to spatiogeometric representation, which this dialectic returns to its originary abstractness.

Sixth Rule of the Code of Appropriation:

> *The process of everyday appropriation of a built-up and developed space implies a derealization of this space. Collective ways of being in space do not necessarily privilege the visual order, but also that of the audible, of the tangible, and of the imaginable, all three of these instantiated principles being very active in this deconstruction.*

CONCLUSION IN THE FORM OF A BIFURCATION

Obsolescence of the Notion of Appropriation and Splitting of the Signification of the Code of Appropriation

The code of appropriation is very much the result of a dialectical movement. This dynamism, whose nature had earlier called for further clarifications,[20] is a *force of negation*, of subversion of what are taken to be self-evident territorial facts. The essence of collective life in an urban setting is to be defined not only through the lived experience of oppositions of one social group to another, but also by *a constant tension between constructed spatiality handed over for use and the rhetorical deconstruction of this space, which is done in favor of the expression of styles of inhabiting.* Nothing is ever definitively settled or decided in such a play of oppositions. Reproduced by the dominant representations of functional use, territorial appearance resists; the inhabitants enunciate it in terms of having, of ownership, of spatial boundaries, of territorial solidity. This resistance is incorporated into all the effects of encoding that tend to have some permanency. The effects of decoding, or of counterappropriation, each time express, in their movement of negation, the reality of an ever renewed dynamic. In other words, one day or another, the apparent appropriation of territory is denied, but, in other respects, it is absorbed and preserved[21] in order to be used in some new spatiotemporal configuration. Also, the code of appropriation concerns just as much the social organization as the disorganization of space. It can serve two readings.

The term *code* therefore takes on two significations. On the one hand, the play of encodings and decodings gives itself out to be a system of explanation of collective life over a space that has become the stake in a conflictual affirmation of groups and social aggregates. Yet we are dealing here with a *code of effects,* of signs of differentiation and identification. For, on the other hand, there exists a *rhetorical code,* or metacode, which is for us the condition of possibility for the other one. The moments of its emergence form a discrete sequence that reduplicates the succession of codings and decodings carried out in appropriated sites. This repeated effort of destructuration—which is possible one day or another—of every coded and apparently appropriable space undoubtedly becomes apparent only through careful modal analysis.

In conformity with this perspective and despite the systematic appearance of a statement of "rules," the sequence of the six noteworthy forms of appropriation that have been presented has nothing of an enumeration of explanatory laws about it. If such were the case, the exposition would be but a feeble contribution to the problematic of social codes, which has, moreover, already been skillfully developed in the field of contemporary scientific knowledge. Its sole interest would then be to

4

The Body of Inhabitant Expression

> To return to things themselves is to return to that world
> which precedes knowledge, of which knowledge always
> *speaks,* and in relation to which every scientific schema-
> tization is an abstract and derivative sign-language, as is
> geography in relation to the countryside in which we have
> learnt beforehand what a forest, a prairie, or a river is.
>
> —Maurice Merleau-Ponty, *Phenomenology of Perception*

THE STUDY OF INHABITANT RHETORIC succeeds all too well. The
steps had left traces, stigmata, which permitted the excavation and ex-
humation of something expressed that is obscure and yet marked by
everydayness. As if it were some unknown town—which is here a metaphorical town, the subtext of built-up appearances—here the coherent organization of pedestrian tracks[1] that will satisfy our demand for
knowledge has been brought to light.

Is it not to be regretted that, by retracing too well its structure, by
classifying too well its figures, the act of structuration—the movement
of configuration—has faded away and now escapes us? The geography
of our travels dulls the taste for landscapes we nevertheless *inhabit.* Is
inhabitant expression never but a play of effects, of marks affixed upon
the space? Or will one be able to tell how these steps had a body, how
they signed simply a presence in space capable of a broader-based expressiveness that is also pregnant with other powers?

Already, we had noted a stylistic homology between the narratives
recounted by the inhabitants and their spatial practices. Do not narrative style and ambulatory style emanate from a more encompassing style

of being that engages and commits the whole of our experience of the everyday world? And is not this experience rooted in a lived immediacy, of which we have related only its winding trajectories?

The question of the body of expression invites one to rediscover the experience of the body before knowledge,[2] before the mediation of relations of signification. We shall "reawaken" this experience of the world by rereading the inhabitants' narratives in another manner. The pregnancy of their everyday atmospheres and the immediacies of their sensorimotor activity will be our Ariadne's thread.

CLIMATIC PREGNANCY

What is one to name this set of impressions that surround the lived instant? "Climate," "ambiance," "atmosphere"? The first designation has a meteorological ring to it. The second conjures up too much the idea of some artificially-produced contrivance ("creating an ambiance," "mood music" [*musique d'ambiance*]). The third wavers between the meaning given to it in gaseous physics, Arletty's memorable intonations in *Hôtel du Nord,* and the indulgent smile of knowing arrogance, persuaded that such an object is ungraspable, unclassifiable, psychologically too complex, and sociologically too trifling.

We shall be less attached to words[3] than to the reality they surround, each one in its own way. Indeed, the climate of this or that moment of everyday life always takes on a capital importance for the inhabitants we have questioned. Not easily identifiable, it is quite appropriately felt through an immediate sensory experience. Abortive expressions, imprecise periphrases, suspension points: in language, climate is not separated from its preperceptual characters. Yet how many avoidances, how many redundancies are there in one's walks; how many stops and stays are explained by the pregnancy of a site's atmosphere.[4] How does one avoid for long a site that is nevertheless deserted, where the striking event that has marked it no longer has timely relevance? Why persist in besieging a site into which one cannot really penetrate? Is the obstinate repetition of certain trips just a constant treading over the same ground, when weather and light are always changing, be they ever so slightly? Like

African music, which is heard rising up on hot summer nights and wakes up the inhabitants of one "cove" around midnight, often exacerbates feelings of expropriation or injury (*injuria*, in the sense of ethnic illegality). But for certain inhabitants, an indulgent sense of satisfaction that "there's a party" is awakened at the same time. And perhaps those people are lulled back to sleep with dreams of an unavowed exoticism.

Moreover, collective presences can by themselves alone create characteristic climates. Boisterous invasion or teeming games when the last school bell of the day rings, jostlings and crowdings at the foot of the elevators at these same times, lascivious or bustling times in the market area—these are so many different atmospheres that the auditory and the visual, sometimes the tactile, and more rarely the olfactory senses make one feel and that can bring on opposing kinds of conduct: pursuit or flight.

This boils down to saying that the extreme diversity in the nature of atmospheres and in the way in which they alter the style of one's walks calls for an inexhaustible number of descriptions. Climatic and pathic phenomena seem therefore to have become diversified into a limitless pluralism. And yet, climates and atmospheres are continually instructive, in that they render explicit and explain the qualitative resonance of everyday lived experiences. The same goes for atmospheres that are as peaceful and dull as they are unsayable, those that are unremarkable, those that are repetitive and wherein one day looks like another, and those that one inhabitant labels "gray days [*griseurs*]." And such a gray day also deforms and anamorphoses, as through a mirror whose silvering has crumbled away, the ephemeral monumentality of housing spaces.

Here, then, we have a *first form of derealization* of the built world as it is handed over for use. Here it is that, over the days one lives one's life, an unmeasured separation redistributes the produced space. One term returns over and over again in the interviews, as if it would be the main criterion by which the various atmospheres are to be differentiated from one another: *the inhabitable*, which is defined by the possibility of dwelling, of coming to a stop. *Through the climates of everyday life, inhabiting and walking take on the same lived meaning.* There are walks that inhabit certain sites and other ones that do not inhabit them. The sole difference is this: one must really carry out trips directed by the demands of usage. But as one female inhabitant says, those sites one walks alongside (rather than traverses, for everything slips into indifference, if not into a precipitous effort to be finished with them as quickly as possible) "cannot be called spots." A "spot" would be, in this sense, a site that is appropriable under the sky of an inhabitable atmosphere, that is to say, a site in which one *could* stop. Visiting is possible there; there, one walks willingly.

The climatic allows one to understand how walking and inhabiting refer to each other. Indeed, it envelops every moment of everyday life and is its sky, its horizon. At the same time, it shows how styles of being, styles of inhabiting and walking, are qualified within a habitat-space. It is an *impression,* one might say, in both senses of the term: what is felt and what is imprinted.[12] It encompasses in this way both the acted and the suffered, the reading and writing of one's walks, the static presence of the architectural and the deformation of this built world. The still too brief examination we have been carrying out of this climatic condition allows one to discover two hitherto neglected dimensions: that of dwelling, of stopping, and of pausing, on the one hand, and that of motor movements, on the other.

SENSORIAL HYPERBOLES AND ANTICIPATIONS

Thus, all that seemed structural in rhetorical analysis begins to take on bodily shape in a movement of structuration: the shaping of the inhabited world on the basis of climatic quality. From this point of view, the dichotomies between given (built) and lived, between acted and suffered, between the world of objects and that of subjects, my presence and that of others find themselves shaken up and tend to become like each other. It would be wise, therefore, to find out on what common ground such nonexclusive disjunctions are possible. But first, we may ask, how do these compenetrations occur, how are these mutual assimilations organized, and how are they linked together?

The inhabitant's narratives allow it be understood that there exists a sort of excess of sensory experience. Such excess was condemned by the academic "psychology of faculties" because, from the standpoint of rational knowledge, each sense must remain in its proper receptive place and be, under the command of perception, free from error. But the old textbooks of Jansenist morality, which anathematized this "overflow of the senses," had perhaps better surmised their dynamic and Dionysian nature. Sense impressions already have a power that is to be understood only in accordance with the time involved. These excesses, these hyperboles, these surprising usurpations of synecdoche encountered in walking figures appear here once again through the discrete and scattered expressions of corporeal lived experience. The various sensations picked up in "atmospheres" tend to overflow the site in which they should have been confined.

For all the inhabitants questioned, the colors painted on the central-western facades of the Arlequin herald the fact that "home" approaches. The most oft-cited color is blue, a color that is nevertheless generally viewed as unpleasant: "not very aesthetic," "overwhelming," "disturbing," a "civil-defense blue that makes me sick," a blue that gives a paradoxical intensity to the look of the windows, which become darker by way of contrast (for, "you don't see who might be looking"). And yet seen from quite far away, this color already projects the inhabitant toward his site of rest. Blue becomes the signal[13] of the still far-off environs of this neighborhood. "You're in the New Town as soon as you glimpse the blue from afar." However, up close, the preferred colors are the reds and oranges on the other facade, the one seen from the park side. Blue thus takes on a double meaning: from far off and from nearby, or even from one's abode. As lived in its tonality, it is split in two, depending on the inhabitant's current conduct, depending, too, on what he is doing in such and such a place, and depending on what he is going to do. More than a signal, blue seen from afar acts like a character (and therefore a sign) on whose basis is created a new climate in which spatial forms, topical position, the time remaining for one to travel along one's path, the precise place of one's domicile, and the presence of other inhabitants all fuse together. It engenders a climate that ushers one in as one leaves behind oneself "the town" one has barely yet vacated. Feelings and attitudes find themselves already altered, whereas the outer limits of the neighborhood have not yet been crossed. At the first glimpse of the "reading," the "writing"—that is to say, the action of inhabiting—is already beginning.

Would this be only a fore-seeing? Let us clarify without delay the peculiar status of the visual in urban atmospheres. The concept of readability, which is connected to that of the transparency of forms, comes very much under the heading of a plastic arts' vision of habitat.[14] The visual sense would be directed and led toward the most obvious signifier, attracted necessarily by the spectacular dimension. Thus, from the top of its imposing wall, the "blue cove" so absorbs one's gaze that it turns that gaze into being-gazed-at. This "seeing for the sake of seeing" also rules over one of the ways in which one contemplates the park—which is "simply looked at" because it is "pretty" or even frequented solely via its "belvederes"[15] and which, as beautiful, is precisely for that reason uninhabitable, unlivable.[16] One young female inhabitant evokes with amusement how the postcard then becomes the ridiculous paradigm for finding one's bearings through sight.[17]

But fore-seeing is not only a view from afar and from on high. The topological confusion of colors is often noted because the climate of such and such a moment on one's path was well matched with a single tone. Some inhabitants thus cite colors on the facade that in fact are found on the ceiling of the gallery, and they add that this ceiling is not colored. Their fashioning of space is carried out in perceptual indistinction, in a preawareness of the most pregnant color that took the place of the sky under which they were strolling. In anticipatory fore-sight, motor reaction or action is implied. Let us cite the case of an inhabitant whose body suddenly becomes numb and ill at ease in a part of the gallery where, "with those slabs of concrete, you don't see." Conversely, a young woman remarks that,

> when one takes an octagonal trip, on a visual level . . . you see beforehand. . . . For example, before taking the turn, one already sees the garage or what is going to happen. . . . But, when you have a turn with a right angle, you already stop there, huh? You're blocked by something that stops you, ahead. And for people, it's the same thing. It's important . . . to see a larger space before oneself, to see people coming.

These two expressions do not refer to some spectacular form of objectification. They denote the concern one has to be able to tell in time what the future one will be traveling through is to be made up of, to have some sort of premonition of whether one's encounter with the other will be unforeseen or whether one will be able to ready oneself for it, as well as what walking figure one already has, or does not have, the power to sketch out (figure of redundancy or figure of avoidance).

Sensoriality is doubly "overflowed." The senses encroach upon one another to such an extent that certain colors are expressed only through their form and certain forms only through the mediation of olfactory or tactile perceptions.[18] Yet, on the other hand, the motor order is inserted within the sensorial order and works to select tangible qualities. A site will thus take on the tonality of the effort spent to travel through it. Someone will say:

> It's the terrace that . . . you go up the stairs. . . . You must go up the stairs to get to the first level.

Or:

> On the terraces, the stairs are inconvenient. The steps are too long or too short. If you take two steps at a time, it's too long. If you go up one by one, it's too tiring. So, in general, I go by way of the smooth part.

The kinesthetic quality is antecedent to all others. The space is also fashioned when one stumbles around, prospecting the situation.

In short, it is unknown which one precedes the other, what is suffered or what is acted. Sensed climates already sketch out the conduct of one's action. Spatial distances contract along with the time; the here and the there are narrowed into an "already."[19] Bearing witness to this are numerous expressions gleaned from inhabitants in which the description of sensorial experience is expressed through some motor conduct. Climates differ according to these various ways of "passing through" the park, which is so large in geometrical reality and yet "soon crossed" or apprehended only through the "short promenades" it offers for one's steps. The mounds are qualified essentially by an upward climbing movement and the tactile sensation of the grass. As for the "terrace" of the silo-garage, it has no meaning as a visual composition, for one is surprised by those rare plant stands, looking so ridiculous and so lonely, that are crushed by the high rectilinear facade assailing them. The collage of a meaningless decor superimposed upon a function to which it remains absolutely alien (roof of a silo for automobiles) and which it never succeeds in covering up was conceivable only according to the order of the plan. The meaning of the landscape composition appears only from on high, forty meters aloft. This terrace where adolescents are happy to hang out finds quite another meaning in the terms of one's lived motor experience: the stairs one can climb up, the recesses in which one can sit down, the spaces "where the kids play," and, above all, the fact that it is a favorite inhabitable crossing area, even if sometimes a few worries are mixed in (the oppressing view from all the windows). Such is, however, very much the dynamic nature of the lived experience of inhabiting, which endlessly re-creates, in its own way, given spaces and preconceived uses.

And in order to cast radically into doubt the received notion that first we perceive and then we react,[20] one must recall the ways in which the figure of bifurcation and that of digression arrange [*décident de*] the space on the basis of the movement undertaken. When an inhabitant passes to the right or to the left of obstacles set in the middle of his path, any rationalization of one's conduct comes only after the fact. Motor function decides when one's foresight allows itself to be surprised. This was also the wholly preconscious way in which inhabitants stepped over the "holes" created in the walls that hold up the gallery.[21] Let us listen to their silences as well as to their utterances: "Sometimes, I find myself in front of . . . and I pass through." The three suspension points denote perfectly well the immediacy from "feeling" to "moving." Between the feeling and the movement, there is no antecedence, nor any consequence. The motor act does not follow the sensation, nor does it precede it. *Anticipation makes what is still far off feel close.* And already, the movement is sketched out. Such sketches are reactivated at certain moments in the narrations we have heard, as when the inhabitant, no longer finding words of his own to recount what happens during a trip, draws on a scrap of paper, configures something through a gesture, or points with his finger. He sketches with a gesture in the present what he had felt and thus reproduces as closely as possible the lived instant.

With this motor anticipation, one will come to have a better understanding of several phenomena of spatial practice that were sidetracking us when we undertook the rhetorical approach. Territorial limitations are split into two opposing varieties: on the one hand, limits represented (and reproduced) according to the planned order, which are geometrically spatialized into routes, breaks in architectural forms, differences in material, various closures (porticoes, gates, barriers), and, on the other, limits as they are lived through the very act that transgresses them or readies itself to transgress them, in the tension from near to far. Why do limits not have the same spatial assignment depending on the direction one is walking, unless it is that the climate for entering and the one for exiting always differ?[22] Through motor anticipation, the inhabitant is already "inside" or "outside," whether the site in question is his lodging, some part or other compared to the rest of the neighborhood, or the neighborhood itself.

It could no longer even be stated that urban atmospheres induce alterations in bodily attitudes and conducts. Is not the climatic also a form of action, since it is immediately composed by potential motor responses, based on what is possible? The feelings of exaltation from on high or of crushing heaviness, as were expressed in the figures of polysemy,[23] imply motility. It seemed that the dimensions of height and depth should have remained the prerogative of architecture—which, having laid down elevated forms, would have given them only to be *seen,* shifting all motor conduct into the horizontal dimension. And yet the elevator itself, which was to have turned the vertical dimension into an abstraction, brings to life through motor response (one's apparent bodily immobility changing nothing about this) lovely as well as terrifying imminent prospects of plummeting.[24]

Let us recall, finally, how certain atmospheres are lived and are engendered through one's very contact with a material: the "ramp," whose uneven height is combined with a "granular and unpleasant" floor surrounded by "repair-work mud," and "wild" paths where one's pleasure in treading on the grass is barely disguised. The possibility of walking on laid-out and developed paths (concrete, tar) or on better equipped, or grassy, or truly muddy ground allows a variety of motor conducts— from following along charted paths to the most unexpected sorts of trailblazing—at the same that it serves to differentiate one's climates.

Through these climates and by the power of motor anticipation, our everyday steps take on a new meaning. They were simple schematic traces, rhetorical figures; here they are now as operative movements. The work is the way, said Paul Klee.[25] This affirmation, it seems to us, holds not only for the "artistic" production of space but also for the inhabitant who reorganizes it after his own fashion. The work is the walk, and the act of walking is the work, configuration.

Every walking, every inhabiting gives itself out not only as structures, figures, but also as *configuration, structuration*, that is to say, deformation of the built world such as it was conceived and re-creation of space through feeling and motor function. The "overflow of the senses" [*débordement des sens*] (of the sensible) therefore produces an overflow of the meaning [*débordement du sens*] (formal significations) set in the edified world. Against the "real" as conceived, the power to orient *otherwise* the edified world remains ever active. Each direction of meaning derealizes all that does not enter into the climate of the lived instant.

A second form of derealization now comes into view. On the basis of the site traveled through and inhabited, everything that is neither near nor far has no consistency and finds itself literally "marginalized."

And yet, in this "between near and far" in which all walking is organized, anticipation still appears only in the form of a shortcut, of a forward projection, of a rather spatial gait whose temporal nature is not yet apparent. Moreover, does the rest of the space the inhabitant will be able to travel through tomorrow or later on have no value just because today no lived movement is animating it? Will these absent sites not be present one day or another? The space configured here and now is not a reductionist gathering of all the other spaces. For, then it would turn out like some magic crystal ball that contains the world but whose description in successive stages does not end. Let us reread the strange story by Jorge Luis Borges.[26] The "Aleph," a mirror of the universe, at first provokes the marvelous illusion of a simultaneity of all spatially contiguous entities.[27] Disillusion then sets in: nothing has been seen without the passage of time and without forgetfulness entering in.[28] The gathering of the universe into the lived present was possible only upon a ground of absence. Is that how it goes perhaps for the atmosphere of the everyday world that envelops each lived moment? Would not asyndeton (absence of conjunction, "holes") prove to be the condition for synecdoche?[29]

whose actors would be the inhabitants. Now, it is the powers of our corporeal being that go to make up the way in which this expression occurs: the power to be in affective resonance with an ambient atmosphere and the power to anticipate our motor reactions. *The particular tonalities of our surrounding landscape are the mirror of our sensibility of the moment as well as of the project of our action or of our relaxation.*

2. Between suffering and acting, there is neither logical sequence nor confusion but, rather, degrees of tension. We all have in our memory the immediate experience of these fairly retentional moments (when action is deferred) or, instead, protentional ones (when one's sensibility, lying in wait, tends in the direction of our action). Also, every strolling has meaning only in relation to stopping, and vice versa. *The articulation from walking to abiding* [séjour] *defines what inhabiting is.*

3. Fundamental figures of walking rhetoric, synecdoche and asyndeton emanate from lived sensorimotor experience. A sign of our capacity to qualify space in a singular way, *synecdoche expresses the immediacies and discontinuities of lived time over against the linearities and transitivities of chronometric time.* The spatial contiguities and conjunctions that seem to ground the existence of laid-out and developed space upon connections between homogeneous parts remain abstract fictions. The near and the far as well as the high and the low exist in a relation of heterogeneity; for, in conformity with the power of the body, everyday rhythm proceeds from the interval [*écart*], from rupture. The "blanks"—the "holes," as the inhabitants say—allow for a lived instant that would be similar to no other one. *Asyndeton inserts absence into space and into time.*

Faced with such a criterion of heterogeneity, an urban territory would be split in a qualitative way along two types of spaces: on the one hand, a set of sites that are inhabitable because they leave to strolling and to abiding the power to configure them, to re-create them, to articulate them in a play of absence and presence or, on the other hand, a set of uninhabitable sites (sorts of nonplaces, in this sense)[36] because between walking and abiding there is no possible articulation: these are instead mere crossing areas or places "where one has to go." Such wholly homogeneous sites offer no place for sensorimotor configuration to get a foothold in them, and they are lived in the mode of an absent presence; they correspond not only to the unfrequented parts of the neighborhood but also to those parts that leave one indifferent. They bear witness to a space that is conceived in homogeneity and yet, through lived sensorimotor experience and "atmospheres," melts into insignificancy.[37]

4. Upon this concrete condition of absence, "inhabiting" has nothing of an abstract or static concept about it. It is always born of something possible: the inhabitable. Its dynamic nature appears in the tension between the absent and the present. Absence is combined either with forgetting, rejection (or the attitude of indifference the inhabitable puts on), or with possibility and project. The present exists only between these two forms of absence that permit what we have called *structuration, configuration.*

Instating absence is the third way of derealizing the real. As such, it subsumes the first two: climatic transformation, overflow and anticipation. It tells us about the condition through which what is built up is deformed into an "atmosphere," that is to say, is formed otherwise, according to feeling and motor function. It indicates to what extent the lived present is to be evaluated in terms of force and not of a state.

Understood through the body of inhabitant expression—that is to say, through the powers of the body[38]—rhetoric then becomes "generative and transformational."[39] Against the container state some have wanted to assign to it, corporeal being retains the power to reform, to deform, and to develop. From this standpoint, the word *derealization* might still be deceiving. Where, indeed, is the "real"? In the habitat as it is produced or in one's sensorimotor way of inhabiting? Inhabitant expression does not "derealize." Rather, it "realizes" in its own way. And this way radically contradicts the current postulate of how to build, namely, produce space according to chronometric time and foresee usage according to purely spatial considerations. Inhabitant expression shows us, on the contrary, that *inhabited space is articulated according to lived time.*

5

On the Imaginary Ground
of Inhabitant Expression

As we rise higher in the triangle, we find that confusion in-
creases, just as a city built on the most correct architectural
plan may be shaken by the uncontrollable force of nature.

—Wassily Kandinsky, *Concerning the Spiritual in Art*

THUS, the everyday strolls by which we come and go, hastening us
to the point of running, delaying us elsewhere to the point of taking a
pause or even making a visit, took on the air of obeying the silent injunctions of the urban space. The architectural forms and functional
uses these injunctions try to give out to be read seemed to propose an
inevitable text, a program to which we cannot but conform.

Yet here it is that, step by step, the tracks configured according to the
whim of ordinary preoccupations bring the city into a state of decay and
undermine the foundations of the representation one usually gives of it.
An unforeseeable force "defying all calculations" asserts itself.[1] And the
nature of this upheaval has just become apparent to us: lived time invali-
dates the rules of rationally composed space.

Suddenly, the question about the ground of inhabitant expression
becomes only that much more insistent. If spatial totalities lose all
meaning of their own and are but the occasional material and pretext
for deconstruction, for derealization, what is the field of reference for
everyday action? What is the basic ground brought into play by expression, when laid-out and developed space finds itself relegated to an accidental modality?

The question can be posed in another way. Inhabitant rhetoric
made us understand that our walks move about over a space that has
come undone and been dispersed. We inhabit a discontinuous space in

accordance with a time of *differance*. Is this to say that everyday actions correspond to an inhabitant stochastics? And yet, from one moment to the next, from one place to another, between the visit and the walk, between my way of inhabiting and that of the other inhabitants, everyday life does not unfold like a Brownian motion in which, over a given field, one grasps only the feverish and random traces of particles that otherwise allow themselves to be defined only in the contradictory terms of immobility. The ways of inhabiting are located through their *discretion,* less in the sense in which they allow themselves only to be glimpsed—and is not discretion connatural with everydayness?—than in the sense in which they exist only at the pinpoint. We thus rediscover an older acceptation of the term: the *discretum*.[2]

Now, the fact that inhabitant expression manifests itself only "discretely," in a scattered way, here and there, does not imply the absence of qualitative unity. There thus exist a stylistics and a process of sensorimotor articulation that give an overall coherent meaning not only to the lived experience of a single inhabitant but, also, to the whole of coexistent everyday lives. In other words, one must ask oneself how unity concretely circulates between each "discrete" manifestation, and how each of these manifestations refers to a never clearly expressed common ground.

Does there exist an instantiated principle whose omnipresence would have already been indicated to us by prior observation of walks—one that would be able, on the one hand, to explain in a concrete way the connections between each discrete expression and, on the other, to characterize the nature of the ground from which all everyday expression proceeds and from which it draws its expressive force? And would perhaps inhabitant expression, which is both incorporated and grounded, merit then a more theoretical definition?

BETWEEN THE PRESENT AND THE POSSIBLE, THE IMAGINARY GROUND

Beyond all the varieties of spatial practice that manifest it, inhabitant expression has two basic ways of breaking up the representation of the continuities and homogeneities that belong to laid-out and developed space. In anticipating action, it renders present what "really" is not yet so (we have already sketched out in this way both avoidance and the search for a site that is not yet but on the horizon of our stroll). In derealizing large fragments of space, it renders absent what representation would judge to be "really" present (thus, those "blank trips" lived in the mode of absence, or asyndetons that insert discontinuity into our everyday travels). In both cases, *the imaginable* overflows the limits of a spatial "reality" that is otherwise represented in terms of two contradictory characters: on the one hand, the real corresponds to the present; on the other, the real is defined in relation to a totality of which it is a precisely assignable part.

In this sense, the instantiated principle of the imaginary, whose discrete existence we have often pointed to in the course of reading walking narratives, seems to respond to our expectations. Does it have the power to produce those fundamental connections that would give coherency to the functioning of inhabitant expression?

Instead of a formal definition of the imagination that would risk reproducing the foibles of that psychology of the "faculties" in which mental operations are divided up, taken apart, and hierarchized (perception, memory, "the" imagination, etc.), in which the form is substituted for the force, and in which what is organizing power is given as a mere instrument, we prefer an a posteriori definition that is engendered little by little through empirical illustrations. It is the lived imaginary that we are to understand, and it is its modalities of appearance, between the present and the absent or the possible, that we will have to carefully note down.

Nonetheless, a brief reminder on the theoretical level will allow us to evaluate how, within the process of inhabitant expression, the place of the imaginary has pertinence. Several times in the history of thought, the imaginary has been considered neither as one of the lower faculties, archaic in origin and confined to the production of images, nor as too confused a faculty to be able to attain the empire of reason, too uncultivated and too uncontrolled in its sudden appearances to be a bearer of truth. Each time our "imaginary" capacity has been taken into account as a whole, it was in order to point to its operative function: *imagining is the power to connect*. The imagination is the *medium* par excellence.

Thus, Kantianism—which, two centuries ago, did not immediately preoccupy itself with the instantiated principle of the imaginary—nevertheless conferred upon it the threefold role of reproducing, synthesizing, and creating. If deprived of the connections the imagination afforded them, the understanding and sensibility would never meet. Experience of the world would not have any meaning, and knowledge would have no concrete application. It is to be understood that, far from being a simple and passive reservoir of images, the imagination possesses an activity and a capacity for synthesis.[3] Thanks to these, the manifold and the singular can find unity and universality (which is the essential feature of Kantian concerns). But is it not by this same power that the acted and the suffered, sensation and motor function, the present and the absent are tied together in a process of articulation we were evoking just a few pages ago?[4]

Certainly, the Idealism that centered on the problem of knowledge developed this capacity of the imagination to synthesize only to the extent that the functioning of the understanding was clarified by it. To judge from a short statement by Immanuel Kant in his *Critique of Pure Reason*[5] and by the pages devoted to the analysis of the sublime in the *Critique of Judgment*,[6] the at once obscure and overflowing aspect of the imaginary, which literally outstrips the understanding, is clearly indicated.

In an entirely other epoch, the dynamic aspect of the imagination was even more clearly accentuated. Developing the contributions of the Neoplatonist current of thought, the Renaissance was already familiar with this power of connection, but it understood that power as the manifestation of a force that spans the universe and constitutes its very texture. The imagination connects the manifold and the scattered because it animates and grounds at the same time.[7] (And under this heading, we prefer to designate henceforth such an instantiated principle by the word *imaginary,* which takes on a less restrictive meaning.) The imaginary would have not only the force to unify discrete pluralities but also the force to make opposites coincide (the *coincidentia oppositorium* is, in the Renaissance, a central notion in the interpretation of the world), which give it a surprising importance. Its faculty of conferring unity of meaning upon instantiated principles as contrary as the universal and the singular does not just have the merit of making it an instrument of noteworthy value. The set of connections is more significant than the set of connected objects. In synthesizing, the imaginary first of all signifies itself. Through the omnipresence of this activity that gives it its eminent quality, it becomes the common ground and the field of reference for all that it sets in a relation of coincidence.

These indications can relevantly guide our final reading of walking narratives, which is now coming up. The power of the imaginary takes on coherency only at the end of our path. It does not allow itself to be grasped with ease. Does not such difficulty stem from its highly *peregrine* nature? The imaginary voyages. It does not hold topical assignments in place but, rather, defies them. It accepts the paradox of being at once the fundamental instantiated principle and the instrument of connection. The concept of *vicissitude*,[8] which the Renaissance proposed as a key for the interpretation of the world, splendidly expresses the imaginary's dynamic: making very different things alternate in an ever mobile reciprocity.

Such a circulation of the imaginary,[9] which runs the risk of irreverently transgressing the clear distinctions we claimed to establish between the particular and the general, as well as between space and time and between the individual and the collective, will be illustrated thanks to the reversibility between the present and the absent and between the lived and the possible. And perhaps we will finally come to know whether the inhabitants whose narratives we have listened to do indeed *practically* live in the same world.

Evocation of the Imaginary: The Present according to the Possible

Each urban atmosphere lived by this or that inhabitant at such and such a moment is never absolutely alien to what the other inhabitants are living. The various narratives of everyday life in one and the same neighborhood demonstrated homologies and similarities between the deformations and new structurations the space undergoes. In other words, in disqualifying the laid-out and developed space, each lived present substitutes for that space an imaginable possibility, whose active power we have noted; indeed, the inhabitant's conduct can be deeply affected by it. All the styles of inhabiting have at least some points in common.

It could therefore be assumed that the inhabitants' everyday fashionings are based on a common expressive ground. Now, the narratives we have gathered explicitly evoke an overall imaginary climate that arises from time to time and in whose name spatial derealizations are possible.

The most apparent vehicle for this imaginary ground is to be found in all the common rumors that are passed by word of mouth. Most often, inhabitants place responsibility on those who do not live in the neighborhood. Here are three examples.

> In Grenoble, they say: How can one live in the New Town! Aren't you overrun by the filth yet?

> New Town! It has a bad reputation, between us, huh?

> People who don't know say, "You oughta be careful." . . . Their impression is that there are muggings, stuff like that.

These particular turns of phrase, these ways of hiding what was felt and what one does not dare to admit clearly, demonstrate quite well the imaginary essence of these "they say" expressions, whose force of impact is not negligible. Circulating in people's speech, rumors that are only hinted at seem hardly distinguishable from a local form of ideology that stigmatizes the Arlequin neighborhood and is trying, in political terms, to exorcize the "socialist myth." But in addition, the rumors are grounded in sites, and it is unknown whether they are felt impressions that are masked behind the rumors of the "they"—that is to say, of the others—or whether it is these "they say" expressions—collective delegation—that allow individuals to specify more sharply their own lived experiences. Whatever it turns out to be, the following remarkable cases will demonstrate that the atmosphere of sites goes well beyond the power of rumor and that, in the lived present, everything is reactivated in accordance with the force of the imaginary.[10]

The Diurnal according to the Nocturnal

The nychthemeral (night-day) cycle does not yield a simple and regular rotation of daily atmospheres. We have seen in the figures of polysemy[11] its instrumental form as well as the everyday use one makes of it. In rereading the numerous excerpts from inhabitants' narratives that illustrate staggered polysemy and appropriation by dislocation,[15] one will discover how the imaginary ground surfaces. It is an imaginary ground that combines the sensations of imprisonment with an imminent sense of free fall, the "infernal noises," similar to some sort of bestial possession and ready to seize hold of someone ("like jaws") as well as to perform a metamorphosis ("you're trapped like wild animals. . . . Bam!"). All these powers of the night play at ceaselessly driving away and bringing near the unspeakable subterranean world. This fateful game of cat and mouse is well described in graffiti repeatedly engraved on the doors of the elevator: "rat trap."

The Ordinary according to the Alien

The preceding examples already serve to illustrate precisely how the form of the present is lived according to the force of the possible. Here are some other examples in which the imaginary evokes—as if at the surface of one's walks, one might say—alien forces that may possibly be encountered. Territorial appearances—which correspond to an attempt to assign a group onto a site in a fixed way[16]—take us back to an effort to exorcize all that is imaginary and confused in the identificatory movement of social aggregates. The force of all the afflictions that one believes to be possible, even though they have not actually been felt, is confined within the apparent limits of a site. One tries to represent as perpetually distant that which in one's premonitions may imaginarily be approaching. All sorts of eclectic, symbolic collages are possible for those who wish to safeguard their "ordinary existence," their familiar world. Some point to the "stairwells" of the North Africans, others the fancy apartment stairwells. Tunisians identify typically Algerian sites. Messy or dirty space is associated with the space inhabited by the "foreigners," but equally well with spaces in which too many children hang around, and also with sites where "there is too much concrete." Alien sites are apprehended in confusion, in a "mixed-up" sort of way, as inhabitants so often say; these are sites in which one does not make out very clearly what is going on and in which one does not quite know what might happen. A sign suffices; a signal, rather: an odor from a foreigner's kitchen or intense traffic circulation of children in the passageways is sensed by one's sight or hearing and amplified by rumors. Through these signals, the foreigner finds himself fingered, indexed, and, starting from these indices, which are often quite slender, all the rest is left up to the imagination.

Projected onto the topography of an urban map, this imaginary topology would be incoherent. There would be double or multiple contradictory meanings for one and the same site, a general polysemy for one and the same signal. The intense traffic circulation of children within a passageway may signal a North African mode of life or a style belonging to those "student households where everyone lives together, they say." Homologous interactions between signifier and signified (foreigner:dirty, dirty:foreigner) will put causal links off track, for the meanings of sites are superimposed, one on top of the other, and territories become fluidified.[17] Understood in terms of force and not of fixed boundaries, these contradictions nevertheless coincide. Appropriation has any force at all only through the force of its contraries. For, what is contradictory according to a clear-cut spatiality becomes contrariness in the lived present. The ordinary is dynamized only through the evocation of the possibility of the alien, the strange, and the foreign. Without a recognition of the dynamic ground of the imaginary, the only meaning this play of forces will ever have will be that of *epiphenomenon* of a social mechanism according to which everyday lived experience is an insignificant accident.

THE EVERYDAY ACCORDING TO THE EVENTFUL

In its everydayness, the ordinary is a present that is repeatable each day. Beneath the storied finery of the event, the possible corresponds to what would happen a single time. In the ordinary present, this extreme singularity of the exceptional event is imagined as something eventual, or else it is reactivated—reimagined, if we may put it that way—as a unique fact from the past and an unreality from the present. There is nothing in from partial deterioration to cataclysmic disintegration: a "disaster," a "pigsty," "everything fallen apart." Physical deterioration as well as a deterioration of the social climate seem like they are going to arise little by little of their own accord. One then imagines the forces that might be able to check such a decline through a reinforcement of social activities. Yet then trivialization would become inevitable: "It would become a housing development like the other ones." Now, the various forms of deterioration as well as the kinds of forces capable of "restoring discipline"—or of better supervising the maintenance and upkeep of the neighborhood—presently exist within everyday life. The way of imagining Arlequin's tomorrows is organized on the basis of the present.

Facts lived everyday feed the possibilities envisaged. Filthiness here promises to be filthiness everywhere. And, as one inhabitant notes, disaster is already conjugated in the present tense:

> If there are some people who are a bit filthy, later, there will be a disaster. Sometimes, you see old armchairs, stuff lying about, it's a disaster. [. . .] If this became really unpleasant, you could no longer live here.

A female inhabitant who said, "When I'll go everywhere [. . .] I'll be myself," has too great a fear that the overall atmosphere might change in the meantime. One keeps an eye out for the first signs of abstention or abandonment on the part of the activity coordinators and the municipality, the two major guarantors to whom, through the deliberate choice of making the neighborhood an ongoing creation, this neighborhood finds itself tied.

> I feel a bit apprehensive for the New Town of tomorrow, because I find it really nice, very colorful, and I like it a lot . . . and I would be quite afraid if the municipality abandoned it. It would be a pigsty in no time at all, huh? Because the New Town, if abandoned, would be horrible! It would be a labyrinthine pigsty.

Reading these statements from the inhabitants, it appears that the sometimes fantastical evocation of the future brings us back to a way of living the possible in the present. The apparent evocation of a future destiny is imperceptibly turned around into an immediate presence of the imaginary thus being convoked. The Arlequin is already, according to certain signs, what it could be tomorrow.

The Whole according to the Part

The process of synecdoche manifests itself again as these evocations and convocations of the everyday imaginary unfurl. Synecdoche was presented as a fundamental figure of a walking rhetoric. Here we find it in the process of organizing the latent yet fundamental presence of the imaginary in the lived experiences of inhabitant expression.

Three heuristic examples will clarify straightaway how the imaginable is convoked in one's ways of inhabiting frequented sites.

Three inhabitants repeat each day the same short trips. Whatever the variations in atmosphere might be, they occupy only a very small part of the neighborhood, spatially speaking. None of them has gone even once into the park, and they are unfamiliar with most of the buildings. But this ignorance implies nothing unimaginable. Each of them evokes in his or her own way the rest of the neighborhood, and these modalities are qualified according to the style of inhabiting belonging to each one. For the first inhabitant, the neighborhood in its globality is evoked as a possibility that is appropriable little by little. She hopes it will always be "nice" and "colorful"—whence her understandable fear that the nocturnal world, the windiness outside, and maintenance neglect might come to impede her project of inhabiting the area and confine it to what she calls "my corner that I've made for myself."

Another inhabitant lives according to a style that is decidedly voluntaristic. A regular at various activities, she imagines the rest of the neighborhood as a space that is to become appropriated more and more by everyone and to be lived in the mode of "encounter." The enormous qualitative charge affecting such brief trips (the narratives are quite long and always different from one day to the next) highlights her walking as a way of inhabiting the whole neighborhood.

The third inhabitant, who is very disturbed by his short daily trip in the mezzanine, has no project for a more expansive appropriation. Each day he traverses his daily hell, and the Arlequin neighborhood as a whole is evoked for him by the "garbage and vomit, the carcasses of bicycle frames and the shells of old cash registers" he steps over each day.

For these three inhabitants, the rest of the neighborhood is evoked and convoked in the present. The uninhabited elsewhere stands out already as inhabitable possibility, or as uninhabitable. And these observations hold for the inhabitants as a whole, who are split between two extreme cases: that of the voluntaristic project of appropriation and that of fascinated abandonment. The style of the first inhabitant offers the example of an intermediate case: that of a rather balanced articulation between her project and the resistance it encounters. No inhabitant, not even one who travels widely across the territory of the neighborhood, succeeds in making his everyday life coincide with the spatial totality. One's steps cite and configure at the same time a space whose nature is nontotalizing yet globalizing.

Such a globality, which gives itself out as the common ground of inhabitant expression, is constituted through the evocation of the possible and the convocation of the imaginary within the atmosphere of the present act of inhabiting. This twofold movement—which, in the narratives we have gathered, accentuates sometimes the evoked, sometimes the convoked—refers us back to one and the same imagining power in which the possible and the present are mutually responsive. The same outstanding common characters—the nocturnal, the accidental, the alien, the eventful, and their contraries—are also found to be convoked or evoked. These characters are capable, each in their own moment, of insinuating themselves into those particularities that will predominate in this or that present and in such and such a possibility. If inhabitant expression deforms and derealizes planned urban totalities, is this not, in fact, on account of the implementation of this imaginary ground in which the lived present draws its corrosive quality? Why are harmful characters experienced in places the designers of the spaces, in their representations, thought would be pleasant, more propitious for encounters with others, and even favorable to the blossoming of a genuine "social life"? Why is the color not necessarily cheerful; why does it not render forms light and "transparent"; why are the volumes not always reassuring? Yet all that took on meaning only in an overall project in which everything was all too well tied together. Given in homogeneity, equivalency, permeability, and transparency, *the real totality offers no foothold; it is radically unimaginable. In everyday life, the "real" is the presently lived site. And, through it, the totality is reimagined as globality.* Moreover, the disturbing possibilities the process of conception-production had evacuated reappear all the more in one's not represented, but rather lived, usage. Against the diurnal transparency of a techno-logical habitat, the imaginary can still, through lived experience, set in opposition the forces of the accidental, the unforeseen, and the noctur-nal, in the sense in which the imaginary has "an autonomous symbolic existence."[19]

Three Powers of the Lived Imaginary

The imaginary does not have the phantasmagoric and unstable charac-ter one ordinarily assume it has. A study of everyday life that is attentive to singularities and to details would show that in it lies a power whose import is ill evaluated by the universe of technical production.

Presented as one of our psychological faculties, the imagination looks like it is abiding in a space of its own, a sort of mental territory that is not to surpass certain limits and that is called upon during quite a specific set of activities: connecting perceptions, preparing the genesis of concepts, being the compost of artistic and technical creation. It is conceded a single liberty: it is allowed to go at will into the seemingly incidental field of aesthetics. From this perspective, the imaginary would be the mere complement, the facile foil, of the real. Everything that the former would not accept would be thrown out as dross in the latter domain. Is not this reduction of a concrete power into a psychological faculty, this way of confining the irrational and the polysemous in the seedier parts of town, in the suspect "zone" of the city of knowledge, a strategic effect? Yet, by hurling into the vacant lots of the irrational all that might cast doubt on rational rules and the clear and distinct con-ceptions governing both thinking about space and its planned produc-tion, so many additional attributes have been given to the diffuse and subterranean force of the imaginary.

Examples of social deviance, unco-optable forms of urban conduct, and everyday practices that remain inexplicable[20] no doubt share a com-mon bond. They manifest in a point-like way and with a peculiar sort of irruptive violence the hidden presence of a forbidden imaginary of abid-ing. We have studied some of the most commonplace expressions of this way of being, which is characterized by the following modalities: refusal of ongoing connection, or conjunction, and rejection of exclusive disjunction. These two characters, which are entirely suitable to a logic of the imaginary,[21] are to be found again both in ordinary urban practices and in exceptional ones. Rational urban thinking will be scandalized by them. One willingly grants the existence of heuristic and "marginal" cases, those accidents and imponderables that readily justify the contention that one must always plan more. But it can hardly be granted that the essence of lived everydayness is grounded upon these same irrational instantiated principles and that, in this sense, the system of our certainties might be shaken to the core.

And yet the two principal walking figures—asyndeton and synecdoche, those spatial derealizations on whose basis the social code of appropriation and the articulatory process that defines the act of inhabiting are structured—signify, each in its own way, the fundamental presence of these two imaginary instantiated principles in every inhabitant expression.

Instead of a formal definition of the imagination, we have preferred a genetic definition of the imaginary. The first kind of definition would have straightaway put forward one function among others. In that case, we would have appealed to it in order to clarify some spatial practices that were too vague. Such a theoretical option—which, moreover, is quite common—will always demonstrate the incidental role of the imagination. The second one, which prejudges nothing, establishes itself bit by bit along the line of a concrete examination of everyday actions and until it reaches the point of the hitherto improbable affirmation of its decisive import. The term *imagination* conveyed too much the classical distinctions among various functions for us to have been able to use it here. The imaginary is a domain, a field of action and of passion that spans the whole of our existence in space and in time. We never completely leave its soil. In its insistency beneath the apparent solidities of planned spatiality and functional uses, it exhibits the tenacity of that nocturnal realm we evoked earlier. Indeed, it is always ready to disturb the diurnal certitudes that feign to ignore it. And this paradigm illustrated better than any other in what sense the lived imaginary is the ground from which inhabitant expression draws its three principal powers, which we now recall:

1. *Power to exceed.* Thus, all ambulatory figures border on synecdoche—which, thanks to the absences and breaks made by asyndeton in planned space, make the part stand for the whole. But in order that a site might take on such an importance that the rest of the neighborhood or the city would be canceled out, a particular sensorial condition is required. One sensation sets the tone for all the others and overflows the apparent spatial limits that, in addition, motor anticipation transforms into a tension between near and far. Everyday conducts introduce chaos into the spatial organization produced by the developer and excess into foreseen functional operations. They configure the space in their own way by first rendering it heterogeneous. In this sense, the imaginary upsets constructed spatialities and derealizes them by the *power to give the whole in the fragment.*

2. *Power of reversibility.* The reversals between whole and part, between present and absent, between acted and suffered affect the most fundamental ways of living space according to time. Thus, the total is not suppressed. Evoked in the partial, it is convoked also under the form of an atmosphere enveloping the present. The climate of such and such a lived moment substitutes a sensorial and imaginary globality for the representation of the spatial totality. But the quality of the present action that is to come, or is deferred, determines the tonality of this atmosphere. Likewise, the evocation of a possible future on the basis of the present reduplicates the convocation of tomorrow in today's inhabiting.

   These reversals pertain to a process of symbolization that is peculiar to the imaginary and that outstrips what received knowledge says about it when it defines the symbol: "every concrete sign evoking something that is absent or impossible to perceive."[22] In everyday life, the process of symbolization convokes at the same time that it evokes. Graffiti that are not understood, the cardboard box of garbage half strewn across the floor of the gallery, the still-green edge of lawn or some striking color—all these evoke in their own way absent possibilities of which they are discrete signs. Each one symbolizes in this first sense (evocation in a shortcut form) something imaginable with indefinite limits. And yet, spanning affectivity, feeling, and motor function, these same symbols produce imaginary resonances that are capable of mobilizing the presently lived act. Reversibilities indicate that the evoked imaginary and the convoked imaginary are caught in a mutual genesis, this "incessant exchange that exists at the level of the imaginary between subjective and assimilative drives, on the one hand, and objective summonses emanating from the cosmic and social setting, on the other."[23]

Finally, a linear representation of time is absolutely alien to the lived modality of inhabiting. If an image must be provided, that of the circle would be more fitting to illustrate such circulations that carry the present toward the possible and bring the possible back toward the present through the vehicle of symbols. The power of reversibility implies the rupture of chronological continuities and spatial contiguities.

3. *Power of immediacy.* One has rightly attributed to the imagination the functions of connection, assembling, and synthesis. It engenders an imaginary field that is the medium par excellence, the site of exchange between the drive-induced gesture and the environment, between the plurality of styles of inhabiting and commonly held modalities. Yet the imaginary connections hardly use conjunction and logical sequence at all. The imaginary is lived according to immediacy. The pregnancy of the imaginable in the climates of this or that moment, the superimpositions between the convoked possibility and the evoked possibility, the convocation, in the act of configuring space, of an evocable climatic globality—all these processes show that inhabitant expression lived in space and in time skips causal or rational sequences and does without streams of representations. There is nothing about it of a "relation" of part to whole or of a "relation" of the individual to the "socius"; the same goes for rationalizing explanations that would yield on the one hand the subject, on the other hand the object, on the one hand knowing, on the other hand the world in itself. To the extent that everyday life can find meaning qua expression, the imaginary proposes itself as the essential referent to which the moments of inhabiting, and all the spaces inhabited, relate. The imaginary weaves beneath each present lived experience a ground the imaginary immediately gives to it as world.

At the outset of a patient reading of narratives of everyday life, we were seeking a change of scenery. The progressive appearance of the global power of the imaginary leads us quite far afield. Are we rambling? On the one hand, one will have had an adequate glimpse now of how everyday conducts are not forms of occupying a space that has been proposed to one but, rather, forces for reorganizing a lived space-time. One will also have glimpsed that this dynamism emanates from the imaginary. This would thus be a contribution to present-day research on the imaginary roots of collective life. But, on the other hand, can the lived experience of inhabiting be told and understood only in the trace of a pure practice, with only snatches of it being grasped and its empirical examination never ending? Is it only dispersal, and is its unity of meaning simply hypothetical? In short, in overflowing the boundaries of the well-known and reassuring structure of the relation of signifier to signified, inhabitant rhetoric would lead to a set of remarks that, from errancy to errancy, might end up straying into the realm of the arbitrary. Is inhabitant expression but a series of rejections, or just some babbling provocations launched against urban planning? Has it no internal necessity? Can it not be rephrased into a theory?

Toward a Theory of Expression

Just as the inhabitants whose steps we have followed sometimes stop in the course of their trips and look back on something or toward someone, so, along the itinerary of our investigation, have some noteworthy points interrupted our forward bound [*élan*] and invited us to take a look around. These theoretical adjustments have taken place four times:[24] when two fundamental figures, synecdoche and asyndeton, referred ambulatory rhetoric back to a poetics rather than to prosaic statement; when spatial derealizations brought to light by the code of appropriation scrambled the order of clear significations and indicated that everyday rhetoric also signified itself; when the body of inhabitant expression showed that acting and suffering are not two distinct instantiated principles but, rather, that they are lived through a process of articulation, in a rhythmic manner; and when, finally, in the preceding pages, the ground of inhabitant expression proved to be imaginary and was to be characterized by the three powers of excessiveness, reversal, and immediacy.

On four occasions, everyday practices have expressed a rejection of the self-evident truths of planned space. And the four forms of interpretation they called for seem to call into question the certainties of our knowledge of social space and to disturb our overly inured habit of seeking general causes and clear significations. Is there, however, nothing in common among these four theoretical sketches of inhabitant expression that, as against determinate space and knowledge, plainly persist in stating the existence of the polysemous and the arbitrary?

Yet, as a matter of fact, *the status of expression outstrips that of binary-structure signification in that it never functions in an arbitrary way.* Everyone knows the two principles on which the theory of the sign is grounded: the arbitrary relation between signifier and signified, on the one hand; the linear character of the signifier, on the other.[25] Now, one need only bring up again the figures of inhabitant rhetoric in order to grasp that "expressers" outstrip the order of "convention" and that they are far from "unmotivated." Also, walking rhetoric clearly differs from a linguistic process. Even if the space "traveled through" were the same, one never walks exactly in the same way. However unremarkable our ways of inhabiting might be, they would never depart from a climatic pregnancy that never leaves them totally "unmotivated." The atmosphere brings together a veritable network of significations that envelop the lived presents. Of the convocations and evocations of the imaginary that are mingled with "climates" and that ground the articulations of each inhabitant expression, as well as of collective relationships, it could not be said, they are "a line."[26] Finally, the fundamental presence of the imaginary in the regulatory system of lived inhabitant expression appears not only likely but necessary. It makes one understand that, at the level of the process of symbolization (which becomes concretized in spatial configuration through synecdoche and asyndeton), expression is never carried out according to an arbitrary relation and does not unfold in a single dimension.

In everything that inhabitant expression has manifested, no expresser remains the arbitrary instrument of what is to be expressed. The signifier holds and is valid only by virtue of the signified content. It already "holds" and "is valid" for itself, qua mode of expression already loaded with meaning. What is expressed (for example, avoidance or the seeking out of a qualified site; ease of habitation or inhabitant malaise) refers back to the mode of expression. And in its way of configuring the inhabited space, the mode of expression implies straight off what it endeavors to express.

No doubt, the narratives of the inhabitants, like our ways of reading them, are hampered by the linguistic process one must indeed use. And in its linear stretch, this linguistic process has a hard time accounting for the expression of a practice that is itself already lived as an expression. The narratives turn back around and take up in another way what was said, move about from one detail to another, colliding against and shaking up the linearity of the statements made. The same goes for our attempts at analysis. And yet, if one does not succeed in making a complete tour around this inhabitant expression and exhausting its expressive force, is it not that its nature has nothing linear about it and that it must be understood, rather, in its multiple dimensions? Is it not true that each lived moment in this or that site implies and convokes, in a manner that is not arbitrary and yet is pregnant in its concrete plural forms, the globality of the inhabited space? One never finishes recounting the modalities of any one inhabiting. There is still and always something else to say.

This "nonfinite" character of the narrative of everyday life, as well as that of the analyses made about it, can be exasperating from the "scientific" outlook, which likes to tour all the way around questions and put a decisive full stop. As for us, through our understanding that the modes of inhabiting have meaning only under a regulatory system of expression, we come to suspect that the study of such modes finds no decisive end. In addition, the strangeness of such expression, which functions in an immediate as well as mediated manner, sidetracks our habits of thinking in terms of exclusive disjunction, or binary principle of noncontradiction, through which an object is this or else that and cannot be qualified in a contradictory way. Yet in the end is it a matter of contradiction or of contrariness?

It is not contradictory that there might be at once a relation of the expresser to what is expressed and, on the other hand, a reversal from the expressed to the expresser that can be contracted into immediacy. It is quite difficult to give a theoretical representation of this, and we lack the notions to do so. Or rather, the theory of expression no longer exists. It offers no operative interest; it is not usable in any production technology.

As a test and in a transitional way, can we find a way of thinking that accounts for expression's status and presents it in a theoretical form?

Examined in its concrete operation, the lived practice of inhabited space displayed itself in accordance with two movements. The most evident one is *developmental movement,* a movement of unfolding in spatiotemporal succession by which one step follows another, a path ends in a stationary position, and a configuration is displayed in figures. Having "unfolded" in this way, the various modes of inhabiting allowed one to see the elements of their composition and authorized the disjoining of this or that figure from some other one, of such and such an aspect of movements of appropriation from another, of the acted from the suffered, of the present from the absent, of the possible from the present, of the eventful from the everyday. The connections, like the absences of connection, could thus appear at all levels of analysis. The second is an *enveloping movement,* a movement of constriction, one could say, in which the elements developed in the preceding movement convoke one another mutually: from expresser to expressed, from expressed to expresser. The whole was given in the part, the possible coexisted beneath the present, the imaginary ground was convoked immediately in this or that lived here and now.

And yet these two movements thwart each other, because the first goes from immediacy to the exposition of mediations and distinctions and the second from the mediated and the successive to immediacy. This contrariness nevertheless has permitted us not to betray the lived experience of various particularities and to spurn hastily arrived at abstractions. It has also allowed us to sift out the shared principles involved in multiple ways of inhabiting. These movements of explication and implication that appeared in our attempt at an approach in fact make up the fundamental mode of inhabiting that gives itself out as expression. *Although they are contraries, these movements are lived simultaneously.* What is this third movement?

A theory can account for this coincidence of contraries only by appealing to a third term. One must go back rather deep into the history of thought, back to the Renaissance, in order to find a triad of notions capable of giving coherence to the representation of the status of expression. These three specific notions have been borne by a—nevertheless suspect[27]—current of thought that became established especially with Nicholas of Cusa and Giordano Bruno. Whatever the object to which they may be applied, one can preserve the meaning of these notions, which are eminently suitable for thinking expression. We are talking about *explication, implication,* and *complication.*

Explication corresponds to the movement of modal exposition, of successive development, of an expression that configures and allows how expression configures itself to appear. *Implication* is the movement in which modal particularities convoke one another, the expressed referring back to the expresser with each expression wrapping itself up in the others. *Complication,* which here has the meaning of global inclusion, of totalizing union, is at once the state of envelopment expressed through implication and the movement that expresses itself through explication. Simultaneity and succession as well as immediacy and mediacy coincide there in the same sense. Both ground and power at one and the same time, complication seals the status of expression.

This triad probably provides the most pertinent means for giving theoretical unity to all that the lived modes of inhabiting have allowed to appear in the diversity of their articulatory forms. It accounts for what we named the process of sensorimotor articulation, but also for the cohesion of walking figures in spatial configuration, for the meaning of these at once contrary and concomitant movements of differentiation and identification, which manifested themselves in the code of appropriation, and for the diverting and paradoxical powers of the imaginary. Finally, it accounts for the way in which the part gives itself out as the whole and the whole can be convoked in the part. All these processes have, in short, the same meaning: *lived experience of inhabiting does not have to express anything other than itself.*

Everyday existence expresses itself *practically* in the modes of inhabiting that express in turn an autonomous power of expression. This autonomy, which can be defined in theoretical terms by the notion of complication, is not an everyday delusion that would be superimposed upon the prosaic "usage" of the laid-out and developed space. Quite to the contrary, when recognized as expression, a lived experience of inhabiting *has the power to deform* these habitat situations one hardly chooses, to remove from them the unimaginable reality with which they are adorned. A collective habitat is perhaps even a matter of choice—yet, it is inevitable in present-day building production— about which everyday lived experience can manifest its buried and unnoticed powers.

Why, finally, does a theory of inhabitant expression seem barely conceivable today? The notions that would allow such an approach have been emptied out.[28] But furthermore, the approach remains particularly difficult. It cannot be performed with clarity and binary distinctions. Indeed, theory brings "expressions" back up to the expressed—the expressed being, in short, the meaning of being-able-to-express. Now, the expressed has a very paradoxical status. This is because, as Deleuze notes,

> "what is expressed" *has no existence* outside its expression, yet bears no resemblance to it, but relates *essentially* to what expresses itself as distinct from the expression itself. Expression thus bears within itself a double movement: one either takes what is expressed as involved [*on enveloppe*], implicit, wound up in its expression, and so retains only the couple "expresser-expression"; or one unfolds [*on développe*], explicates, unwinds expression so as to restore what is expressed (leaving the couple "expresser-expressed").[29]

One grasps clearly only one or the other of the two movements. And yet the attentive analysis of one of the two must not lose sight of its complement. Otherwise, the complication that gives coherence to the status of the expression comes undone and is split up, the expressive power will not allow any meaning to appear, and one will no longer understand what was to be expressed.

It is precisely the paradoxical status of the expressed that would show how an act of inhabiting, grasped as expression, can be deleterious if it itself recognizes itself and that would show what threat it would then evoke. Indeed, this paradox exceeds the dualisms and the properly distributed conjunctions that govern a dominant mode of thinking-producing. Let us cite Deleuze once again:

In short, what is expressed everywhere intervenes as a third term that transforms dualities. Beyond real causality, beyond ideal representation, what is expressed is discovered as a third term that makes distinctions infinitely more real and identity infinitely better thought. What is expressed is sense: deeper than the relation of causality, deeper than the relation of representation.[30]

We have proceeded from the most spatial forms of everydayness to the sketch of a theory of expression. Here we are at the end of our change of scenery. Borne by the inhabitants' narratives, our approach has bided its time, in envy, perhaps, of the time of inhabiting that it has taken pleasure in making apparent, abandoning itself to the "gray tones [griseurs]" of the everyday, allowing itself almost to be surprised by events, and thus playing at varying the paths it takes. While the lived experience of inhabiting now gives itself out as expression, the wealth of inhabitant expressions has hardly been exhausted at all.

We have been told over and over again that all capacity to inhabit space in an active way has by now disappeared, that, despite its sporadic efforts, inhabiting power is henceforth impotent, that the soul of our cities is dying. But has inhabitant practice been able already to express itself? Would we not have betrayed its ingenuity in favor, rather, of a discourse that reproduces categories that would not in the least be disavowed in the universe that makes a profit from the production of space? Although concerned with fidelity, our very approach will have related only one "story" of everyday life among others. In order to make one and the same final discovery—namely, that inhabitant expression expresses first of all itself—many other approaches would have been possible and they remain so, under the heading of one and the same fundamental similarity. Let us therefore finish up without ending by referring to a few lines from Samuel Beckett that will translate the lived experience of the climate surrounding our own itinerary:

Dawn was just breaking. I did not know where I was. I made towards the rising sun, towards where I thought it should rise, the quicker to come to light. I would have liked a sea horizon or a desert one. When I am abroad in the morning I go to meet the sun, and in the evening, when I am abroad, I follow it, till I am down among the dead. I don't know why I told this story. I could just as well have told another. Perhaps some other time I'll be able to tell another. Living souls, you will see how alike they are.[31]

Conclusion

A Cosmogenetic Point

The space open before you does not have any
other measure, any other quality,
Than that given to it by the form and
the rhythm of your steps.

—Traditional Vedic saying

THERE ARE CONCLUSIONS that, in ending a book, put a *full stop* to
the question being treated and offer it up as a finished object. Such a
procedure would have no meaning here. This book remains a rough
draft, a preliminary sketch; it ends nothing. On the contrary, our wish
is that it would invite one to return to this infinitely more precious and
rich text on which ambulatory practices write without their tiring and
which they recommence each day upon an urban space that seemed to
reject them or remove all signification from them.

Before formulating this invitation more fully, we shall take *stock*
[*nous ferons* le point] *of the situation*. One of the great concerns of our
time is to know for how long, in our cities beset by an unprecedentedly
vast undertaking of planning, the inhabitants will still be able to "find
themselves" within it.

In a way, the answer is simple. If the "constraints" and the "imperatives" in whose name development is carried out are really necessary,
the preconception of spatial practices in the form of functional usages
would have to keep on growing. The process of urban production (ren-
ovation, restoration, new neighborhoods, traffic plans) will have to add
up an increasing quantity of parameters and, for this very reason, secure
for itself a more and more general mastery of space. The singularities

lived by inhabitants who are isolated or in small groups (for, the social unit of everyday life is the aggregate, not the class or the social group, which are real, but abstract, entities) have no weight. Not only that, they are reduced in advance, codified in the profile of the typical inhabitant, and classified in general terms. When a new neighborhood rises from the ground, everything essential is *stated*. Thus do we believe that concrete is steeped in ideology as well as in economics. The singular "occupants" are to be satisfied with architectural forms and are to satisfy a way of life largely prepared in advance. *Lived space seems to become an accident of conceived space.*

In another way, the answer is undecidable. Indeed, if we wanted the point of view to change, if the requirements of economic imperatives were to be bracketed, be it only for the time of conducting an analysis, if we were to take into account everyday existence in town not as it is represented but as it is lived, we would see that the categories of *"use"* and of *housing* [*logement*] correspond only very partially to our ways of inhabiting. The production of planned space has its own rhetoric, a particular way of forming space and qualifying it. We would summarize this way in the following proposition: *Planned space is conceived and is achieved only on the basis of a representation of its totality. The "real" is the territorial whole and the functional partitions that are arranged therein. All the rest is but imaginable.*

Now, inhabitant expression proposes an entirely different configuration of space. A housing complex can be lived only partially, in a discrete manner, with absences that render the space heterogeneous. *The "real" is the presently lived fragment of space. All the rest is grounded in a globality that is imaginary in nature.*

These propositions are antithetical. It is hard to see how they could be reconciled. There exists but one actual state of fact: the planning imperative of urban space *reduces*[1] the power of inhabitant expression. Yet, this reduction is again reduplicated through an epistemological choice that gives out the totality as essential and the fragmentary as accidental or incidental. Depending on the capacities, the limits, and the degree of rigidity extant in the field of knowledge in which an analysis of spatial practice is conducted, inhabitant expression will be apparent there or will not. Let us examine one final example, taken from within the neighborhood we have studied, which will illustrate this determining factor. Everything depends on the way in which the questions are posed.

During the spring of 1974, drawings done by neighborhood children appeared in the windows of local businesses. Noteworthy is the fact that all these drawings represented the Arlequin neighborhood as seen from rather far away, the buildings blocking out the horizon, and with, of course, the interesting deformations peculiar to children's sense of graphics: a window standing out in a close-up and certain anamorphoses of architecture regularity. But no building "interiors" were to be seen, none inside the passageway, nothing within the apartments, not even under the gallery. Only two drawings depicted the interiors of the studios of the "Video-Gazette" and the judo classroom. How had the organizers of this competition billed the topic? "The New Town, the Inhabitants, Games"—a proposition that was as abstract and reifying as could be and one to which these children from six to eight years old responded to the best of their abilities, shunting into a far-off *view* what they were living every day. The "first prize" is described in the following terms by one of the competition's organizers:

> Very interesting, with this universe of concrete which seems to be falling to the side in which it is leaning, and with, in front, by way of contrast, the grass and the flowers.

This was the best "landscape."

Other children's drawings were exhibited in the same storefront windows in late 1979. Quite different, these later drawings allow us to glimpse gestures, sketches of some lived relationship to this or that part of the space. No longer do we see those ridiculous stick figures that had been pushed so far back; the figures are now quite filled out. This time, the proposed theme was no longer spectacular in character. It was now aimed at inducing the inhabitants to be more concerned about cleanliness in the public spaces of the neighborhood. The children no longer had to illustrate, to account for something, but, rather, to propose, to convince. Also, the expressiveness of their drawings stuck much more closely to everyday lived experience. It no longer was a matter of representing a totality but, rather, of giving voice to a space that was familiar to them and that they drew *as* they were configuring it every day. They were no longer required to fill in the space; they had to mobilize it.

Our interpretive essay on everyday life does not claim to resolve the contradictions that render urban life difficult. Nor is it trying to substitute itself for the kinds of investigations that have been conducted since the mid-sixties by researchers who are worried about the evolution of our world and who have taken great care to dismantle, in a lucid way, the mechanisms for the production of planned space while keeping in mind the psychological and social consequences such mechanisms can entail. But by repeating too often that the lived dimension is scoria, dross, a useless discarded by-product that cannot be assimilated by the present-day system of production and management of space, is one not likening [*assimile*] it to an insignificant *remainder,* something simply left over? One wonders whether this inhabitant power still exists, when it has been so well demonstrated time and again that it has been reduced, "dominated," "co-opted."

Perhaps it is sometimes necessary to shift the emphasis, to treat as not necessarily fundamental this chronologically primary and spatially dominant instantiated principle we would call *the order that proceeds from construction to renting*. Perhaps a commentary—however modest, however inaudible, however limited in its means as it might appear—ought to underscore, across the very, or too, real production of the built world and the preconceptions it induces, the tenacious persistence of a power of inhabitant expression. Would it not be fruitful to accept, finally, that beside, before, and beyond an epistemological choice that has always made it its goal to focus back on [*recentrer*] representations and concepts, the lived experience of inhabiting might lead us toward the outlying [*excentré*] and the excessive, toward the empty and the polysemous?

What is most unforeseen and what is most diverting risks shaking the convictions and certainties of the order that reduces the powers of inhabiting. In this sense, three main directions begin to take shape, three surprises provoked by the evocation of an inhabitant expression whose discrete existence seemed to us not to signal the obsolescence of a now-censured power but, rather, to point to the possibility of another interpretation of the urban universe. So, this is not some full stop [*point final*] that we shall be placing at the end of our essay but, rather, a *cosmo-genetic point*.[2] Starting from this point, our understanding of the city would develop differently. We shall broach its movement in three ways.

An Inhabiting without Building

The concept of building and the reality it designates have disappeared or are on the way to disappearing. The kind of edifice that could be called an oeuvre, a work, has become a *product* of the commercial economy, an object to be filled in. In the past, an edifice indicated of what people, of what classes, or of what social castes it was the work. It seems that today the domesticity of the home and the monumentality of the palace or of the temple have been reduced and assimilated into the concept of one's "premises" [*immeuble*]. What is certain is that the disappearance of an act of building as implantation, as configuration of space on the basis of the forms and functions of an immediate necessity (shelter against the cold, rain, wind, and sun), is characteristic of "advanced" technological societies in which the edifice becomes an object for sale. Reading an eminently enlightening yet still quite descriptive work that is lacking in theoretical pretensions such as Pierre Desfontaines's *L'Homme et sa maison* suffices to shake up, in a healthy way, our universal convictions. There exist throughout the world some medium-sized towns that are still unscathed by the influence of urbanism and, especially, there are some countryside areas where architecture shows us that building depends on inhabiting, that it is constituted as a space of tensions in which functional necessities (shelter formed in accordance with the region's climatic conditions) as well as symbolic instantiated principles (earth-sky, diurnal-nocturnal, near-far, indigenous-foreign) are given articulation.

So, contrary to the kind of constructing that produces abstract "housing-cells" dimensioned in "ratios," building is directly expressive of inhabiting. It incorporates ways of being. It is itself a modality liable to variations, implying time; it is socially oriented (and not merely a support for the juxtaposition of social elements) and open to tension and to conflict.[3] *Building is already inhabiting*; it is qualifying, in a lived way, a singular space and a singular time.

Because both bring into play the same articulatory process, there is a connaturality between the act of building and that of inhabiting. In this sense, the proposition is also reversible. *Inhabiting is configuring space.* And every inhabitant produces, without knowing it, an organization of space. Such an organization is ingenuous, but also indicative of a fundamental power that architectural science merely exploits through the skills of its technical prowess.

If the power of building has been occulted and the term *inhabiting* has become a doublet for *housing,* the play of transformations brought on by economic considerations is not the only thing at issue. The change that has been carried out has taken place through an objectifying representation of housing, one's habitat becoming a housing-object. It has made it possible to think in terms of a standardized product constructed in a repetitive manner. Even more than that, this change has relegated the appearance of the habitat, properly speaking, to the end of a long series of distinct sequences that extends from conception (from *projectation,* as one says in the world of urbanism) to the delivery of the product. Whence a limitation of respective responsibilities: each contributor (urbanist, architect, financier, and then manager and owner) can avoid his own duty to respond and can hand over to the other "responsible parties" any discontented "occupant" who might contact him. Whence, also, the denial of all genuine mastery[4] and the referral of the housing question back to some mysterious and fateful "social mechanisms." It has become all too obvious that *the process of construction always precedes the process of inhabiting or housing.* In other words, on the one hand, the ways in which one makes use of one's housing have been preconceived as soon as the urbanistic and architectural project begins; on the other hand, the concrete act of housing is never taken into account in the production process as a whole. Reduced to a "being housed," excluded from the productive act, the lived experience of the inhabitant is ultimately handed over to the vagaries of the "housing market." Thus, in the representations of the ideology of urbanism, what the economic and functional imperatives of production had implied from the start is treated merely as an unfortunate accident.

Recognition of inhabitant expression thenceforth entails an inevitable corollary we must underscore, however utopian it might be. The process that goes from constructing to housing is grounded upon a split. The process that goes from inhabiting to building is grounded upon an organic correspondence. Cut off from building, inhabiting retains its power to configure and to imagine by foiling what is implanted as thetically real in our "modern" cities. In this sense, we will offer no backward-looking conclusions. Building is missing-in-action, not dead. And its potentialities are still exercised in a virtual way in the obscure confrontations between *inhabitant* expression and constructed space. We would say, rather, that the "modern" is what has just died; it is already conceptuality, already fixed in place. It is dead absolutely, that is, as soon as one lays down the first stone, as soon as its first object is sketched out, for it has rid itself of lived time. And rather than calling for a return to the past, we would prefer to grant, as a plausible outcome, self-construction.

But this outcome will remain an exotic dream for most inhabitants of high-density housing complexes. We are speaking about those for whom utopian syntheses are beyond their ken; those who do not have the power to manipulate easily discursive codes, be it only in order to subvert them; those who undergo or suffer the forms of fashion but hardly create them at all.

There is another consequence, more modest and more immediate. It is one that might beneficially upset the instituted categories, if inhabitant power were recognized as a configurative force and a virtual potentiality of building and if the housing question were posed on the basis of lived modes of inhabiting rather than in the representation of an object to be filled in. To point out that every edifice is overdetermined on an everyday basis (that is to say, that all everyday lived experience convokes the other and the world in each inhabited site—and to refuse to represent this overdetermination as some sort of dysfunction, a semantic mix-up, or a defect in the perception of the "legibilities" of architecture): this is the sense in which an interpretation of everyday life, one attentive to its expressive features, might deconstruct the trivial and too convenient dichotomy that equally dismisses both urbanistic production and the inhabitants. If one no longer knows what building is, one will at least really have to ask oneself one day no longer, "What is housing?" in the sense of mere lodging but, rather, "What is inhabiting?"

An Inhabiting without a "Why?"

This question, which has been examined concretely on a precise "terrain" following a method that is as attentive and faithful as possible to the myriad detours and the many moments of spatiotemporal practices, does not culminate in a system of primary causes. When it comes to everyday life, to practices lived upon a group-housing space, the choice of one *modal lane* limits the transcriptions and betrayals of that at which observation aims. There really is not a tropism, but rather a similarity of nature, between the observed and the observation. The interpreter is to blend into the everyday and to refrain from making any premature analytic divisions, any hasty abstractions, waiting upon and staying near to these expressions of everydayness, lingering amid what is intimate and familiar, and, finally, leaving to the narrative of "lived experiences" the expressive form that is peculiar to it, and without which it would have no meaning. Before looking for the "whys," ought one not allow the "hows" to express themselves in the style that is peculiar to them?

It will, however, be surprising, and perhaps scientifically scandalous, that our comments would venture no further than this intermediate zone. Not that the project would fail to culminate in a few propositions, but that, speaking of inhabiting, that project "would never reach the end of them." Settled into this intermediate realm, our change of scenery does not exit therefrom. Should it have found the causes of the "mechanism," trivializing in the view of scientific knowledge, by inserting within some causal system these sometimes surprising and "savage"-looking everyday banalities? By refusing to stick to a formal ending, to the overall metaphorization of inhabiting into a "housing," and by grasping modes of living other than through "why" questions, other than through categories familiar to the very actors who produce the built world, our investigation, which has privileged an approach to intermediate sites (walking paths) and a study of details, of accidents and irregularities, and of small variations over time, nevertheless ends up allowing a regulatory system of expression to appear, one that this investigation has not finished "touring around."

Must one deduce from this that—setting aside the functional aspect (housing), which alone is taken into account in the listing of necessary causes (the economic, the political)—the everyday practices we have been tailing behind are pointless [*gratuits*] objects? Will one ascribe to them what Angelus Silesius said of the rose: "The rose is without a why"? Although the poetic nature of the act of configuring space has become apparent to us, inhabiting has to be understood rather as a movement than as an aesthetic object. Yet, in any case, it is averse to the "why," because the "why" no longer intends anything but representations, whereas the "how" intends things.

In order to illustrate this radical difference in orientation and to signal at the same time another opening indicated in the modal study of inhabiting, we must mention here the formidable question of *needs,* which for several years has cluttered up research in the social sciences and which barely conceals a return to the old debate between vitalism and mechanism. Are needs "natural," signs of vital appetites, or else products of social change conditioned by the relations of production? Do they refer back to a "deep-seated" desire that takes form in accordance with the conditions of the moment, or else are they historically created? The problematic of needs includes, in any case, a logic that is heavy with consequences:

> It leads to resolving inequalities, deprivations, and contradictions engendered by capitalism through a vast welfare apparatus [. . .]. It does not suffice to "house" people; people must be able to "inhabit" an individual or collective space.[5]

This logic practically lays down the answer before the question is asked; and under its cloak, the most glaring needs are satisfied along the way. In the process, the power of the giver is reinforced and the necessity of his presence is confirmed. Moreover, how are needs apprehended and interpreted? You look at the "masses," the "users," and, on the basis of social movements and their dynamic, you extract a social content: needs. Social life is abstracted into the notion of need, just as people's practices are reduced to various functions. The abstraction of "functionality" is inserted into a logic that is grounded on the relation of container to contained. Thenceforth, every sort of manipulation is, if not easy, at least possible. The logical presuppositions involved authorize a *logistics,* in the sense of an operational strategy, which includes anticipations of people's use. The new conformism passes through the filter of needs:

> The happy consciousness—the belief that the real is rational and that the system delivers the goods—reflects the new conformism which is a facet of technological rationality translated into social behavior. It is new because it is rational to an unprecedented degree.[6]

The rehabilitation of a status for expression in the social sciences may invite one to think in another way, to cast into doubt a methodology that separates the content from the container, to advance an understanding that everydayness holds more than a "social behavior" obsessed by the search for its wants and its satisfactions, and to refer this occulting problematic back to those who are the masters of the question and who have, at the same, produced the answer.

There is a way of thinking that is expert in the mechanisms for a domineering sort of production of urban space. Such a way of thinking will always keep one from recognizing that what inhabitant expression expresses first of all is itself. The logic of urbanistic thought grants only a transitive causality. The effect always has to be distinct from the cause, and the signified from the signifier. Thus, housing is represented as the product *ad extra,* the effect cut off from the cause, over which one no longer has any grasp. Thus, lived experience would be only the accidental signifier of much more general and essential instantiated principles. In this sense, short-circuiting the modal, the intermediate, and the unstable is equivalent to objectifying inhabiting, and it is so as much through the mechanisms of construction as through the ways of defining "housing-objects," "short-term objectives," and pairs of concepts of the need/satisfaction type by means of which one turns out "household objects" and those ridiculous "subjects" of use that are so many individual props for consumption.

The first advantage of our lingering over the modalities of lived experience and of our pursuing the discovery of them would be to dismiss such abstract objectifications that slice up, a priori, all concrete sociability and lead one to consider the instantiated principle of the collective as a collection of juxtaposed individuals whose unity would reside in the Establishment,[7] with its cohort of (legal, economic, sociocultural, etc.)

establishments. The second advantage of such an approach would be to deliver inhabitant expression to us in the immediacy of its tensions, of its conflicts, of its not yet reduced, not yet "resolved" possibilities.

AN IRREDUCIBLE IMAGINARY

The third surprise will come from the excessiveness, from the ambiguity, from the overflowing nature of a rhetoric of lived inhabiting. "The fear of meaning—and especially of double meaning!—is the major terror of our intellectual pedagogy," Gilbert Durand points out.[8] And if the imaginary appears to be the common ground of these excesses, of these double or multiple meanings, the resulting surprise could verge on perplexity. One will be surprised that an imaginary whose mischievousness, whose reveries, and whose outbursts can be accepted in a pinch as quite natural diversions—as escapades that, when all is said and done, actually favor the reproduction of the labor force—might overflow its confines and give itself out as the ground of the lived experience of inhabiting. It will be doubted that such a power to imagine—about which one knows only its momentary and fleeting role as an intermediate faculty in perceiving and knowing—might appear as the force by which we do not live the fragmentary as it is given to us. How could the abstract principle of homogenization not be the only way of reading identities and convergences of meaning? And how—opposite, or alongside, this thetic principle—could an imaginary persist in its irreducible power of expression and insist upon proceeding through homology rather than through clear-cut divisions and distinctions?

But does not such a surprise also conceal a fear? This would be the fear of the possible sudden emergence of a groundswell that no measuring stick succeeds in gauging and that no reason is certain to be able to contain.

The devaluation of the imaginary and the will to reduce its force barely conceals a vague, yet still disturbing, memory of the powers of which it is capable. For, in order to limit onself to the Western orbit, only five centuries separate us from a culture in which the imaginary (*phantasia, spiritus phantasticus,* as was said at the time) had been recognized as the fundamental intermediary, on the near side of conscious perception as well as on the far side of rational knowledge. It was not so long ago the key to the understanding of the world and of multidimensional man.[9]

Today's rejection of an irreducible power of the imaginary manifests itself though the way in which the creative imagination is annexed and is, at the same time, reduced to the domain of productivity. The imaginary becomes an instrumental moment in the production of the edified space. This moment, on which the most creative writers lay stress and whose brevity and limits they regret,[10] brings into play the pregnancy of archaic space, the drive to play, the ornamental drive, and the drive for order.[11] Crossed with the drive for imitation, these drives nevertheless deteriorate into divisions and fixations: forms and functions are conceptualized separately, and the force of the schematism becomes fixed in set schemata. The form no longer is configuring but, rather, posited in order to figure. For whatever they are worth, designers of urban space figure into their consumer product the image of a world that implies nothing other than filling in, contiguity, and distribution.

And yet, from the conceptual designer's imaginary to the inhabitant imaginary, a spontaneous analysis would not be loath to underscore the unevenness, the deterioration. The conceptual design would exploit the imaginary all more actively as it produces a material reality that occupies the space (and the ground of this space gives itself out as "real-estate" reality, "landed" reality) and as the use is anticipated, preconceived, implicitly or explicitly imagined when there is a "social project." Among inhabitants, the imaginary would be liberated in a superfluous sort of way in leisure (*otium* or opium?). While thus reduced and desiccated, such an imaginary would nevertheless have more effective value than a merely suffered imaginary or one in which its activity is represented as defenseless and contingent.

The study of everyday walks indicates, on the contrary, that there really is much more creative movement, configuration, and dynamic tension going on in the humblest acts of inhabiting than in the very process that produces the contemporary built world. This points to an opening and to an investigative lead in which, on the basis of the lived experience of inhabiting, and not of conceptually designed housing, the imaginary functionally utilized in the production of laid-out and developed space might be confronted with an imaginary the inhabitant actually lives. A certain number of received values would then most likely be overturned, and this expressive power of an irreducible imaginary (one ignored for this reason by discourses on construction and housing) would appear as *a cosmogenetic point.*

In making the universe of everydayness begin on the basis of what is *given,* the world of manipulated technology is posited as the first cause. And so, even the most lucid critics render those who no longer know how to inhabit responsible for those who no longer know how to build. Scrupulous conceptual designers bow under the burden of an enormously bad conscience. Everything is still played out in terms of "knowing" and of "conscience." It is said, "The world we have been given is bad. The forms in which the dominant powers are set are deadly but fated."

In understanding everyday activity on the basis of its *imaginary ground,* the world begins in another way. It is seized as a structuration and not as structure, as functioning of configured forms and not as simultaneous positing of preconceived functional forms. The inhabited world, with or against other worlds, is convoked and reactivated in the realm of the conflictual and not in these falsely homogeneous "fillings-in" wherein each ends up representing himself in solitude and the expletive, as if one were mere "filler."

The imaginary is, in short, the cosmogenetic point on the basis of which an inhabitant expression still exists and endeavors to fashion its world. It is the strategic point, too, from which the study of urban existence could come to consider, in terms of force, movement, and expression, what in received ideas are represented to us as forms, positions, and pure signitive relation. As Paul Klee said:

> Nowhere, ever, is the form to be considered as achievement, result, final term, but as genesis, as becoming, as essence *in actu.* The form as achieved appearance is a bad and dangerous specter.[12]

In offering this passage for the reader's contemplation, we shall apply it to the end of the present work in two senses.

These formulations—namely, that the form would be formation and configuration and that, on the other hand, "achieved appearance" would be a "dangerous specter"—sum up in an aphoristic way our intention here by giving a literally more *operative* sense (qua *oeuvre, opera, opus*) to the lived experience of inhabiting than to the production of the built world and by overturning the vice of making all too obvious evaluations.

The same remark also applies to our own itinerary. Faithful to the nature of inhabitant expression, we have refused to give an end term [*un terme*] or a conclusion to it. We wanted only to propose a transitory and transitive way of formulating the question of inhabiting. The time of this writing and the modes of inhabiting we had described have already been altered. Here, as elsewhere, inhabitant expression is a far cry from having said its last word.

In this sense, the way that turns its back on definitive "terms," on established relations, and on dogmas, the one that opens itself out toward the eccentric, the intermediate, and the ambiguous calls for another future as well as for other investigations. The initial, uncertain project has made its way, gained its ground, and its end is only temporary. What we have discovered in the lived experience of inhabiting, and the way in which we have done it, end up being brought together in the same idea of an oeuvre, a work that is already "along the way" and that calls for other variations. Let us understand in this sense another phrase drawn from the same text by Klee:

> Through the identity of way and work, the work becomes articulated "along the way," in passing from a uniform gait to varied gaits.[13]

Here we are already "along our way" at the invitation of everyday walks grasped in their movement, the rhythm of their gaits. Because they have the secret power to break up uniformity, because their variations sidetrack and will still evade our certainties and our self-evident truths, the paths of expression do indeed seem to lead somewhere.[14]

Appendix A

Synoptic Table

A formal conclusion would have been possible in the form of a synoptic table. We attempt a sketch of such a table here.

It seems to us that two powers, two different orders, are in constant confrontation with each other in everyday life. One of these establishes itself through general representations (which are reproduced by the "user" and the "consumer"). The other one, which is buried and goes unnoticed, is rooted in the lived experience of the inhabitant.

The order of constructing-housing, which stretches from the layout and development of space to the delivery of housing, enjoins a representation of both the production of space and the usage of the spatial product. This representation is reproduced even in the general speech patterns of the inhabitants.

The order of inhabitant expression, or of inhabiting, subsists under the first of these and is grounded on an active sense of inhabitant action.

On the one hand, the modalities of inhabitant expression and the representations of constructing-housing stand in contradictory relation to each other. (And one will have glimpsed in what sense these contradictions can hardly be "resolved.")

On the other hand, the order of constructing-housing covers over that of inhabiting and reduces it in two ways:

- the constructed product *is represented as bringing about* housing usage;
- everyday details, modalities of lived experience, and the forces of inhabiting *are reduced to representations* that are conceptualizable and manipulable.

This set of reductionist processes implies the convergence and the identity, on the conceptual level, of the *mode of producing* and the *mode of thinking* producing and usage.

The foregoing can be read in two possible directions. Either:

- one takes the point of view of the reductionist order (the order of constructing-housing), and then the habitual process by which one buries the power of inhabiting can be rendered explicit. In that case, one must begin by reading the pages that inventory the principal categories of the reductionist order (odd-numbered pages of the table); or

- one "takes a plunge" and one takes the point of view of the order of inhabiting. The reading can then begin with the third principle of this order of inhabitant expression, since it is the most inconceivable one for the logic of the reductionist order (last even-numbered page of the table).

Yet, every reading of the table in this second direction would show, in short, that the power of inhabitant expression remains irreducible and that, on account of this fact, no attempt to resolve the basic contradictions between the two orders is viable.

Let us note, finally, that the arrangement of the table, which is organized into three series for greater "clarity," by itself betrays a problematic that does not succeed in ridding itself of the spatial paradigm cluttering up our thought. In this sense, inhabitant expression remains alien to the logic of such a confrontation, as well as to the metaphor of synoptic arrangement. Also, such a table interests us only to the extent that it manifests this ultimate disavowal.

Practical Hints

In the double-paged tables that follow, each numbered proposition stands in contradictory relation to the proposition bearing the same number on the facing page.

In italics, one will read the logical and ideological reductions the

order of constructing-housing tries to apply to the noteworthy characteristics of the order of inhabiting. (The indication *Reduction,* which
will be found on the even-numbered pages, refers one back each time
to the text in italics that is to be found on the respective odd-numbered
page and in the same row.)

ORDER OF INHABITING

First principle: Inhabited space is lived partially, in a discrete way (with absences), and in a heterogeneous way. The representation of the globality of this space is imaginary in nature.

EXPRESSIONS OF THIS PRINCIPLE

---

1. Globality takes on meaning in each concrete *articulation* of inhabiting, which convokes it and evokes it.

   Reduction :

---

2. Inhabiting expresses itself through *breaks,* cuts, and opacities; also through excesses and through overflows of the fragmented onto the constructed totality. In deforming the latter, it gives itself out as *movement of configuration.*

   Reduction :

---

3. The rhythm of everyday life comes from the eventful. Inhabited space is configured and marked by eventful memory.

   Reduction :

---

4. Articulating the heterogeneous, inhabitant expression lives appropriation through the evocation or convocation of a conflictual sociability. A space is *appropriable* only on the ground of its strangeness, its foreignness, its alienness.

   Reduction :

ON HOMOGENIZATION

ORDER OF CONSTRUCTION-HOUSING

First principle: The space of the habitat is constructed only on the condition that there is a representation of homogeneity. It is handed over to use as a rational and real totality.

OPERATIVE PROCEDURES AND REDUCTIONS OF INHABITING

---

1. The part has meaning only in its *relation* to the totality that "really" grounds it.

   The moments of everyday life are reduced to partial uses, to territorial assignments related to the abstract identity of the total territory.

---

2. Housing depends upon a state of planning in which each part receives its rightful place and finds itself juxtaposed to the others by virtue of an abstract delimitation of boundaries and upon a ground of *continuity*.

   Themes of transparency, of fusion, and of the opening of sites. Leveling of differences through the metaphors of "audible" discourses.

---

3. In its system, which tends toward closure, planned space grants as an event only what is foreseeable, conceivable, and re-presentable.

   Theme of the preconception of "social life." Only what arises with at least a minimal form of organization is possible. In production itself, there is an absorption of the overall and primordial event: How will produced space be inhabited when it becomes use-space?

---

4. Appropriation is conceived as juxtaposition of *appropriated* sites, as partition within homogeneity, and as repetition, in various parts, of the same relation of the subject to the object.

   Themes of integration, of fusion, and of mixture. Identification and establishment of a common denominator (spatial homogeneity) for all that can be alien (social differences, ethnic differences, differences in everyday practices) leads to a process of abstract assimilation that tends to give itself out as real.

ORDER OF INHABITING

Second principle: Space is articulated through time.

EXPRESSIONS OF THIS PRINCIPLE

---

1. Articulation of retention and protention. Convocation of the sensorial totality that qualifies a multidimensional climate. Lived time configures space through the possibility of the project and upon a ground of absence.

Reduction :

---

2. —Movement of motor configuration.
   —Appearance and disappearance of lived space.

Reduction :

---

3. Articulated through time, space opens itself up to the possible, to the unforeseeable, to the imaginable, to repetition in difference, to motor anticipation, and to the pregnancy of variable atmospheres.

Reduction :

---

4. The raw material of a regulatory system of inhabiting appears in those modalities of lived experience that are one's everyday ways of being in space according to the time.

Reduction :

ON ABSTRACTION

ORDER OF CONSTRUCTING-HOUSING

Second principle: Time is structured and mastered through spatiality.

DEFINITIONS OF SPACE
AND REDUCTIONIST COROLLARIES OF INHABITING

---

1. A space to be seen (perceived), capable of being put at a distance, always referable to in terms of spatial simultaneity.

   —*Reduction of tension through objectification: distancing "on the opposite side"; self-reduction, always including a variable degree of the spectacular. The project becomes fixed in an object.*

   —*Reduction of absence through the filling in of spatial permanency; substantification of spatiality.*

---

2. A thetic space: space to be "posited" through permanency.

   —*Reduction of configuration into postures (stroboscopic representation);*

   —*Reduction of the articulation of the movement to a pause and of the articulation between appearance and disappearance into representations of poses and positions.*

---

3. A space of functional uses, grounded upon conceptual oppositions (leisure-labor, consumption-play, circulation-withdrawal).

   The vacuities, equivocalities, and "unrealities" of a lived experience of inhabiting are made up for through a preformation of usage in accordance with the succession of contiguous operations. Induction of a repetition of the identical, of an abstract anticipation of "social life," and of a homogenization of the "social climate." Inductions are inscribed in the architectural forms and the codes of use. Reductions are conveyed through the abstract concepts of professional discourses.

---

4. The abstract representation of space yields spatiality as raw material.

   —*Reduction of modes into concepts;*

   —*Isochronic reduction of lived time, through which each instant has to be equivalent to every other one.*

ORDER OF INHABITING

1. As analyzed in the situation of multiunit housing, inhabiting expresses itself through a clash between the lived and the given as conceived. As mode of inhabiting, walking configurations are as much result as movement, initial meaning as ultimate meaning of this clash. They express inhabiting and inhabiting expresses itself in them.

2. Inhabiting alters the representations of given dualities in space and displaces their signification without denying their existence (outside-inside, public-private, etc.). Inhabitant expression proceeds through resonances, echos, and pregnancies by which the inhabitant convokes the inhabitant universe, and vice versa.

3. Inhabiting can be grasped in its concrete movement only in the form of an expression. Yet, more than a mere form, expression is given as the nature of the lived experience of inhabiting. In an investigative project, what is lived and what of it is expressed are inseparable. For, the memorable and the recountable are already inscribed in the lived configuration of space, along with the forms and forces of sociability. Between the fact that, on the one hand, the lived experience of inhabiting can be grasped only through its expressions and, on the other, the very nature of the lived experience of the space of one's habitat is a force of expression, there is no tautology as between two propositions. There is a mutual referral of meanings between different movements over time and in accordance with the modal variations through which they express something and express themselves.

Third principle: The order of inhabiting is grounded upon a ternary articulation between expression, expresser, and expressed.

ON BINARY DIVISION

ORDER OF CONSTRUCTING-HOUSING

Third principle: The productions, inductions, and repro-
ductions implied in the first two series are grounded on
a logic of binary division. Divisions between cause and
effect, container and contained, conceived and lived, outside and inside, public and private, individual and social.

REDUCTIVE EFFECTS PRODUCED BY THESE ABSTRACT DIVISIONS

---

1. *Reduction of the system of inhabiting to a conceived/lived split. Inhabiting understood as a housing consecutive to the production of constructing. The conceived-
lived difference can be abstracted in various ways and be represented either as a
necessity (causality of a variable nature, depending upon one's analysis) or as a
contradiction one underscores and attempts to reduce.*

---

2. *Reduction of movements to becoming and of forces to forms via:*

*—subject/object division, which privileges the point of view of objectifying
knowledge;*

*—causal representation, wherein only one relation between two fixed and defi-
nite terms is conceived at a time;*

*—representation in terms of "contradictions" that dissolve the concrete modality
through which contraries are lived.*

---

3. *Reduction of the lived experience of inhabitant expression through the split between signifier and signified: the significations apprehended (as much in the preconception as in the analysis of "social life" as it is given) are polarized around univocal meanings. They become incidental accessories of a representation of signifieds
that are regrouped into abstract concepts: "conception," "realization," "usage,"
but also "social life," "social project," and "social confrontation." In an investigation of inhabiting, one applies the same process of division and abstraction: on the
one hand, perception, on the other, memory; on the one hand, lived experience,
on the other, signification; on the one hand, the individual, on the other, the social;
and, finally, the contained ("content analysis"), cut off from the container, becomes
an abstract material.*

---

*(The third principle of the order of inhabiting is not reducible as such. Inconceiv-
able in the dominant code of knowledge and of the production of space, it is reduced into the modes that express it and is represented in a binary division that will
never allow inhabitant expression's own force to appear.)*

Appendix B

Map and Toponymic Lexicon of the Arlequin Neighborhood

The Arlequin neighborhood is the terrain from which the illustrations of walking rhetoric have been drawn. This neighborhood was constructed between 1969 and 1972 in the New Town Priority Development Area[1] of Grenoble, France.

This neighborhood map will allow readers to visualize schematically a quite peculiar kind of spatial organization. It represents the neighborhood at the ground level, with the most essential information concerning either the basic functions or the "landscaped" features of the space surrounding everyday strolls.

This lexicon provides definitions for the unusual terms that the neighborhood planners used to designate certain sites, often with new conceptions.

Toponymic Lexicon

gallery   main pedestrian lane that passes underneath the buildings. Including its various branches, its "linear" measure is nearly a kilometer.

mezzanines   pedestrian landings that duplicate the layout of the gallery, connect to the elevators on this story situated right above street level, and lead to certain places that lie beyond yet are still neighboring the gallery (the roof level of the garages, elementary schools, park entrances)

ramp   sloping segment of the gallery that corresponds to a rise in all the floors of the apartment complex

coves   spaces bordering the gallery that are in the shape of the buildings' characteristic forms (hexagonal module)

passageways	corridors for entry into apartments. These are sometimes quite long, about fifty meters, and they regularly branch out into small lobbies that provide access to two or three front doors of individual apartments.
silos	half-buried garages whose roofs serve either as gardens or as a location for an elementary school
mounds	artificial hillocks installed in the park. They are fifteen meters high, covered with grass, and almost hemispherical in shape.
lake	a human-made expanse of water, one-half-meter deep, situated in the park
Community Center	building and institution comprising the junior high school and neighborhood sociocultural activities

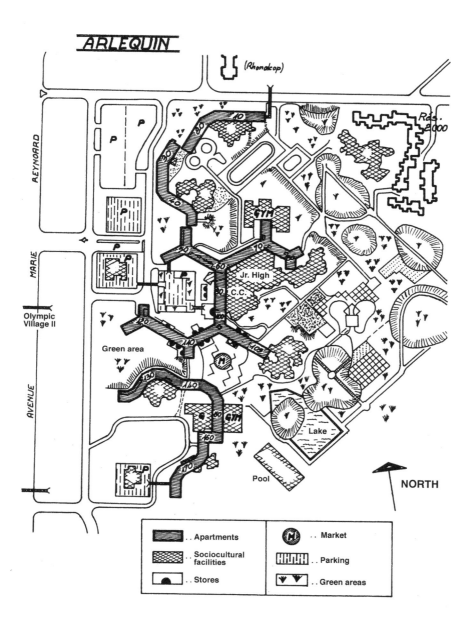

Walking Together, Three Decades Later

DAVID AMES CURTIS

To return to things themselves is to return to that world which precedes knowledge, of which knowledge always *speaks,* and in relation to which every scientific schematization is an abstract and derivative sign-language, as is geography in relation to the countryside in which we have learnt beforehand what a forest, a prairie, or a river is.

—Maurice Merleau-Ponty, *Phenomenology of Perception*

But the thing is not really *observable*—there is always a skipping over *[enjambement]* in every observation, one is never at the thing itself.

　—Maurice Merleau-Ponty, *The Visible and the Invisible*

I wanted you. And I was looking for you.
I wanted you. And I was looking for you all day.

But I couldn't find you. I couldn't find you.
You're walking. And you don't always realize it.
But you're always falling.
With each step, you fall forward slightly.
And then catch yourself from falling.

Over and over, you're falling.
And then catching yourself from falling.
And this is how you can be walking and falling
At the same time.

　—Laurie Anderson, "Walking and Falling," *Big Science*

DAVID AMES CURTIS

ON A BRIGHT AND BRISK LATE SEPTEMBER DAY in 2004, a quarter-century after he had featured the site in his book *Pas à pas,* Jean-François Augoyard kindly offered me a tour of the Arlequin "new town" on the outskirts of his hometown of Grenoble. Having translated this book over the preceding months, I had already shaped in my mind a picture of this fascinating housing complex, about which you have read here. My preformed image of the site—an outgrowth of my act of translation—began to be confronted by another reality, the one formed as we strolled the grounds. Augoyard pointed out, off in the distance, the three main mountain ranges surrounding Grenoble, which I had known previously as the settings for Jean-Claude Killy's 1968 Olympic exploits. Now, climbing one of the three "mounds" (artificial hillocks) described in his book, I realized for the first time how the planners perhaps had fabricated them to mimic visually and physically the environing landscape, with its high peaks—a contextual point not brought out in *Pas à pas.* But as I struggled up a slope, I had to contend not only with the (mild) difficulty of the ascent but also with how that ascent differed from how I had imagined it, each step unsure as I set one foot after the other on an anticipated but unaccustomed slant, the path being more a synthetic version of the winding Heidelbergian *Philosophenweg* than steps up a Mayan temple mount as I had fancied. Words like *lake* did not answer to my promenade past the small but not negligible man-made expanse of water set before me but rather troubled my vision and slowed my pace; and neither did the "silos" for cars, when I passed by, appear as crushingly high above my slightly bowed head as I had envisioned them in my translation, even though I already knew from the book that these and other ersatz terms devised by planners were surely *misleading.* Once we arrived at the "gallery" of this housing complex on International Style stilts,[1] I was surprised to find in the fresh breezes how open and airy it seemed in comparison with the overhang of the impression I was under until then. We never attempted what I had expected would be an infernal rise in one of the complex's reputedly treacherous elevators, but when we did go up an apartment building stairwell, the "passageway" on the mezzanine level that opened out before me set me off balance as it seemed more luminous and less hazardous than I had thought it would be. Finally, I was stopped in my tracks by what was *not* there; the "Maison du quartier," whose name I was still unsure of in translation, no longer existed as it had three decades before, being the casualty, in the interim, of reconstruction plans and right-wing budget cuts about which Augoyard filled me in. I stood looking at the built configuration that now stands in its place, but looking for what could only be sketched out vaguely for me by a few choppy waves of the author's arms as I sought to transform these rough gestures into a satisfactory translation of a now-departed construction-function: "Community Center."[2] Just as I had laboriously retraced the steps of *Pas à pas* in translating the book, carefully attempting to set my own "wordprints" into each of the writer's own and thereby hoping to re-create the same gait, make the same impressions, achieve the same depth, disturbing neither their sense of flow nor their appearance and yet finding myself trudging over markedly different linguistic ground while attempting to do so, so did I proceed hesitantly, almost trippingly, over an imagined yet physically real builtscape I was now traversing unsteadily for the first time and yet had seen rather clearly in my mind's eye for several months.

Whether he considers himself a great artist, a moonlighting writer,[3] an occasional dabbler, a yeoman in the field, a proletarianized intellectual, or a temporary wetware replacement for the future universal translation machine, the human translator is always faced with *choices*—pretty much all of them imperfect and not fully satisfactory. These choices are not only about the selection of individual words or phrases but also regarding the personality and voice of the author one is translating: his vocabulary, phrasing, tone, pacing, and, last but not least, his background.

In the case of *Pas à pas*, the question of background is a particularly rich and varied one, retrospectively quite challenging to catch sight of in its breadth, for large swaths of postwar French intellectual history (such as that of urban studies, linguistics, rhetoric, and Structuralism, as well as of such thinkers as the existential phenomenologist Maurice Merleau-Ponty,[4] the Marxist urbanist Henri Lefebvre,[5] the deconstructionist

Jacques Derrida, and the philosopher of expression Gilles Deleuze),[6] along with foreign influences and prewar precursors (the ontological phenomenologist Martin Heidegger and his student, the Freudo-Marxist critic of modern technology Herbert Marcuse—as Françoise Choay rightly notes in her introduction—along with the creator of modern linguistics Ferdinand de Saussure), definitely come into play.[7] Like the rhapsode Ion in the eponymous dialogue written by Plato, the translator must not only give the distinct impression of, but also endeavor as much as possible to achieve in fact,[8] a complete understanding of the text under interpretation as well as of what the author of the text himself knew and was thinking about—all of this rendered, however, in a context one step removed from the original linguistic setting.[9]

Now, such choices concerning *influences*—one's understanding of what other discourses are also speaking through the text—also involve *decisions* on the translator's part: determinations as to how and to what extent additional voices intrude upon, harmonize with, or simply accompany the author's own as well as proposed solutions as to how to give voice to them in another tongue. To take an illustrative example, Heidegger—author of "Bauen, Wohnen, Denken" (in English: "Building, Dwelling, Thinking")—certainly seemed to me, as he did to Choay, a key reference for Augoyard, who himself cites a passage from *Being and Time* about the temporal manners in which "Dasein goes along its ways." Should Heidegger be deemed such an important influence that a major term in the book, *habiter,* must be translated as "dwelling" (*habiter* is indeed the term found in the French translation of Heidegger: "Bâtir, habiter, penser")?[10] Besides the fact that such expressions as "dweller rhetoric" and "dweller expression" would seem even more clumsy than the distinctive ones ultimately chosen—"inhabitant rhetoric" and "inhabitant expression" for the key terms *la rhétorique habitante* and *l'expression habitante*—it seemed to me that, while Heidegger was still a prime reference, Augoyard's urbane language could maneuver through the translation on its own, not entirely beholden to concepts from the Black Forest philosopher. Indeed, as a final translator's note in the present volume points out, the last lines of Augoyard's book pose a clear challenge to a key Heideggerian text—something that may become apparent to the English-speaking reader, however, only through knowledge of the French translation of the title to Heidegger's first postwar volume, *Holzwege*. (While making no claim to have completely circumnavigated the topic at hand, namely, "everyday walks in an urban setting,"[11] the author states with some conviction that he has blazed his own trails well enough and far enough to establish that "the paths of expression do indeed seem to lead somewhere." The French title of *Holzwege* is *Chemins qui mènent nulle part,* Paths that lead nowhere.) Moreover, *dwelling* evokes a lived state over time (associated by Heidegger with building and thinking), while *inhabiting* can, and does here, connote a mobile, dynamic, and reversible—though not necessarily symmetrical—relationship to home and neighborhood characterized not only by "numerous occasions for pauses and stays" within and beyond one's domicile but also by excursions and explorations, as well as by more or less typified and set patterns of movement in and out of one's dwelling, that relate also to practices offering silent but salient resistance to certain forms of building.[12] Similarly, elsewhere in his tome Augoyard conveys his skepticism about the "static architectural thought" of Le Corbusier, as expressed in the latter's "modulor," which had erected *postures,* not "gaits," into paradigms for an inhabitant's lived experience of "everyday comings and goings."

As it turns out, Augoyard himself has something to say about translation. Near the outset, while reviewing possible leads, subsequently rejected, for ways of investigating how one might account for quotidian strolls through parts of the city, he writes, "A topographical translation, like any interpretation based on continuities and contiguities, . . . seemed to us an improper way of accounting for spatial practices as they are lived day to day." (Topography had at first seemed likely to provide him with the analytic tools for which he was searching: "For a daily stroll, what is more metaphorical than a map?" The related field of *topology,* it should be noted, was then in vogue in Structuralist circles.) This brief statement is in fact expressive of a broader viewpoint, for throughout the book Augoyard is more than suspicious of the one-to-one, univocal, linear correspondences of classical, Saussure-inspired Structuralism. Such an attitude might at first seem surprising, since walking is such an apparently straightforward activity and a "step by step" approach, taken in a usual sense, would therefore seem particularly well matched here. Nevertheless, we shall subsequently arrive at the place where these steps, full of gaps and in their meandering succession, will be conceived in an entirely other manner.

As he already warned a few pages earlier, "there is always a 're-mainder' in analytic operations that involve division." His turning away from "topographical translation" leads him to assert that "daily strolls . . . belong to that class of overlooked practices that apparently cannot be co-opted by the commercial economy and that are, in the view of sci-entific knowledge, insignificant."[13] Augoyard opts for the less trodden road,[14] for it offers him an alternative to the broad and well-worn path of a traditional scientific-analytic approach designed to discount any "remainder" that cannot precisely be resituated within clear-cut and well-established divisions. Indeed, discussing this nontopographical ap-proach to his chosen topic, he explains that

> the referent for one's walks is not the simultaneity of a planned spatial whole but, rather, at each moment of the stroll, the coexistence of the different instan-tiated principles involved in everyday life. The explication, the development in movement of this coexistence, resembles a sort of creation, and through this creation the space into which one has gone takes on this or that quality, de-pending on the occasion, but no longer has any permanency of its own (except in representation and on maps).

Augoyard goes so far as to talk, in chapter 2, about the "creative gait of lived space-time." As will be fathomed later on, the imaginary plays a deeply original role in this creation not only of one's gait but also of the shifting ground upon which that gait is expressed.

How, then, to account for this ambulatory invention of a lived world? Returning to the limits and drawbacks of topography, he asserts that, "better than topographical observation, oral expression has appeared to us to mimic quite closely the act of strolling." Yet here we notice a key, and oft-repeated, gesture in Augoyard's own expository move-ment, one that I have myself been at pains to re-create in translation. While conceptions of urban planning, the language of linguistics, and the terminology of rhetoric are integral moments of his overall exposition, his forward motion through and beyond them is quite distinctive and thus worth retracing, for it is the movement itself, not the positions taken up in succession, that, according to my reading via translation, seemed most significant.

Augoyard does state that "the analogy with graphic expression is unendingly striking."

> Just as a book is read in company with a motionless (re)writing and is written at the same time that it is read for oneself and for others, *walking resembles a reading-writing*. Sometimes rather more following an existing path, sometimes rather more hewing a new one, one moves within a space that never tolerates the absolute exclusion of the one or the other.

He follows up this statement, however, with another one: "This analogy is to be pursued so long as it does not betray the lived quality that is of interest to us and so long as it does not reduce the traces of pedestrian activity to a prosaic linguistic system." Mimicry, resemblance, and analogies may indeed serve as temporary guideposts for understanding ambulatory orientation, but the poetic and the creative recover from the descent into the prosaic and the analytic and then overtake them with each new step. One is reminded here of the lyrics to Laurie Anderson's *Big Science* song "Walking and Falling."[15] The tightly constructed format of this book—which, despite an early dismissal of the idea that any "prosaic linguistic system" might account for the creativity of walking practices, could have misled one into thinking of it as straightforwardly "systematic" in conception—eventually comes into focus as a sort of endless rocking motion in a continually off-center forward movement, constantly falling, as if into indefinitely deep holes, and then righting itself in time for the next step.

Step by Step might as a consequence appear to some readers to embody an early example of the "poststructuralist" texts that began to proliferate in the aftermath of Structuralism's wholesale discreditation at the time of May '68. Are we, more than a quarter century later, reading here (in translation) merely one more instance of a rather outdated fashion in Continental thought, now often characterized by undiscerning eclecticism and rampant irresponsibility, that has itself become increasingly discredited of late—without, however, much of anything substantial filling its shoes? Is this another irrelevant hodgepodge of the "French Ideology," about which University of Minnesota Press author Cornelius Castoriadis wrote so discerningly?[16]

One facet of post-Structuralist thought, Jacques Derrida's, does indeed surface on several occasions in Augoyard's book, with a half-dozen uses of the verb *deconstruct* and its derivatives as well as an enunciation of the concept of "differance" ("this movement, as retention of the other as other in the same").[17] "Inhabitant activity," Augoyard observes, "displays . . . properties [that] cannot be integrated into a systems model that tends toward closure. This is the resolutely disruptive function of everyday events and the fundamental role of spatial deconstruction." "What is heard," for example, ". . . covers over and deconstructs the visual realm, which ordinarily is predominant." He goes on to assert that "the essence of collective life in an urban setting is to be defined not only through the lived experience of oppositions of one social group to another, but also by *a constant tension between constructed spatiality handed over for use and the rhetorical deconstruction of this space, which is done in favor of the expression of styles of inhabiting.*"

These mentions of deconstruction, it may be suggested, can be *taken in stride.* For, one notices that they are but one (though several times repeated) step in a trajectory that includes other steps—as when Augoyard speaks of a "constant tension" of which the moment (or movement) of deconstruction is but one term. With the overturning of the usual terms of analysis employed to describe pedestrian movement, he asks, "If spatial totalities lose all meaning of their own and are but the occasional material and pretext for deconstruction, for derealization, what is the field of reference for everyday action? What is the basic ground brought into play by expression, when laid-out and developed space finds itself relegated to an accidental modality?"[18] It is rather in the elucidation of this "basic ground" and in the scrutiny of "modalities" that we might discover where the author is headed and how far he gets.

Early on, Augoyard hypothesizes that "it would be necessary . . . *to postpone for some time the repetition of our 'why' questions and to give free rein to the 'how'*—that is to say, to substitute a modal type of interpretation for a causal type of explanation." His "methodological approach" is therefore one "that has chosen the path of *modal analysis* (one oriented by the 'how' rather than by the 'why')."[19] This "modal" emphasis on the "how" over the "why" can be said to be inspired by a phenomenological approach in general—which is characterized by description of experience without reference to causality—and not especially by Derrida's idiosyncratic commentaries thereon in his discussions of Edmund Husserl. Indeed, the only chapter of Augoyard's book with an epigram written by someone other than a poet (René Char and Francis Ponge) or an artist (Wassily Kandinsky) is the fourth one, which cites Merleau-Ponty's early philosophical work *Phenomenology of Perception* (1945). There, the phenomenologists' rallying cry, "*Zu die Sachen selbst*" (To the things themselves), is curiously repeated as a "return to things themselves."[20]

What may be gleaned especially from Augoyard's work is the opportunity, and indeed the necessity, of closely following movement in words as well as in things and people. Merleau-Ponty's odd *return* turns out to be disorienting, but also indicative of larger trends in postwar Continental thought. An existential phenomenologist should have understood that such a "return" is, to say the least, exceedingly unlikely, if not downright impossible, in light of *Repetition,* a key early work by Søren Kierkegaard, the first existentialist to have irrevocably chosen to build his shelter outside the Hegelian system. But it should have already been obvious to any philosopher who has read Heraclitus's twelfth fragment, often loosely translated as "You can never step into the same river twice," let alone his student Cratylus's radicalizing reply that one cannot step into the *same* river even *once*.[21] Indeed, at the other end of his philosophical trajectory, in the "Working Notes" to his posthumously published volume *The Visible and the Invisible,* Merleau-Ponty in effect grants the failure of the entire phenomenological project: "But the thing is not really *observable*—there is always a skipping over in every observation, one is never at the thing itself." This implicit set of admissions—that one never gets "to the things themselves," that one must inevitably "skip over" things in order to observe them, and that observation of things is itself somehow always (already?) deficient[22]—trips up phenomenology at the level of its deepest, most underlying intention (intentionality and its object) while straddling unsuccessfully a key issue in its overall history but also offering itself to further reflection.

One cannot be "at the thing itself" via observation, for observation involves or entails a "skipping over" movement (*enjambement*). Now, in French, *enjambement* has two main senses. *Enjamber* means to stick one's leg up, above, and beyond something, to step over it, to stride forward or stride toward, to span a gap. But *enjambement* also, significantly, has a literary meaning expressed in English by a direct borrowing from the French, spelled "enjambment" or "enjambement." *Wikipedia* (q.v.) defines it as "the breaking of a syntactic unit (a phrase, clause, or sentence) by the end of a line or between two verses. Its opposite is end-stopping, where each linguistic unit corresponds with the line length." Moreover, in enjambment, "meaning flows from line to line, and the reader's eye is pulled forward. Enjambement creates a feeling of acceleration, as the reader is forced to continue reading after the line has ended." Remarkably, we are witnessing here a mutual accompaniment of motion and meaning[23] that might even drive us to think that understanding comes in strides of movement rather than settles into fixed positions.[24] Such a discovery would be as profound as it is moving: the "point," so to speak, is not at point A or point B but in the act of traversing from point A to point B, and beyond.[25]

Of equal significance, and here we ourselves are trying to wend our way back to what might be taken as Augoyard's own winding path through and beyond phenomenological description, Merleau-Ponty's unconscious epitaph to phenomenology was jotted down in the "Working Notes" at precisely the place where he was attempting to come to grips, though not very successfully, with *the imagination*.[26] By way of contrast, after an initial mention of Derridean "differance" the imagination becomes Augoyard's point of departure for the fifth chapter of his book. There, he endeavors to make good on his early promise that walking practices and the act of inhabiting would testify to a creative accomplishment and ongoing force of resistance not wholly reducible to an effect in the preplanned production of space.

In this final chapter, "inhabitant expression" is treated as not only "incorporated," in the Merleau-Pontean sense of embodiment, but also "grounded" in what Augoyard will call "the obscure and overflowing aspect of the imaginary"—therefore, a ground that is as shrouded in darkness as it is slippery, unstable, and not confined to fixed boundaries.

"In anticipating action," inhabitant expression "renders present what 'really' is not yet so." This anticipatory capacity to *bring into being what is not (yet)* introduces the major themes of what have been, in Greco-Western thought, the repeated discovery and covering back over of the imagination since it was first discovered, out of place, in the last book of the treatise *Peri psuchēs*. There, Aristotle says "Never does the soul think without phantasm."[27] Augoyard begins his own exposition with Kant's (re)discovery of it in the *Critique of Pure Reason*—there, the latter says, significantly and mysteriously, "This schematism of our understanding applied to phenomena and their mere form is an art hidden in the depth of the human soul, the true secrets of which we shall hardly ever be able to guess and reveal"—and with Kant's subsequent hints at an elaboration in the *Critique of Judgment*. Kantian imagination, he says, connects "understanding and sensibility," gives meaning to "the experience of the world," and allows knowledge to have "concrete application." For Augoyard, "*the imaginable* overflows the limits of . . . spatial 'reality.'" For, "far from being a simple and passive reservoir of images, the imagination possesses an activity and a capacity for synthesis" that "literally outstrips the understanding." Indeed, as Augoyard had himself found earlier and now summarizes here his discoveries, it is by "this same power that the acted and the suffered, sensation and motor function, the present and the absent are tied together in a process of articulation." Instead of *imagination,* he "prefer[s] to designate henceforth such an instantiated principle by the word *imaginary,* which takes on a less restrictive meaning" by comparison.

As antecedents to his own exploration of the imaginary, Augoyard cites in a note the names Sigmund Freud and Gaston Bachelard, who "agree on this industrious circulation of the imaginary that defies the apparent distinctions in whose name mental functions are doggedly separated from one another and our psychosomatic entity is torn asunder."[28] Such a "circulation" takes us back to Augoyard's initial point of departure: the expressive errantry of walking narratives. For him, however, "the power of the imaginary takes on coherency only at the end of our path." And yet his *approach* will be crucial to the outcome: "Instead of a formal definition of the imagination, we have preferred a genetic definition of the imaginary." Closely accompanied along this path by Gilles

Deleuze, Augoyard eschews "theoretical representations" of the role the imaginary plays in human expression, preferring (or enunciating the necessity of) a detour through Renaissance articulations of imagination and expression. He concludes that "the imaginary is a domain, a field of action and of passion that spans the whole of our existence in space and in time. We never leave its soil." Significantly, the word *spans* translates here the French *"traverse."* Augoyard is articulating, in a way, the mobile meaning-creating process of *enjambement* upon an ever-shifting imaginary ground.

Halfway through his Conclusion—in a section titled "An Inhabiting without a 'Why?'"—Augoyard's previously temporary "postpone[ment of] the repetition of our 'why' questions" (in order to pose "how" questions that uncover the expressive creativity of walking practices) is waived in favor of a more long-term suspension, ascribed to the very nature of inhabiting.

> Although the poetic nature of the act of configuring space has become apparent to us, inhabiting has to be understood rather as a movement than as an aesthetic object. Yet, in any case, it is averse to the "why," because the "why" no longer intends anything but representations, whereas the "how" intends things.

It should be noted without delay that, had *habiter* been translated as "dwelling" instead of as "inhabiting," the reader herself would have been stopped in her tracks and unable to proceed, no matter how long and how deeply she might have dwelt upon the possible meaning of the statement that *dwelling* could be encapsulated as *movement*. But *why*, we are tempted to inquire here, is it said that inhabiting resists "why" questions?[29]

Temporary postponement becomes indefinite deferral as phenomenological intentionality metamethodologically remakes an entrance: "the 'why' no longer intends anything but representations, whereas the 'how' intends things." We have trod this ground before and found that we must skip over things in order to observe them:[30] observation goes too far for phenomenological intentionality to live up to its motto, "To the things themselves," and thus the latter ultimately falls short of its own mark. The justification for this backtracking is itself methodologically inspired by a certain view of phenomenology: the one in which "everyday existence in town" is to be investigated, as Augoyard says, "not as it is represented but as it is lived." Whence this simple binary opposition between lived experience and representation?

The former term comes from the late Husserlian notion of the *Lebenswelt* (life-world) and is expressed in French as *le vécu*—a general term, meaning *real-life* or *personal* experience, given philosophical import primarily by Merleau-Ponty as a way of talking about the subjective side of experience without appearing to indulge in the Cartesian subject–object dualism he had sought to go beyond. The (wholly negative) understanding of "representation" stems here from another of Heidegger's *Holzwege* texts, "The Age of the World Picture."[31] Descartes is considered the culprit by his having brought about this "age" in which "subjects" said to *represent* beings as "objects" triumph as part of an unquestioning technological attitude characterized by wholesale calculation.[32] Curiously, in the penultimate published note to this 1938 talk, when Heidegger envisions a time after this age has expired and the attendant overcoming of Western metaphysics is achieved, man will, he affirms, no longer represent being as an object ("wenn er das Seiende nicht mehr als Objekt vorstellt"). If representation (*Vorstellung*) is, intrinsically and always already, the *placing* of an object *before* a subject and a debased re-presentation in the form of a representational picture (*Bild*), as Heidegger claims, why does he have to add *als Objekt*?

It might seem that we are *going too far afield*, in a translator's Afterword, to concern ourselves with *représentation*'s obvious translation as "representation," let alone with its usage in a third language not mentioned directly in the translated text. Yet it may prove useful to provide the reader with authorial background information—that is, information on the author's background, the steps he has taken previously as well as the voices he has heard along the way, and that continue to speak within him, *even and perhaps especially when he is challenging one of those voices*, as we may hear Augoyard doing vis-à-vis Heidegger at the end of *Step by Step*.[33] Indeed, the ambiguity or reduplication we found in Merleau-Ponty's "return to the things themselves" and in what, for Heidegger's "epochal" reading of Cartesianism, is the pleonasm "represented as an object" is itself repeated by Augoyard himself in his Conclusion—in a passage about repetition:

If the power of building has been occulted and the term *inhabiting* has become a doublet for *housing*, the play of transformations brought on by economic considerations is not the only thing at issue. The change that has been carried out has taken place through an objectifying representation of housing, one's habitat becoming a housing-object. It has made it possible to think in terms of a standardized product constructed in a repetitive manner.

If, for argument's sake, one accepts Heidegger's conflation of objectification with representation as such,[34] Augoyard's phrase "an objectifying representation" is equally pleonastic. And it is just as necessary, for reasons we shall explore.

For Augoyard, this lived experience certainly includes intention (understood phenomenologically to embrace also protention and retention). He also accepts the vector of affect or feeling ("the present takes on an affective tonality that differs according to whether the eventuality in question is imagined in a harmful or a favorable light"), even if inhabiting, as he said, is not to be envisioned especially as an "aesthetic object."[35] Representation, however, remains for him lived experience's direct opposite: "Inhabitant expression lived in space and in time skips causal or rational sequences and does without streams of representations."[36] But once one has rediscovered *the imaginary,* can one completely "do without" representations (*Vorstellungen*) as well as images or pictures (*Bilder*)?

In *Being and Time,* Heidegger was in a less unilateral and restrictive *mood,* one more inclined to an open-ended *ambulatory* investigation that takes the Peripatetic Philosopher as its point of departure:

> What has escaped notice is that the basic ontological Interpretation of the affective life in general has been able to make scarcely *one forward step* worthy of mention since Aristotle. On the contrary, affects and feelings come under the theme of psychical phenomena, functioning as a third class of these, usually along with ideation [*Vorstellungen*] and volition. They sink to the level of accompanying phenomena. It has been one of the merits of phenomenological research that it has again brought these phenomena more unrestrictedly into our sight.[37]

But there, the imperative was to avoid the psychical in order to concentrate on Dasein's basic affective structure—care (*Sorge*)—to the detriment of considering the world also as will and representation. In inhabitant expression, "what is expressed (for example, avoidance or the seeking out of a qualified site; ease of habitation or inhabitant malaise) refers back to the mode of expression. And in its way of configuring the inhabited space, the mode of expression implies straight off what it endeavors to express." Thus, intention ("avoidance or . . . seeking out") and affect ("ease . . . or . . . malaise") combine without difficulty in imagination. But what of the representation (the "qualified site") itself?

"Let us," Augoyard proposes, "be even more specific":

> Urban atmospheres are born in the crisscrossing of multiple sensations. In this immediate experience of the world, the rain, the wind, and the night hardly have any value of their own. What the inhabitant retains therefrom is the raininess, the windiness, the "fearfulness," that is to say, the affective tonality. Thus, raininess (coldness, dampness, desire for shelter) will qualify the lived world in that very moment. An everyday ambiance takes on a consistency on the basis of a focusing, of a valuing of one element in the environment that will symbolize and reduplicate in an expressive way the atmosphere in which one is bathed.

So, we are to begin with "sensations" (*aisthēseis*). The Merleau-Pontean thesis of the "primacy of perception" is reaffirmed. In lived experience, it is especially an "affective tonality" that is retained, along with and via "focusing" (intention). Curiously, such "focusing" brings about a "symboliz[ation] and reduplicat[ion]" of the basic sensual affects (which supposedly came first, though it is unclear how, before some intentional focusing, there would be any affects in the first place). "There is," says Augoyard citing Pierre Sansot, "a 'reduplication' of urban sites." It is at this point that representation and image make their reappearance: "This color or that coldness will set the tone for all the rest of the sensations and will even enlist, as if by a never extinguished resonance, cultural images, social representations, and ideological reflexes."[38] The primary "sensations" and then a focus-induced "affective tonality" are said to, after the fact, "enlist" such *Vorstellungen*. The origin of representation, its co-originariness, is itself occulted.

"Here," Augoyard, continues, "is one example from the world of sound":

North African music, which is heard rising up on hot summer nights and wakes up the inhabitants of one "cove" around midnight, often exacerbates feelings of expropriation. . . . But for certain inhabitants, an indulgent sense of satisfaction that "there's a party" is awakened at the same time. And perhaps those people are lulled back to sleep with dreams of an unavowed exoticism.

The world of lived experience, an ever *qualified* world, cannot be construed as a "world of sound" in general. In our everyday social world, "North African music"—a "social representation," surely—is experienced just as directly as chirping crickets, grating elevator noises, or any of the other sonorous examples the author provides. Why this reduplication that is, at the same time, a denial of the equiprimordiality of (social) representation and the latter's inevitable reappearance as merely a secondary quality of lived experience?

In between *Being and Time* and *Holzwege*, Heidegger published another book. Castoriadis, the foremost contemporary philosopher of the imaginary, has commented:

> No doubt it is to Heidegger, with his *Kant and the Problem of Metaphysics* (1929), that we owe both the restoration of the question of the imagination as a philosophical question and the possibility of an approach to Kant that breaks with the somnolence and aridity of the neo-Kantians. No doubt, too, that Heidegger reintroduces in his turn and completely on his own—an impressive spectacle—the successive movements of discovery and covering back over that have marked the history of the question of the imagination. . . . Let me simply note here, with respect to the "recoiling" Heidegger imputes to Kant when faced with the "bottomless abyss" opened by the discovery of the transcendental imagination, that it is Heidegger himself who in effect "recoils" after writing his book on Kant. A new forgetting, covering-over, and effacement of the question of the imagination intervenes, for no further traces of the question will be found in any of his subsequent writings; there is a suppression of what this question unsettles for every ontology (and for every "thinking of Being").[39]

No doubt, Kant himself "recoiled" from the principal and preponderant role he himself had attributed to the Transcendental Imagination in the first edition of the *Critique of Pure Reason* and subsequently decided to suppress by backtracking in the second edition . . . because the "bottomless abyss" would have otherwise eventually upset the ambulatory routine of his daily constitutionals. Heidegger's recoil movement in "The Age of the World Picture" is, by way of contrast, exceedingly reduplicative. The end of his eighth appended note reads: "Man as a representing subject [*vorstellende Subjekt*], however, phantasizes [*phantasiert*], that is to say, he moves [*bewege sich*] within the imagination [*in der imaginatio*], insofar as his representing [*sein Vorstellen*] fancies [*einbildet*] being as the objective [*das Gegenständliche*] in the world as picture [*in die Welt als Bild*]."[40] The "representing subject" is already a redundancy for Heidegger. Its act of representing would be quite literally, with respect to the world, that of a "picturing as picture" (*als Bild einbildet*). The overkill is fatal. For, it is only in a reduplicative language of picturing, imaging, imagining, representing that Heidegger is able to critique the Cartesian dualism of the "representing Subject" and of that subject's particular imaginary view of beings as separate objects. It is also disingenuous, for the "insofar as" (*insofern*) slyly attenuates the otherwise overstated claim that representation is always and everywhere carried out in the form of objectification. Notwithstanding the claim that the Greeks were (or we, once saved by a Heideggerian God, would be)[41] attending to Being when allowing beings to appear as they are in a "clearing" via *phantasia*, we must walk away from this flight from representation once it is recognized that observation never places us at the things themselves, that to go "to" them is also to go over and beyond them, and that the proclaimed "return" thereto has to itself be revisited.[42]

Thus, when Augoyard says, "spanning affectivity, feeling, and motor function, these same symbols [namely, graffiti] produce imaginary resonances that are capable of mobilizing the presently lived act," we find that, *at the very moment he articulates the imaginary in terms of a "spanning,"* he himself has returned in fact to the near side of the *produktive Einbildungskraft* (productive imagination) of Kant's first *Critique,* let alone the idea of a creative imagination at work from the outset. What is imaginary here is *produced* instead of producing, even when it is itself declared to be "capable of mobilizing"; its being is but that of acoustical "resonances" or pale visual copies. That is to say, these attenuated replicas would be of a secondary, merely reproductive, and enfeebled status in comparison with their sensational originals. It was the author himself, however, who had previously complained, near the start of his chapter on imagination, that in the history of thought the imaginary has often wrongly been "confined to the production of images."

It is not surprising, when one is struggling with a rough and formidable predecessor—as the municipally based Augoyard is with the woodsy Heidegger—that one might sometimes stumble or even on occasion be drawn backwards. Our goal is not to *trip up* our author but, rather, to see how he fares in this struggle, perhaps to lend him a hand here and there from the standpoint of elucidating problems of translation. There are indeed many gaps in Heidegger's thinking, and it is understandable that Augoyard might eventually fall into a few of them. As Castoriadis remarks about Heidegger, "Here we have the bizarre spectacle of a philosopher talking interminably about the Greeks, and whose thought draws a blank in the place of *polis, eros,* and *psyche.*"[43]

What struck me as I translated this text was instead how well Augoyard negotiates an intellectual terrain he was not, by far, the first to cross. His final chapter offers in fact an exceptional elucidation not only of the unsettled imaginary ground of the inhabitants' expressive lived experience at the Arlequin housing complex but also of that ground's (almost haunted) subterranean underside.[44] There are a specificity and a remarkable quality to these investigations, almost invariably backed up by narrative speech issuing from the residents themselves. As a former community and then labor organizer from the early 1980s, I very much regretted that I had not read *Pas à pas* at the time in order to have benefited from his example as a careful listener of his neighbors' utterances and an attentive companion to them along their peregrinations. And he ends by situating the imaginary as a generative "cosmogenetic point," thus hinting at a genuine ontological basis for this disturbing and disruptive (one is tempted to say *uncanny*) human power within the universe. The "cosmogenesis" of which Augoyard speaks in his Conclusion now inspires the original French editor of the book to talk pertinently in terms of an "anthropogenesis" as well.[45]

The absence, in this book, of an examination of psychical phenomena cannot, I believe, be attributed primarily to Heidegger's Dasein-centered philosophy but, rather, to Augoyard's own stated and quite understandable reluctance to add to or otherwise countenance a literature that attempts to analyze urban residents' experiences in purely psychological terms. Surely he is correct that residential housing and comportment are social phenomena that cannot be reduced to psychical contents. Instead,

Augoyard appeals directly to Freud, among others, when he delineates the "industrious circulation of the imaginary."[46]

Similarly, a certain doubt as to the pertinence and benefits of "scientific" studies is evident in this tome. No doubt, some of this distrustful attitude can be traced back to Heidegger's (and his student Marcuse's) views on technological thinking, as well as to Merleau-Ponty's phenomenology, with its critique of the abstractness of "every scientific schematization." Indeed, a certain conception of "lived experience," seen as opposed to Cartesian geometrico-scientific thinking, nearly displaces the study of "everydayness" at several points in this work. "Daily strolls," for example, reveal "overlooked practices . . . that are, in the view of scientific knowledge, insignificant."[47] And of "the descriptive study of everyday comings and goings," he says, "we are hardly talking here about a sociological study in the scientific sense of the term." Yet, at the same time, Augoyard's language expresses a certain science-based rhetoric that cannot be overlooked and should not be misrepresented. I have, for example, carefully and closely translated some phrases that in the original French bordered on scientific jargon, yielding "nychthemeral cycle" and "auditory apparatus," whereas "night and day" and "hearing" would have been the more appropriate "everyday" expressions. There are, I believe, professional reasons involved in this complex self-articulation vis-à-vis the sciences. A philosopher by training who became the author of a French state thesis on urbanism that was turned into a volume edited at a prestigious Paris publishing house, Augoyard navigates between a healthy distrust for a purely objective, technical approach to the study of people's everyday activities, on the one hand, and a need to communicate, in a way viewed as legitimate, with an audience still often imbued with such an approach, on the other. We may note that the circumstances surrounding this complex self-articulation continue today, for he was subsequently named a director of research at the French National Center for Scientific Research (CNRS) and became a founder of its CRESSON (Research Center on Sonorous Spaces and the Urban Environment) unit, whose Architectural and Urban Ambiances group he leads at the Grenoble School of Architecture. Still today, Augoyard directs scientific research and student theses with an eye toward illustrating what traditional scientific approaches leave out and what an attentive study of people's actual everyday activities and experiences in an urban environment (especially acoustical ones)[48] might reveal. One could recap this admirable endeavor with Aristotle's acute observation that it is not the expert maker of an object, but the *user* thereof, who is the best judge of its utility.[49]

Eros as well as gender considerations do appear largely absent from *Step by Step*. Surely, "the body of inhabitant expression" is a *gendered* one that, in its everyday walking practices, leans on sexed anatomical differences, especially a different configuration of the hips, as well as on socially instituted responses to and expressions of power in relation to erotic life and relations. In a city located in a Western country, especially one situated as Grenoble is in the Alps, this body is a *clothed* one, too. Rereading through the published narrative extracts, one is struck by the consistently expressed concerns of female walkers, from the problem of finding places to rest and sun themselves outside without feeling watched too closely to a sense of imminent danger that is articulated more often (to judge from the available testimony) than is the case with their male counterparts. Augoyard takes passing note of these differences but does not highlight them or provide any specific thematic treatment that would account for such basic and relevant variations.[50]

In this case, however, the void could easily be filled, I believe, by an honest application of what Augoyard himself teaches us about the need to be attentive to everyday walks—and here, especially, in relation to the aforementioned "nychthemeral cycle." By the early 1970s, "Take Back the Night" marches had already been organized by women in several European countries as a response to precisely these sorts of concerns about *freedom of movement*.[51] The first such event on American soil had just taken place in San Francisco in 1978, a year prior to *Pas à pas*. It was not until 2003 that a specifically French version of this trend made its appearance—based, as a matter of fact, to a large extent on the cares of women and girls in outlying housing projects who are faced with (often violent and threatening) traditional and often specifically Muslim male attitudes toward their comings and goings, as well as toward their attire and behavior. This movement took the name "Ni putes, ni soumises" (Neither whores nor submissive) and eventually mobilized a well-attended national demonstration in the wake of grass-roots organizing and consciousness-raising efforts in largely immigrant and second-generation communities. It would be interesting to apply Augoyard's interview practices and investigative tools to a site-specific sampling of participants in these *marches* in order to see how their everyday walks may or may not have been transformed thereby.

The polis issue is a bit more complicated. On the one hand, for understandable reasons he himself articulates at the start of his book, Augoyard's micromethodology opts for a study of inhabitant narratives in only one strictly delimited part of the city, not the municipality of Grenoble as a whole. On the other hand, it is a municipally instigated housing *policy*, concretely instantiated in actually constructed architectural forms and expressing a certain ideological conception of planning and building with national and global implications, that Augoyard pertinently presents as being challenged by "users'" real walking practices, now rendered explicit and examinable through carefully scrutinized first-person participant narratives.

A bit of extratextual historical background information Augoyard shared with me may be of assistance. Similar to what happened in Burlington, Vermont, where a democratic socialist–led election coalition eliminated an entrenched political machine in 1981 and instituted community-trust housing along with many other innovative reforms, the conservative political forces that had ruled Grenoble in the postwar period were overturned in 1965 by a Socialist-led coalition spearheaded by community associations that sought to reenergize the city via a number of new municipal measures, including the creation of the Arlequin complex. It was a time of policy experimentation; and the Arlequin, combining in one large housing project lodgings adapted to a variety of income levels, was planned as one of the city's showcases. Indeed, Augoyard reports that the Arlequin, begun in the late 1960s and completed in the early 1970s, was viewed as a "utopian" creation designed to manifest and to support a broader effort to change society. From its inception, the author lived there with his wife and child. His knowledgeable, innovative, open-ended method of interviewing fellow residents made him an active participant-observer who was willing to experiment with the latest theoretical techniques and trends in order to bring out, in great detail, conflicts between users and their built environment as well as to reveal an elemental power to resist and to reshape to which the inhabitant practices thus gathered and discussed bear witness.

Augoyard does address political considerations directly in his Conclusion—in fact, immediately after his declaration that "inhabiting is averse to the 'why,'" as methodologically contrasted there with more fecund "how" questions. "In order to illustrate this radical difference in orientation and to signal at the same time another opening indicated in the modal study of inhabiting, we must mention here the formidable question of *needs*. . . . The problematic of needs includes . . . a logic that is heavy with consequences." To illustrate these consequences, Augoyard quotes an astute comment from former Unified Socialist Party (PSU) presidential candidate and future prime minister Michel Rocard that perfectly illustrates the "being housed" versus "inhabiting" dichotomy so central to the author's argument: "It leads to resolving inequalities, deprivations, and contradictions engendered by capitalism through a vast welfare apparatus. . . . It does not suffice to 'house' people; people must be able to 'inhabit' an individual or collective space."[52] In relation to the logic of needs, Augoyard summarizes the results of his own investigations and explores their broader political implications:

> This logic practically lays down the answer before the question is asked; and under its cloak, the most glaring needs are satisfied along the way. In the process, the power of the giver is reinforced and the necessity of his presence is confirmed. Moreover, how are needs apprehended and interpreted? You look at the "masses," the "users," and, on the basis of social movements and their dynamic, you extract a social content: needs. Social life is abstracted into the notion of need, just as people's practices are reduced to various functions. The abstraction of "functionality" is inserted into a logic that is grounded on the relation of container to contained. Thenceforth, every sort of manipulation is, if not easy, at least possible. The logical presuppositions involved authorize a *logistics*, in the sense of an operational strategy, which includes anticipations of people's use.

It is here that Marcuse's critique of "the new conformism" and, more generally, of the misdeeds of a "technological rationality" gone wild makes its explicit appearance in *Step by Step*.

These critical political considerations are extratextual, however, in the sense that they cannot be gleaned directly from residents' narratives but rather from a certain reading thereof that brings in formulations not expressly articulated by participants themselves in their narratives. As a category for study, "everyday life" allows one, via narratives thereof, to explore inhabitant practices down to the level of "the tiniest gesture made," detecting therein and sketching therefrom a concrete overall form of resistance to a modern objectifying rationality that both upsets one's usual way of conceiving such a rationality and overthrows that rationality's own usual conceptions.[53] Here is how Augoyard expresses this opportunity made possible by his modal methodological study of everyday lived experience:

> The study of everyday walks indicates . . . that there really is much more cre-
> ative movement, configuration, and dynamic tension going on in the humblest
> acts of inhabiting than in the very process that produces the contemporary
> built world. This points to an opening and to an investigative lead in which,
> on the basis of the lived experience of inhabiting, and not of conceptually
> designed housing, the imaginary functionally utilized in the production of laid-
> out and developed space might be confronted with an imaginary the inhabitant
> actually lives. A certain number of received values would then most likely be
> overturned, and this expressive power of an irreducible imaginary (one ignored
> for this reason by discourses on construction and housing) would appear as *a
> cosmogenetic point.*

And yet narratives of "everydayness"—especially when opposed (perhaps too unreflectively) to reflective thought and, more generally, to "rationality"[54]—do not easily lend themselves to a sustainably articulated political response, and in any case not to one the participants themselves have actually articulated in their narratives.

Augoyard is not the first to have faced this dilemma. The American "Johnson-Forest Tendency"—led by Trinidad-born revolutionary C. L. R. James and Leon Trotsky's former secretary Raya Dunayevskaya, and which became the Detroit-based Correspondence group—published *The American Worker* in 1947. This narrative written by an autoworker pseudonymously designated as "Paul Romano" and accompanied by a political-intellectual analysis from "Ria Stone" (the political activist and trained philosopher Grace Lee Boggs)[55] was later translated into French and serialized by the Socialisme ou Barbarie group in the first eight issues of its review (March 1949 to January 1951). It was Merleau-Ponty's former high-school philosophy-class student (and later his literary executor) Claude Lefort who proposed, in *Socialisme ou Barbarie*'s eleventh issue (November 1952), a phenomenologically inspired method for analyzing worker narratives. This programmatic text, "L'Expérience prolétarienne" (Proletarian experience), is quite instructive. As the historian of the group Stephen Hastings-King reports,

> Lefort, in keeping with the group's anti-Leninism, argued that only workers could know, and write about, their experience. Lefort's essay posed the theoretical questions to be addressed by Socialisme ou Barbarie's projected collection, publication and analysis of autobiographical worker narratives. He situated these questions relative to two exemplary texts: Paul Romano's "The American Worker" and Eric Albert's "Témoinage: La vie en usine." Lefort used these narratives of worker shop-floor experience . . . as primary data in a phenomenological investigation of "the proletarian standpoint." The goal of this investigation was the isolation and description of the "significations" or games that structured proletarian comportment. The full project would have relied upon phenomenological procedures (reductions) that were never carried out because, despite the solicitation for writings which frequently appeared in *Socialisme ou Barbarie* (as well as in related projects like *Tribune Ouvrière*), workers simply did not write.[56]

In relation to this precursor effort, Augoyard can be said to have made two positive advances. First, in the related field of working-class habitation and habitat, he discovered and developed a way of soliciting significant numbers of first-person participant narratives of everyday struggle.[57] Second, his application of literary techniques of analysis fostered a critical and reflexive approach to these narratives while he himself remained an engaged participant-observer. Noting the rhetorical basis for any recounting of even the "tiniest gestures," the author of *Pas à pas* highlighted a feature that had remained obscure or underthematized in Socialisme ou Barbarie's uncritical take on workers' narratives as straightforward and transparent accounts unencumbered by the mediated labor of writing or recounting.[58] And finally, Augoyard's movement-centered elucidation of narratives of everyday walking practices brought out homologies between words and actions without ever reducing one to the other or prioritizing one over the other.

A few words should also be written about Augoyard's theme of *everydayness* in relation to its theoretical precursors as well as to its political implications. In a French postwar context, the obvious initial reference is to Lefebvre's three-volume *Critique of Everyday Life,* the first volume of which appeared in 1947. This effort started out, in part, as a critique of *Being and Time*'s conception of the "everydayness" (*Alltäglichkeit*) of the "they"'s ontologically unaware fallenness. Lefebvre, a Marxist philosophical-sociological critic of both rural and urban life, sought to unmask the everyday alienation inherent in a cityscape inundated with rural outcasts and transformed by urban capitalism. Owing in part to this critique, Lefebvre exercised an influence on Situationist International members from 1958 until 1962, "when there was," as *Not Bored!* editor Bill Brown explains, "a nasty falling-out."[59] Raoul Vaneigem's 1967 text *The Revolution of Everyday Life* nevertheless testifies to an ongoing Situationist interest in this theme, linked, as in Lefebvre's work, to the category of *lived experience*—but with a connotation to "everydayness" that seems more positive and actively involved in political and social struggle:[60] "Revolution is made everyday despite, and in opposition to, the specialists of revolution. This revolution is nameless, like everything springing from lived experience. Its explosive coherence is being forged constantly in the everyday clandestinity of acts and dreams."[61] Nonetheless, it would be exceedingly difficult to trace a direct line between Situationist *dérive* and what we have called the "expressive errantry of walking narratives" studied and revealed in Augoyard's work. And both of the operative terms in Situationist "psycho-geography" seem alien to Augoyard's anti-psychological and anti-topological methodological practice. Nor do either a philosophy of desire or any grand pronouncements figure in *Pas à pas,* whereas Vaneigem took the time to declare: "The complete unchaining of pleasure is the surest way to the revolution of everyday life, to the construction of the whole man."[62] What Augoyard contributes is a positive and precise understanding of the role of everyday struggle, as exemplified in people's actual walking practices within a preplanned built environment. And this is precisely what Michel de Certeau picked up and borrowed in his book *The Practice of Everyday Life.* The already established author de Certeau nevertheless turned down a request to preface Augoyard's maiden volume before publishing, one year later, his own tome, which was indebted to Augoyard's groundbreaking thesis and which received greater attention.[63]

A final contextual note. When I visited the Arlequin with Augoyard in September 2004, it was a quite different place from the way it was twenty-five years earlier. With the intervening installation of a right-wing municipal government, the extensive set of social programs, services, and amenities that were conceived as an integral and ongoing part of this showcase housing project had been cut drastically in the interim, just as residents had feared. The "power of the giver" has withdrawn along with the welfare-state giver. Vandalism was on the rise, Augoyard reported, and had become more invasive and irrational—door locks, for example, filled with glue, necessitating purchase of new locks—to the point where the Augoyard family, who had been contemplating this move for nearly a decade, finally decided to move out. (My tour began at their new home in a low-rise apartment building at the edges of the Arlequin's grounds. What is notable is in fact how long they lived at this housing project that was the inspiration for Augoyard's first book, before moving out when their child became an adult.) Always a significant presence, the North African and Muslim communities had grown, and there were signs of fundamentalism—though, Augoyard observed, such signs are fleeting and ambiguous: the head of household who might one day be wearing a long beard could and sometimes did cut it off and switch allegiances the next. The general municipal neglect of such outlying housing projects, the widespread discrimination suffered by immigrant and second-generation communities in France, and the poor overall economic situation of left-out segments of the population in a deindustrializing Western country had been evident and were taking their toll for many years. Finally, the situation exploded into violence across France in the fall of 2005, with mass car burnings, confrontations with police and other authorities, and extensive vandalism often aimed at symbols and buildings of the state.

What are the methodological tools that might be employed today for someone who wishes to address the situation at Arlequin or in other poor and working-class communities in France and elsewhere while still giving direct voice to participants and offering pertinent analysis of their experiences and ongoing self-activity? In what ways might the methodological contributions and, more important, investigational leads offered by *Step by Step* help to advance such an endeavor? It goes beyond the confines of a translator's afterword to prescribe for the reader what she should make of what has been read in the present volume. For my part, I have confined myself to offering what might be pertinent background information while conveying the problems a translator faces and the reflections he has had in the actual practice of making a text available to persons who will now themselves attempt to inhabit this text critically in another language within the International Republic of Letters.

My thanks to Catherine Porter, for recommending me for another collaboration with the University of Minnesota Press; to my editors there, first Carrie Mullen and then Jason Weidemann, for their support and their patience; to Beau David Case, for his exemplary librarian research skills; to the Augoyard family, for their hospitality and helpful suggestions; to Françoise Choay, for her continued participation in a book project she first made possible more than a quarter-century ago; and to Alex Gezerlis, whose kindness and generosity are matched by his keen and critical eye for my literary weaknesses.

This translation is dedicated to Clara Gibson Maxwell, my companion on the road of life, whose dancing and choreography continually teach me the meaning of an existence in movement.

Notes

FOREWORD

1. [*Grands ensembles:* Large-scale high-rise public housing projects that were built with a sense of urgency at the periphery of major French metropolitan areas during the 1960s in order to provide living quarters for an influx of generally low-income families from a variety of backgrounds.—*Trans.*]

2. See, in particular, chapter 7 ("Walking in the City") of Michel de Certeau's *The Practice of Everyday Life* (1980), trans. Steven Rendall (Berkeley: University of California Press, 1984), 91–110.

3. See "Sensorial Hyperboles and Anticipations" in chapter 4.

4. On the nontrivial character of walking and of taking steps in their twofold relation to man's animality and to his specificity as a speaking being, it might be intriguing to make reference here to a little known text written by Honoré de Balzac, "La théorie de la démarche" (Theory of the step). This article, published in the August 15, 18, and 25 and September 5, 1833, issues of the review *Europe littéraire* (and republished by Échoppe in 1992), contains in embryo the ideas, developed by François Delsarte between 1833 and his death in 1871, that constitute the theoretical basis for the school of American modern dance founded by Ted Shawn and Ruth St. Denis (see Ted Shawn's *Every Little Movement: A Book about François Delsarte, the Man and His Philosophy, His Science and His Applied Aesthetics, the Application of This Science to the Art of the Dance, the Influence of Delsarte on American Dance* [Pittsfield, Mass.: Eagle Printing and Binding Co., 1954]).

5. *Pas à pas* could be read as a sort of counterpoint to and complement of the analysis Günther Anders offered in the first volume of *Die Antiquierheit de Menschen* (Munich: C. H. Beck Verlag, 1956; First Part, "Über die Prometheische Scham"), which Augoyard had not yet read at the time.

6. See the first page of *Step by Step*.

7. See the third paragraph of the Conclusion (emphasis added).

8. See "Arteries" in chapter 1.

9. See "An Irreducible Imaginary" in the Conclusion.

1. ARTERIES, IMPASSES, SIDE STREETS

1. Medam, *La Ville-Censure.*

2. Ibid., 172. See also, apropos of these examples of hypertely, Simondon's *Du mode d'existence des objets techniques.*

3. Let us cite just three of the many works that have offered assessments of these issues: Choay, *L'Urbanisme, utopies et réalités: une anthologie;* Castells, *La Question urbaine;* and Medam, *Conscience de la ville.*

4. We have heard this attitude voiced often enough and its written expression can be found in Françoise Lugassy's *Le Discours idéologique des architectes et urbanistes.*

5. See the analyses of and connections between works made by Henri Lefebvre in *The Production of Space,* 364ff.

6. We shall cite only the henceforth classic analysis of Henri Lefebvre in *Critique of Everyday Life,* as well as the meticulous and little known analyses of CRESAL (Centre de Recherche et d'Études Sociologiques Appliquées de la Loire, Saint-Étienne) brought together in various research papers, such as *Production de l'espace urbain et idéologique* (1972); *Le Fonctionnement de la mobilité résidentielle intra-urbaine* (1974); and *Les Processus d'évolution des grands ensembles* (1974).

7. See François Ascher's thesis, *Contribution à la critique de l'économie urbaine: Essai d'analyse économique de la production d'un élément urbain: le cadre bâti.*

8. Such as that of Françoise Lugassy, Jacqueline Palmade, and Françoise Couchard, *Contribution à une psychologie de l'espace urban: La Dialectique du logement et de son environnement. Étude exploratoire.*

9. Research papers in applied psychosociology that are most aware of this methodological problem write their conclusions in the conditional.

10. Ἀπορία (aporia): a deadlocked or embarrassing situation that, in Platonic thought, brings up new questions.

11. *"Travers"* in Émile Littré's *Dictionnaire de la Langue française.*

12. We are referring here to our detailed methodological study in our thesis, "Le Pas: Étude de la vie quotidienne dans un habitat collectif à travers la pratique des cheminements."

13. See Janet, *L'évolution de la mémoire et de la notion du temps.*

14. In this neighborhood, the place-names are often unexpected or puzzling. A lexicon of these names can be found in Appendix B.

2. An Inhabitant Rhetoric: Figures of Walking

1. The high-density housing complex known as l'Arlequin, in Grenoble, France, in 1975.

2. We have borrowed the names of figures from the classical catalog of tropes or from figures of language.

3. As Ferdinand de Saussure designated the originary reality of language (*Course in General Linguistics,* 9).

4. [The reference, of course, is to Roland Barthes's "Le Degré zéro de l'écriture," a series of articles first published in 1953; see now *Writing Degree Zero and Elements of Semiology,* trans. Annette Lavers and Colin Smith (London: Jonathan Cape, 1984). —*Trans.*]

5. [The name of the bar, "Bar-bu," is a play on words, meaning both *bar where one drinks* and *bearded.* A somewhat comparable name in English might be something like the "Bearddrinker." —*Trans.*]

6. We emphasize: "paths" and not "shortcuts."

7. "Digression" in Émile Littré's *Dictionnaire de la Langue française.*

8. At the Arlequin complex, the "streets" are arranged under the buildings.

9. These "passageways" are very long corridors that provide access to the apartments.

10. Several inhabitants have told us how, on a Sunday, they have "shown" the Arlequin Gallery as a sort of curiosity to their friends, "who laughed a lot."

11. In the strictly linguistic sense, "Polysemy [. . .] is an essentially synchronic notion. Through polysemy, language obeys the law of economy; it is able to reuse several times the same sign while making its signified vary [. . .]" (Peytard and Genouvrier, *Linguistique et enseignement du français,* 207).

12. "The practical necessities of communication require that the linguistic form be constantly and on all levels redundant" (Martinet, *Éléments de linguistique générale,* 179).

13. The first among the Aristotelian classificatory principles open to the momentary.

14. [Translation of Figure 9:
Isabelle—The week of the 13th to the 19th
MONDAY
Monday morning:

I left the "2000" apartment complex to go to the junior high; I was afraid of getting there late. XXXXX I was with a girlfriend. I was very hot.

I left the junior high to go to a girlfriend's home at number 60. I reentered the junior high, passing by number 90 with XXXXX 5 girlfriends XXXXX and I XXXXX went out again with a girlfriend to go to my home at number 170.

We were sad; for once I went on the Market -$_\wedge^{\text{Place}}$ to take a short-cut and took the gallery ramp until number 170. I went back to the junior high without any enthusiasm with my girlfriend. I left; I was sick to my stomach for having eaten so fast. I went home, and on the way I met a lady friend of my mother—

Monday afternoon:

I went to the junior high school at 2 o'clock, (I didn't really want to go there). I left at 3 o'clock, and I went with a girlfriend to do some sewing; to do that, I went in front of number sixty, -^{and} number seventy. I left at 6:30 p.m., myself, and I went home, happy.]

15. Excerpt from an interview cited as an example of digression, in the "Peritopism" subsection of the "Elementary Figures" section in this chapter.

16. Sansot, *Poétique de la ville,* 27.

17. Hillocks laid out within Arlequin Park.

18. "Hyperbole" in Émile Littré's *Dictionnaire de la Langue française.*

19. The hyperbole lived in one's walks proceeds like the figure of *amplification* discussed in *On the Sublime* 11.1 by "Longinus": "elevated expressions follow, one after the other, in an unbroken succession and in an ascending order."

20. A joyous sort of barbarism, it would seem, and here we would find another moment of the *barbarous,* analyzed as an imaginary type of inhabiting in Alain Pessin and Henry-Skoff Torgue's thesis "Villes imaginaires: Introduction à l'imaginaire urbain" [and now available in book form from Éditions du Champ Urbain (Paris, 1980)—*Trans.*].

21. Émile Littré's *Dictionnaire de la Langue française:* "Synecdoche: figure by which one takes the genus for the species, the species for the genus, the whole for the part, or the part for the whole. . . . Example: 'the billows' for 'the sea'. . . . In metonymy, I take one name for another one; in synecdoche, the most for the least, the least for the most."

22. See ibid.

23. See *anaphora,* in the "Figures of Redundancy" subsection of the "Combinatory Figures" section in this chapter.

24. See the analysis of the hyperbolic mode, in the "Figures of Redundancy" subsection in this chapter.

25. From quite far away and in a very modest manner, there is a sort of dragon geography as found in the Chinese system of feng shui.

26. Here we have the transfiguration of the neighborhood, the image of which is reflected in the water of the lake, the colors of the buildings thus mixing with the greenery of the park. Such a landscape is seen only from the height of the "big mound."

27. One may reread the page from her notebook that was reproduced for our study of metabole, above, in the "Figures of Redundancy" subsection in this chapter.

28. Very heavy and categorical intonation.

29. Our most recent research, which bears on other urban fabrics (old neighborhoods, single-housing units, squares of nineteenth-century buildings, boulevards), has in no way contradicted these conclusions drawn from an analysis of multiunit housing.

30. See, in particular, Jakobson, "Two Aspects of Language and Two Types of Aphasic Disturbances," 53–82.

31. Jakobson, "Closing Statement: Linguistics and Poetics," 358.

32. Ibid., 357.

33. In the sense of communication theory.

34. Insistence on the plural within the singular, which characterizes the status of narrative. Mutual presupposition of the I and the You. No narrative without a narrator and without a listener. See Barthes, "Introduction to the Structural Analysis of Narratives" (1966), 281–82.

35. See ibid., 282. The problem "is to describe the code by which narrator and reader are signified throughout the narrative itself."

3. An Inhabitant Rhetoric: The Code of Appropriation

1. The history of rhetoric shows a progressive disassociation between knowing-how-to-figure and the life of speech. Among the Ancients, these two instantiated principles were very closely connected. Yet in the course of a long process of theorization that begins with the arts of thinking of the Renaissance, starting from Petrus Ramus (and the thought of the Port Royal School) and culminating in César Chesneau sieur du Marsais (seventeenth century) and Pierre Fontanier (eighteenth century) and, finally, on to linguistics and psychoanalysis (stylistic devices–figures of the Unconscious), rhetoric seems "to lose its voice." However, another line of descent exists, a popular, political, or strategic lineage of "savage rhetoric" that is conscious of the lively power of speech; one only has to listen to the voices of charlatans and grifters, as well as to electoral rhetoric, in order to be convinced of this.

2. See the famous debate about the rhetors in Plato's *Gorgias.*

3. See the comparative study of everyday life across four adjacent neighborhoods, *Situations d'habitat et façons d'habiter,* by Jean-François Augoyard and Alain Medam, a planning-construction research paper.

4. Stairwell numbers, or segments of the building-neighborhood.

5. The hexagon is the archetypical shape that determines all the angles.

6. The "Video-Gazette" is the name of the sector of activity that manages the neighborhood's closed-circuit television system and is responsible for local-access programming.

7. The "Video-Gazette"—"a sort of spider," the inhabitants say. Although not occupying much room of its own, it is nevertheless said to have the power to branch out into each home via the strange influence of cable transmissions.

8. [The phrase *no man's land* appears italicized in English in the original French. —*Trans.*]

9. See the "Figures of Redundancy" subsection of the "Combinatory Figures" section of chapter 2.

10. See the "Figures of Symmetry" subsection of the "Combinatory Figures" section of chapter 2.

11. See the "Polysemous Figures" subsection of the "Elementary Figures" section of chapter 2.

12. [Traditionally, children in France have had Wednesday and Saturday afternoons off from school. —*Trans.*]

13. Heading in this direction, we bring together two statements by Raymond Ledrut: (1) "The connection between social differentiation in the city and the partitioning of space is more or less solid. Local groupings and other groups are often entirely distinct. This is the case of contemporary cities" (*L'Espace social et la ville,* 339); (2) "The field of urban experience is not a field of significations that belongs to a city in itself, to clearly distinct people in the city, or even to mechanical relationships between two protagonists who are external to each other. This experience is that of a time, and it finds itself structured by everything that more or less defines this time" (*Les Images de la ville,* 13).

14. The "park" does not forsake complicities between the concept of nature, on the one hand, and the concept of man who has rediscovered a "self" invested with universality, on the other. Such complicities are sealed together in a residual ideology that is preromantic and romantic origin.

15. See the figures of avoidance in the "Elementary Figures" section of chapter 2.

16. "Here the appearing and functioning of difference presuppose an originary synthesis not preceded by any absolute simplicity. Such would be the originary trace. Without a retention in the minimal unit of temporal experience,

without a trace retaining the other as other in the same, no difference would do its work and no meaning would appear. It is not the question of a constituted difference here, but rather, before all determination of the content, of the *pure* movement which produces difference. *The (pure) trace is differance*" (Derrida, *On Grammatology,* 62 [I have corrected a simple grammatical error—confusion of singular and plural—in Spivak's translation. —*Trans.*]).

17. See the "Polysemous Figures" subsection of the "Elementary Figures" section of chapter 2.

18. See the "Figures of Redundancy" subsection of the "Combinatory Figures" section of chapter 2.

19. See anaphora in the "Figures of Redundancy" subsection of the "Combinatory Figures" section of chapter 2, and paralipsis, in the "Elementary Figures" section of chapter 2.

20. See the question of dialectical movement, which was left hanging at the end of the "Differentiating Appropriations" section of this chapter.

21. See the Hegelian concept of *Aufhebung,* which is constitutive of dialectical movement.

22. To "mix up [*confondre*]" space is to scramble its geometrical appearances—but also to greet them with derision.

23. See, in particular, staggered polysemy, in the "Polysemous Figures" subsection of the "Elementary Figures" section of chapter 2.

4. The Body of Inhabitant Expression

1. As in forests, the existence of animals is read on the basis of the network of traces of their passing: "tracks [*passées*]."

2. See the epigraph to the present chapter, drawn from Maurice Merleau-Ponty's Preface to his *Phenomenology of Perception* (1945), ix, and this book as a whole.

3. We need several words to designate what the German language says in a single word: *Stimmung.* A substantivized adjective would come rather close. This would be the term *climatic,* which we shall sometimes employ.

4. See Sansot, *Poétique de la ville,* passim. (And the term *passim* will never have been so adequate; for, in order to apprehend what the atmosphere of urban sites might be, something quite other than a dogmatic formula is needed there; what is needed here is at least a book, and between each word, the weaving of a fine internal necessity that, in its discretion, is the opposite of seeming and a model of making-appear.)

5. Let us understand this term in the strong sense it had during the Renais-

sance (in the Latin word *character*), namely, a striking, lasting quality, a printed sign, which is never random and which gives access to the thing intended.

6. Text reproduced in the "Figures of Redundancy" subsection of the "Combinatory Figures" section of chapter 2.

7. A careful analysis would note that, in the drawings framing this page, the junior high school is not to be found there at all, but only the residential buildings and the crossing areas.

8. "There's basically the wind . . . [laughter] against one's face! From number 130 to number 140, one's really facing an air current." "That wind! . . . especially in winter, it's another restriction. I heard an old lady say that she was afraid to go out in the winter, because she was scared about being bowled over by the wind. A gust of wind like that, on elderly people who easily lose their balance, that can be dangerous!" "On account of the wind, people are in a hurry; and even more so in the winter, with the cold; except in a few areas, where you have some respite."

9. We understand this term *phantasm* simply in the sense it had in an old litany of the Catholic ritual that was used for conjuring away the fantastic and demonic manifestations of the night: "*Ab omnia phantasmata liber nos Domine*"; something unreal that is posited at the same time as it is exorcized.

10. "When it rains, I don't look at anything. I could care less! At that point, I don't know anyone any longer!" one inhabitant exclaimed.

11. Sansot, *Poétique de la ville,* 18 and 29.

12. "Let us go further: *in a city, one never knows what reflects and what is reflected,* what is the sound and what is the echo, who or what has night fever, whether it is the lights of the city or the busy passersby" (ibid., 13).

13. It is a matter of a signal rather than of a landmark [*repère*]. In conformity with the theory of the legibility of urban forms—a theory that still seems to be in fashion—the designers wanted the *bearing-finding* or *locating* [*repérage*] function to be operational. But what could the "urbeme," the unit of signification of a language (in the strict sense) of urban affairs, possibly be? (See the articles by Raymond Ledrut, "Parole et silence de la ville," Richard Fauque, "Pour une nouvelle approche sémiologique de la ville," and Marion Segaud, "Anthropologie de l'espace: catalogue ou projet?" in *Espaces et Sociétés.*

14. If we are to believe certain architectural discourses, color is supposed to cancel out what would otherwise be the opacity of concrete facades.

15. Let us recall the etymology: "*bel vedere,*" or having the lovely view, is possible only from a distance that leaves the object untouchable.

16. It would be like that fictional sailor's story, which a rich merchant wants to live out himself and make someone else live out, but which, once lived, disintegrates into death and incommunicability. There is no longer any story (see the

wonderful 1967 made-for-television medium-length film by Orson Welles, *The Immortal Story,* which was based on a short story by Isak Dinesen).

17. A fragment from one interview: "On a photograph of the gallery, [. . .] it's hard to find one's apartment. There are three postcards about the New Town [. . .]. It's really quite something. The lake is bluer than blue. [Bursts of laughter.] And the building reflected within it! Oh, I really had a laugh!"

18. Here are a few expressions we have heard: "The colors? How to say it? . . . I don't like the bands; I prefer the rungs." "The buildings altogether . . . it smells like concrete!" "I don't like the pointy tops to the junior high school. I like the school from the lake with its honeycomb pattern; it stings less" (the allusion is here to the roofs on the junior high school, which are in the shape of asymmetrical pyramids).

19. We have often pointed out to the inhabitants that the total route of the gallery covers a good kilometer. Everyone has expressed surprise or incredulity, so much can the lived experience of everyday time be alien to topography. "This even implies that the pathways we take towards desevered entities in the course of our dealings will vary in their length from day to day. . . . As Dasein goes along its ways, it does not measure off a stretch of space as a corporeal Thing which is present-at-hand; it does not 'devour the kilometers'; bringing-close or de-severance is always a kind of concernful Being towards what is brought close and de-severed. A pathway which is long 'Objectively' can be much shorter than one which is 'Objectively' shorter still but which is perhaps 'hard going' and comes before us as interminably long" (Heidegger, *Being and Time,* 140).

20. For the critique of reflexology, we refer the reader, on the one hand, to the works of embryologists (George Ellett Coghill, Leonard Carmichael, and Adriaan Kortlandt) and ethologists (Konrad Lorenz, Niko Tinbergen, Peter H. Klopfer), and, on the other hand, to Kurt Goldstein (*The Organism: A Holistic Approach to Biology Derived from Pathological Data in Man*), as well as to Maurice Merleau-Ponty (*Phenomenology of Perception*). [One of the best arguments against reflexology is to be found in the opening pages of the fundamental and too neglected work of Erwin Strauss, *Vom Sinn der Sinne* (Berlin: Springer Verlag, 1935), which, on this theme and on that of the interdependence between feeling and moving, has broadly inspired perceptual psychology, phenomenology, and ethology—*Author's note, 2004.*]

21. See the figure of bypassing in the "Elementary Figures" section of chapter 2.

22. There is a strangeness to the return trip, where identity wavers from the first step onward: "That night I set out for home. I did not get far. But it was a start. It is the first step that counts. The second counts less. . . . Then I followed more or less the same paths we had taken on the way out. But paths look differ-

ent, when you go back along them" (Beckett, *Molloy*, in *Molloy. Malone Dies. The Unnameable*, 165–66).

23. See the "Polysemous Figures" subsection in the "Elementary Figures" section of chapter 2.

24. These are the ironic ups and downs of a technological medium that is lived in contradiction to the elevator's function; through it, we rediscover the vertical dimension that is essential in human motor patterns (Binswanger, "Dream and Existence").

25. "*Identität von Weg und Werk*." See Klee, *The Thinking Eye: The Notebooks of Paul Klee*, 168.

26. See the final, fantastic short story, "The Aleph," published in *The Aleph and Other Stories, 1933–1969*.

27. On the illusion of spatial simultaneities, see the third rule of the code of appropriation at the end of the "Territorial Appearance" section of chapter 3.

28. "Does this Aleph exist in the heart of a stone? Did I see it there in the cellar when I saw all things, and have I now forgotten it? Our minds are porous and forgetfulness seeps in; I myself am distorting and losing, under the wearing away of the years, the face of Beatriz" (Borges, "The Aleph," 30).

29. See the beginning of the "From Figures to Code" section in chapter 2.

30. See the experiment in continuous reportage (seven months running) that was attempted by an American television network on the Loud family in 1971 and the commentary Jean Baudrillard offers in "The Precession of Simulacra," 28ff.

31. Nor does this definition depart from the quite numerical notion of "measure." The preferable definition (in the sense of a seizure of limits via configuration, rather than formal division) will be the one that presided over the art of Gregorian modal music: sequences of bursts (*arsis*) and rests (*thesis*); death and birth of the impulse (*ictus*).

32. It would be the essence and also the secret of time, if we are to believe Anaximander's statement (sixth century BCE) as reported by Simplicius in his *Physics* (24.13): "And the source of coming-to-be for existing things is that into which destruction, too, happens 'according to necessity; for they pay penalty and retribution to each other for their injustice according to the assessment of time,' as he describes it in these rather poetical terms" (Kirk, Raven, and Schofield, *The Presocratic Philosophers: A Critical History with a Selection of Texts*, 117–18).

33. See the fourth rule of the code of appropriation in the "Differentiating Appropriations" section of chapter 3.

34. One female inhabitant from number 60 says, "The little bit of the neighborhood I frequent, it's mine."

35. "I don't often look through the window [. . .]. Or else, just like that, while passing by it, because the neighborhood is also a bit my home." Another female inhabitant says, "You see, I bring my chair close, like that, near the balcony, to knit. Notice that I don't see very much, because I'm small and because the plant stands are high. But I keep contact with the outside. And the view isn't unpleasant."

36. See the expressions of some inhabitants, reported earlier: "this isn't a spot," "I wouldn't live there."

37. Some sites in the Arlequin neighborhood that planners foresaw would be used as meeting places, sites of collective gravitation (because on the walls have been painted the words "pole 1," "pole 2"), remain obstinately deserted.

38. We speak of the *power of the body* in the sense of the evaluation of what it *can do* (in terms of limits, but also in terms of dynamic capacity). It seems to be of fundamental importance to weigh this evaluation before any ethology of inhabiting, as well as before any production of habitat, just as Spinoza weighed it at the start of his ethic of "feelings" (that which affects), in his *Ethics* (in *Complete Works,* Part 3, 277ff.), which proposes some quite valuable prolegomena to the study of existence in concrete situations.

39. As structural grammar becomes with Noam Chomsky "generative and transformational grammar" (*Syntactic Structures*). Can one imagine a generative and transformational development plan and architecture?

5. On the Imaginary Ground of Inhabitant Expression

1. [In the French translation of Kandinsky, what in English appeared as "uncontrollable force of nature" appears as "une force qui défie les calculs." —*Trans.*]

2. [In French, the meanings of *discrete* and *discreet* overlap in one word: *discret. —Trans.*]

3. This power to produce syntheses is analyzed in the famous pages from Kant where he deals with the Schematism (*Critique of Pure Reason,* 121ff.).

4. See the section "An Articulatory Process" in chapter 4.

5. "This schematism of our understanding applied to phenomena and their mere form is an art hidden in the depth of the human soul, the true secrets of which we shall hardly ever be able to guess and reveal" (*Critique of Pure Reason,* 123).

6. Kant, *Critique of Judgment, Including the First Introduction,* book 2, "Analytic of the Sublime," 91ff.).

7. The *spiritus phantasticus* (a term that is nearly untranslatable, because

it includes ideas that are for us so different, such as those of imaginary power, divine fire, and breath of life) manifests itself in two ways. On the one hand, it animates; it is the breath that gives life to all things and makes significations speak. On the other hand, in the form of the *subjectum,* the field that supports all existence, or else in the metaphorical form of the *atrium* or the combinatory field of second-order significations (interpretorial reproduction of the immediate meaning of things), it grounds. See our master's thesis, "Imagination et Nature chez Giordano Bruno," a 124-page mimeographed document.

8. See in particular Giordano Bruno's "La Cena de le Ceneri."

9. So as not to weigh down our argument, let us simply recall the extreme importance that, in a kind of thinking that is familiar to us, Sigmund Freud and Gaston Bachelard granted to this industrious circulation of the imaginary that defies the apparent distinctions in whose name mental functions are doggedly separated from one another and our psychosomatic entity is torn asunder.

10. The concrete forms by which one evokes the possible in the present pick up on various traits of everyday life that are already present in figures and appropriations—whence the numerous references to narratives already quoted. This final reading, which seeks out the ground of expression, will briefly recall those "traits" of everyday style, along with their most representative expressions.

11. See the "Polysemous Figures" subsection in the "Elementary Figures" section of chapter 2.

12. Mechanical ventilation system for the apartment complex.

13. See Yves Bardin's short film *Quand les poules auront des dents* (When the hens will have teeth). The fantastic and murderous invasion of ferocious hens who take over the Arlequin begins in this film with eggs hatched in the underground areas of the gallery. This film is available at "Grenoble-Information-Animation," Grand Place, Grenoble, France.

14. Cf. the narrative of one mother. In one stairway, someone shot at her son with a rifle. The evidence seems quite convincing: the cake pan he was carrying now strangely resembles a colander. In this case, the horrible persists through eventful marking.

15. See the "Polysemous Figures" subsection in the "Elementary Figures" section in chapter 2, and the "Appropriation via Dislocation" section in chapter 3.

16. See the Second Rule of the Code of Appropriation at the end of the "Territorial Appearance" section of chapter 3.

17. See the cascade of exclusions of which the Community Center is the site in the "Differentiating Appropriations" section of chapter 3.

18. Let us recall the two logical traditions that, each in its own way, have articulated Western philosophy, depending on the different connotations they

give to the modality of the possible: the tradition of paired values: true or false (see the dominant scholasticism of the Middle Ages, the Port Royal Logic, Leibniz); the tradition of unpaired values: true, false, neither-true-nor-false (this tradition, which has always inspired mistrust, stretches from Epicurus to Jan Lukasiewicz).

19. Durand, *Les Structures anthropologiques de l'imaginaire: Introduction à l'archétypologie générale,* 68.

20. We are thinking here of several practices that stretch from the damaging of urban sites to the ironic inversion of their functional significations. We refer to the analyses of André Micoud in his mimeographed research report, *Les Nouvelles Formes du refus de la ville* (Saint-Étienne: Centre de Recherche et d'Études Sociologiques Appliquées de la Loire [CRESAL], 1976), and those of Jacques Ion and Jean Nizey, in *Les Processus d'évolution des grands ensembles* (Saint-Étienne: Centre de Recherche et d'Études Sociologiques Appliquées de la Loire [CRESAL], 1973).

21. If one wanted to draw up the logic of everyday life, it would no doubt be necessary to begin with the covariant of nonexclusive disjunction, replacing the "either/or" of the logic of the excluded middle with the "and/or." This logic of the imaginary has been launched in the field of axiomatic research. See the various works of Stéphane Lupasco, and in particular *Logique et contradiction* and *Les Trois Matières.*

22. Lalande, "Symbole."

23. Durand, *Les Structures anthropologiques de l'imaginaire,* 38.

24. See, respectively: (1) "The Poetic Idiom" at the end of chapter 2; (2) "Conclusion in the Form of a Bifurcation" at the end of chapter 3; (3) "An Articulatory Process" at the end of chapter 4; and (4) "Three Powers of the Lived Imaginary" in the present chapter.

25. Let us refer here to the most memorable source in the history of linguistics, Ferdinand de Saussure's *Course in General Linguistics.*

26. Ibid., 67–69 and 69–70.

27. Such thinking is scandalous because it is grounded upon a philosophy of immanence. In his *Ethics,* Spinoza abandoned the concepts that would immediately denote a status for expression. This status appears only through an almost initiatory reading, the second reading Gilles Deleuze reconstitutes in his *Expressionism in Philosophy: Spinoza* (1968).

28. There is nothing fortuitous, or even contradictory, about the fact that one would have to go back to the Renaissance to find an openly declared theory of expression and that, in the same age, a dominant mode of thinking-producing was firmly constituted on the basis of a certain way of representing space. At that time, methods of combination bore upon a quite precise status for

signification. Significations—each one referring to the others—made up the way of understanding a cosmic order that expressed itself on its own, as well as a way of making that order reexpress itself, and yet that order still had to be convoked through the medium of streams of significations-expressions. The break occurred during the second half of the Renaissance. The methods of thought production and of fabrication (*Ars*) were little by little led astray and turned into pure operative instruments subsumed under a binary structure that went on to disjoin identity *and* difference, which would be split up, the "I think" *and* the world. The triad of expression disappeared like an outdated metaphysics. The representation of space from which the "arts of thinking" drew strength was flattened into "*res extensa*," into representational space, the manipulation of which no longer convokes anything expressive, but simply some immediately beneficial divisions in which the heterogeneous disguises itself as homogeneous. Cf. the remarks of Françoise Choay: "I am more and more convinced that in the West, the great break in urban development and design occurred at the end of the fifteenth century. Before . . . no planning. Not that the urban space included no organization, but such organization was the product of a set of social practices and not that of a specific practice, which is itself the fruit of a break performed on the level of reflection upon the urban object" (interview in *Metropolis*, 67).

29. Deleuze, *Expressionism in Philosophy: Spinoza*, 333.

30. Ibid., 335.

31. Beckett, "The Expelled," 33.

Conclusion: A Cosmogenetic Point

1. We offer, in an appendix, a synoptic table that sketches out the varieties of this reductive process. It is a formal account of the contradictions and reductions that occur between the order of building-housing and the power of inhabitant expression.

2. We use this expression that was favored in the Bauhaus aesthetic. The pictorial metaphor evoked here seems illuminating. The universe of inhabitant expression is engendered on the basis of discretely lived point-like experiences, just as the world of forms tightly bound in the "canvas" is born of a simple graphic gesture or of a colored point.

3. On the question of this necessary involvement of tension in the act of building, the reader is invited to read and reread the pages of Georges Braque's *Cahiers*. [A later, bilingual edition appeared as *Illustrated Notebooks, 1917–1955.—Trans.*]

4. See our analysis of the process of conception-production of a high-density housing complex: "Des opérationnels autour de l'Arlequin."

5. Rocard, "La France en quête d'un avenir."

6. Marcuse, *One-Dimensional Man*, 84.

7. See chapter 1 of Medam's *La Ville-Censure*.

8. Durand, *Science de l'homme et tradition: Le Nouvel Esprit anthropologique*, 143.

9. In the sense in which the one-dimensional false consciousness denounced by Herbert Marcuse as representation of a destiny of productivity did not yet carry weight.

10. Cf. the bitterness and regrets of a frustrated creativity, quite well analyzed in Lugassy's work *Le Discours idéologique des architectes et urbanistes*.

11. See Worringer, *Abstraction and Empathy: A Contribution to the Psychology of Style*, originally published in German in 1908.

12. For this passage, we have borrowed the French translation given by Henri Maldiney at the University of Lyon in 1969 [and then retranslated it into English; for the available English translation, which differs somewhat, see *The Thinking Eye: The Notebooks of Paul Klee*, 169.—*Trans*].

13. Ibid. [English translation again somewhat altered to reflect the French translation from the German.—*Trans*.]

14. [It should be noted, for the reader of the present French-to-English translation, that the 1962 French translation of Martin Heidegger's 1950 volume, *Holzwege* (literally: wood trails; a recent English-language translation has *Off the Beaten Track*), was titled *Chemins qui mènent nulle part* (paths that lead nowhere), and thus is the opposite of what Augoyard affirms concerning the paths of expression at the close of his book.—*Trans*.]

APPENDIX B

1. *Zone d'urbanisation en priorité (ZUP).*

AFTERWORD

The ambulatory dialogue between author and translator, broached on that crisp fall day in Grenoble and continued in the present text (placed most appropriately as an Afterword), has been pursued in an exchange available on the author's professional Web site, www.cresson.archi.fr/sbs.html.

1. I make explicit here my American prejudice against the International

Style, which was reinforced by my 2000–2001 residency at Taliesin West at the invitation of the Frank Lloyd Wright School of Architecture.

2. This experience was the reverse of the one Laurie Anderson drolly described in her eponymous song from *Big Science* (1982) depicting disorientation in a future-dominated builtscape: "Hey Pal! How do I get to town from here? And he said: Well, just take a right where they're going to build that new shopping mall, go straight past where they're going to put in the freeway, take a left at what's going to be the new sports center, and keep going until you hit the place where they're thinking of building that drive-in bank. You can't miss it. And I said: This must be the place." This song includes a sly comment on fictionalized landscaping reminiscent of the Arlequin's mounds: "You know. I think we should put some mountains here. Otherwise, what are all the characters going to fall off of?" I know not whether Anderson ever read Jean Baudrillard on simulacra, but it is known that she studied Merleau-Ponty at Columbia with Arthur C. Danto.

3. Like Proust (translator of John Ruskin) or Paul Auster (translator of Pierre Clastres).

4. But not even a hint of influence, so far as I can tell, from the existentialist philosopher of an absolute freedom Jean-Paul Sartre, who also wrote on the imagination.

5. The University of Minnesota Press originally took an interest in translating *Pas à pas* as an outgrowth from its publication of Lefebvre's *The Urban Experience*.

6. There is in *Step by Step* one late, and quite intriguing, reference to the death of modernity: "Building is missing-in-action, not dead. And its potentialities are still exercised in a virtual way in the obscure confrontations between *inhabitant* expression and constructed space. We would say, rather, that the 'modern' is what has just died; it is already conceptuality, already fixed in place. It is dead absolutely, that is, as soon as one lays down the first stone, as soon as its first object is sketched out, for it has rid itself of lived time. And rather than calling for a return to the past, we would prefer to grant, as a plausible outcome, self-construction." Postmodernism, however, seems absent from the present volume. Jean-François Lyotard's volume on the postmodern condition, *La Condition postmoderne: Rapport sur le savoir* had only come out the same year *Pas à pas* was published; nonetheless, the term had already existed for decades and was popularized two years earlier in Charles Jencks's *The Language of Post-Modern Architecture*. And the "plausible outcome" of "self-construction" seems rather alien to postmodern concerns, being reminiscent, rather, of Cornelius Castoriadis's 1975 major work *The Imaginary Institution of Society* (trans. Kathleen Blamey [Cambridge: MIT Press, 1998]), even though Augoyard, himself work-

ing on the imagination at the time, had not read this volume. Because of similarities of concerns and an overlap of themes between Augoyard and Castoriadis, I have often referred to the latter's work while translating and reflecting upon the former's. It is indeed fascinating to witness these two intellectual trajectories developing at the same time within the context of postwar French thought. I have been helped in my examination of Augoyard's work by Castoriadis's own reading of Yves Barel, another author whose work developed in parallel with his during the 1970s: see Castoriadis's "Complexity, Magmas, History: The Example of the Medieval Town" (1993), in *The Rising Tide of Insignificancy (The Big Sleep)*, available online starting at: http://notbored.org/RTI.html.

Neither does Michel Foucault's name make an appearance. Augoyard's microscopic study of appropriations and counterappropriations—themselves couched in Saussurean terms of mutually generated difference based on the arbitrariness of the sign but being, most proximately, of Lefebvrean provenance—might nevertheless make one think of that theorist of micropowers. On the other hand, it is hard to imagine Foucault, champion of powerlessness, speaking affirmatively, as Augoyard does, about "the power of the imaginary."

7. Not to forget a wealth of premodern and early modern influences: as Augoyard notes, his master's thesis was written on the topic "Imagination and Nature in Giordano Bruno." Those who would take *Step by Step* to be merely a clever text in urban studies or a microanalysis of a particular housing complex would miss a great deal of the philosophical intent and import of this quite remarkable volume.

8. A nearly impossible, not to say infinite, task, given the complexity and overlap of the multitude of referrals involved.

9. In French, *interprète* can mean both "performer" (like Ion) and "interpreter-translator." Nevertheless, to the extent that one can say that a translation is an artistic *re-creation* of voices and significations in another tongue, the term *interpretation,* with its merely *hermeneutic* overtones, seems quite inadequate and inappropriate.

10. In a "Tribune libre" for the December 28, 2005, issue of the Communist newspaper *L'Humanité* ("Bâtir la ville: le désir de civilisation"), Jean-Paul Dollé proposes an amalgam of Heidegger (Dollé cites "Bâtir, habiter, penser") and Lefebvre (he also mentions "the production of space") as a frame for discussing the fall 2005 riots in France. Yet, in contrast to Augoyard, he fails to take as his point of departure the self-articulating position of the inhabitant-user of this space.

11. Augoyard explains in chapter 2: "In any case, one never makes a complete tour around the everyday as it is lived." This apposite claim to, or admission of, nonexhaustiveness is made on several occasions. It is to be noted that "An

Essay on Everyday Walks in an Urban Setting" is the proper English translation of the book's subtitle. A compromise subtitle, "Everyday Walks in a French
Urban Housing Project," was settled on for the present translation.

12. "To dwell" has been reserved, instead, to translate *demeurer* and its derivatives, as in "the possibility of dwelling, of coming to a stop" plus "city
dweller" for *citadin*, and for Choay's use of the term *habiter* when discussing it
in relation to Heidegger. Also, "dwelling" connotes *meditation* on allegedly profound matters, while "inhabiting" indicates a mobile bodily practice.

13. The author wisely added "apparently" with regard to walking practices' assumed resistance to co-optation. For, along with malls (*centres commer-
ciaux*), a major urban planning and design contrivance popularized in France,
as elsewhere, since this book was originally published, has been the deploy-
ment and proliferation of *voies piétonnes*, "pedestrian ways" (generally designated in the States as "walking streets") devoid of cars that funnel pedestrians
and foster shopping in an environmentally more friendly setting, thereby "de-
mocratizing" (to use an abusive, journalistic term) and further commercializing
the experiences of the Baudelairean dandy and Walter Benjamin's flâneur. (See,
on an early-twentieth-century artistic transfiguration of these two nineteenth-
century pedestrian figures, Giovanna Zapperi's "Marcel Duchamp's Dandyism:
The Dandy, the Flâneur, and the Beginnings of Mass Culture in New York during the 1910s," translated by me and available at http://www.artsetsocietes.
org/a/a-zaperri.html.)

14. "Two roads diverged in a wood, and I, / I took the one less traveled by,
/ And that has made all the difference" (Robert Frost, "The Road Not Taken").
As we shall soon see, however, even this mutual exclusion is, according to Augoyard, to be avoided: "Sometimes rather more following an existing path, sometimes rather more hewing a new one, one moves within a space that never tolerates the absolute exclusion of the one or the other."

15. Augoyard immediately and enthusiastically recognized the Anderson
lyric reference when I mentioned it to him; he was familiar with the song on account of his son Erwan, now a filmmaker.

16. See mentions of the "French Ideology" in "Social Transformation and
Cultural Creation" (1979), from Castoriadis's *Political and Social Writings*,
vol. 3 (Minneapolis: University of Minnesota Press, 1988), 304, as well as in
"The Movements of the Sixties" (1986), from his collection *World in Fragments*
(Stanford, Calif.: Stanford University Press, 1997), 51. The obvious reference
here is to Marx and Engels's attack on the irrelevancies of their contemporaries
in *The German Ideology*.

17. An early indication of the limits of a deconstructive approach to walking
practices is perhaps contained in the very citation of Derrida's concept of "differance" (note 16 to chapter 3): "It is not the question of a constituted differ-

ence here, but rather, before all determination of the content, of the *pure* movement which produces difference. *The (pure) trace is differance.*" It is unclear how such a hypostatized notion of "purity" can account for the messy *everydayness* of such movement practices.

18. There are two further mentions of deconstruction.

19. This modal methodological approach, he acknowledges, "comes up right away against a major difficulty": people's tendency to forget. The investigator addresses this problem by asking a "how" question—"How do you walk through your neighborhood; what trips do you take?"—in a protentional rather than retentional mode (the interviewees are to provide their answers only after a suitable lapse of time and after having had the actual experience with this question in mind). Of note, the protentional/retentional terminology stems originally from Edmund Husserl's 1928 work *Phenomenology of Internal Time-Consciousness* (based on his 1905–10 lectures) and is an extension of his method of intentional analysis, derived from the "intentionality" thesis developed by his teacher Franz Brentano.

20. In fact, in Husserl himself, this call was already articulated as a "going back" ("wir wollen auf die 'Sachen Selbst' züruckgehen").

21. Plato *Cratylus* 401d (on Heraclitus) and Aristotle *Metaphysics* 1010a 13–15 (on Cratylus). Perhaps Heraclitus's most famous fragment begins "All things flow" (*panta rhei*).

22. A questionable, but key, thesis in Merleau-Ponty concerns "The Primacy of Perception and Its Philosophical Consequences." This 1946 talk, first published in French in 1947, forms the eponymous text for *The Primacy of Perception and Other Essays*, ed. James M. Edie (Evanston, Ill.: Northwestern University Press, 1964).

23. In French, *sens* means both "meaning" and "direction," an overlap of significations exploited in particular by Merleau-Ponty, as Stephen Hastings-King points out in his 1999 Cornell University history PhD dissertation, "Fordism and the Marxist Revolutionary Project: A History of Socialisme ou Barbarie, Part I," 192.

24. Of course, *movement* here is to be taken in its Aristotelian sense of *change* or *alteration,* of which there are four species, and not limited to its Galilean sense alone of *local movement.* Lest it be thought that I am making a fetish of movement, allow me to recommend, by way of contrast, the work of the late post-Surrealist artist, sculptor, and writer Pol Bury, including his book *Les Horribles mouvements de l'immobilité* (Paris: C. Martinez, 1977); see also my translation of André Balthazar's text for one of Bury's catalogs: "Pol Bury or Murmured Slowness," in *Pol Bury. La lenteur murmurée* (Paris: Galerie Louis Carré, 2004), 9–11.

25. One wonders why Alfred North Whitehead's process philosophy was not an appropriate reference for Augoyard.

26. Merleau-Ponty's May 1959 Working Note, titled "Transcendence of the thing and transcendence of the phantasm," begins as follows: "The transcendence of the thing compels us to say that it is plenitude only by being inexhaustible, that is, by not being all actual under the look——but it promises this total actuality, since it *is there*. . . .

"When we say that—on the contrary—the phantasm is not observable, that it is empty, non-being, the contrast with the sensible is therefore not absolute. The senses are apparatus to form concretions of the inexhaustible, to form existent significations——" And here, still couched in the language of Husserlian phenomenology, is what follows the statement just quoted, about things not really being observable: "What we call the *sensible* is only the fact that the indefinite [succession] of *Abschattungen precipitates*——But, conversely, there is a precipitation or crystallization of the imaginary, of the existentials, of the symbolic matrices" (*The Visible and the Invisible* followed by *Working Notes* [1964], ed. Claude Lefort, trans. Alphonso Lingis [Evanston, Ill.: Northwestern University Press, 1968], 191–92). What Merleau-Ponty describes in static or fixed terms as "concretions" and "precipitation or crystallization" could have been rearticulated in mobile terms by extending his metaphor of "enjambment," meaning-creation through ongoing strides. I believe that Augoyard's book points in this direction.

27. Aristotle *Peri psuchēs* 431a17. See Castoriadis's "The Discovery of the Imagination," in *World in Fragments*. Although he does not present this history as thoroughly and profoundly as Castoriadis does, Augoyard is quite aware of these multiple rediscoveries and successive cover-ups: "Several times in the history of thought, the imaginary has been considered neither as one of the lower faculties, archaic in origin and confined to the production of images, nor as too confused a faculty to be able to attain the empire of reason, too uncultivated and too uncontrolled in its sudden appearances to be a bearer of truth. Each time our 'imaginary' capacity has been taken into account as a whole, it was in order to point to its operative function: *imagining is the power to connect*. The imagination is the *medium* par excellence.

"Thus, Kantianism—which, two centuries ago, did not immediately preoccupy itself with the instantiated principle of the imaginary—nevertheless conferred upon it the threefold role of reproducing, synthesizing, and creating." And Augoyard, author of that Giordano Bruno thesis, offers precious indications as to the historical role of the imagination in Renaissance thought, about which Castoriadis has not written (at least in the extant and posthumous work published so far). On the other hand, with the introduction of *anticipation* as origin of the realization of the real via the imaginary ("render[ing] present what 'really' is not yet so"), the entire basis (ground) for Augoyard's afore-mentioned "protentional" method of interviewing inhabitants is itself tossed up into the air.

28. He also footnotes the work of the philosopher and social theorist Gilbert Durand, founder, in 1966, of the University of Grenoble II's Center for Research on the Imaginary. Augoyard explained to me that the mention of Durand in his thesis (and subsequently in his book) was a late addition made after he had learned that Durand would be on the thesis committee.

29. This consistent denigration of the "why" is particularly perplexing in light of Augoyard's insistence that, "however unremarkable our ways of inhabiting might be, they would never depart from a climatic pregnancy that never leaves them totally 'unmotivated.'" It is perhaps understandable that the author wishes to view inhabiting not only as "movement" but also as *motivated*. (The "power of the imaginary," however, would more plausibly opt, rather, for a present participle with future implications—*motivating*—although the imaginary's interpenetration of action and passion would militate instead for past and present participles combining in an ongoing *Stiftung*, Husserl's German word for "institution.") And he wishes to challenge Saussurean linguistics, which is based, by way of contrast, on linearity and the arbitrariness of the sign: "expression is never carried out according to an arbitrary relation and does not unfold in a single dimension." But what, we may ask, is the sense in saying that inhabiting is *motivated* (taken here by Augoyard to mean the opposite of "arbitrary") and yet eschews the "why"? Augoyard is battling against Saussurean-based Structuralism, and he thereby becomes a champion of expressive creativity. But he has yet to reach the vista where the risky possibility of positing the "why" and the metanecessary arbitrariness of creation themselves combine in, as well as flow from, an unmotivated, self-positing (indeed, self-instituting) imaginary that alters itself not just in time but as time. And yet this is precisely what his "cosmogenetic point," in his Conclusion, could itself eventually generate.

30. The ambulatory act of "skipping over" is not to be confused, of course, with the high-flying bird's-eye or God's-eye view (*pensée de survol*) Merleau-Ponty rightly criticized.

31. One finds the lived experience/representation opposition often in Merleau-Ponty's work, too. The denigration of representation, in this case tied even more directly to causality, also may be found in a passage from Deleuze that Augoyard quotes: "What is expressed is sense: deeper than the relation of causality, deeper than the relation of representation" (Gilles Deleuze, *Expressionism in Philosophy: Spinoza* [1968], trans. Martin Joughin [New York: Zone Books, 1990], 335).

32. In the sixth part of his 1637 *Discourse on Method*, Descartes does indeed talk about "represent[ing] my life as in a picture," and the terms *représen-*

tation and *tableau* (but also *imagination*) do appear a number of times in this and other Cartesian works. For his part, Heidegger provides no textual evidence of his own here.

33. See also the May 1960 Working Note "'Visual Picture' → 'representation of the world' *Todo y Nada*," where, in a line of descent from Heidegger's "The Age of the World Picture," Merleau-Ponty seeks to "generalize the critique of the visual picture into a critique of '*Vorstellung*'" (*The Visible and the Invisible* followed by *Working Notes*, 252). This he does even after his admission that "one is never at the thing itself"!

34. Heidegger could just as easily have understood *Vor-stellung* to mean a "putting forth" of images, their "placing in advance," instead of a static and objective "setting before" (a subject). Many German *vor-* words have the former two senses. See "Merleau-Ponty and the Weight of the Ontological Tradition," in *World in Fragments*, 282, where Castoriadis speaks of "a representation in the 'active' sense . . . that is not placing-something-in-front-of-someone but rather is that by which and in which every placing and every place exist, originary positing starting from which every position—as 'act' of a subject or 'determination' of an object—has being and meaning." Such an understanding and acceptance of imaginary representation could rejoin the meanings of *enjambement* explored earlier and inspired by Augoyard's movement-oriented method.

35. When this phrase was first cited, it seemed that the operative word was "aesthetic," but now it appears that what is being contested especially is "objecthood"—which would be condemned for *representationalism*. That is to say, Augoyard has no objection in principle to *aisthēsis*, so long as the feeling of inhabiting is understood as movement.

36. Here, "skips" and "does without" are translations for the French phrase *faire l'économie de*. Augoyard goes on to state the important points that, in the imaginary realm establishing the ground for real life, neither set theory nor identitary logic operates and that the individual can be opposed to or considered separate from the social sphere only via abstraction: "there is nothing about [inhabitant expression] of a 'relation' of part to whole or of a 'relation' of the individual to the 'socius.'" Despite the dubious Heideggerian pronouncement that "representation" would somehow be absent from "lived experience" (instead of their being, thanks to the imaginary, mutually interpenetrative), we can see that, as with Heidegger and Merleau-Ponty, what is truly being contested is subject–object dualism and a *specific* representational reduction of things, people, and processes to inert and manipulable objects: "the same goes for rationalizing explanations that would yield on the one hand the subject, on the other hand the object, on the one hand knowing, on the other hand the world in itself." The

genuine topic at hand for Augoyard is an elucidation of the imaginary via inhabitant expression: "To the extent that everyday life can find meaning qua expression, the imaginary proposes itself as the essential referent to which the moments of inhabiting, and all the spaces inhabited, relate. The imaginary weaves beneath each present lived experience a ground the imaginary immediately gives to it as world."

37. Martin Heidegger, *Being and Time* (1928), trans. John Marcquarrie and Edward Robinson (New York and Evanston, Ill.: Harper & Row, 1962), 140 (emphasis added). If we take Heidegger's early talk of *Vorstellung* and add thereto his mentions of "affective life" and "volition" (the latter in its most general sense as the distinctly human form of intention and desire), we have, in Castoriadis's terminology, "the three characteristics of the *for-itself,* which were first sifted out as distinct elements during the fifth century B.C.E. in ancient Greece. Everywhere there is the for-itself there will be representation and image, there will be affect, there will be intention; in ancient terminology: the logico-noetic, the thymic, and the orectic. This goes for a bacterium as well as for an individual or for a society" ("The State of the Subject Today," in *World in Fragments,* 146).

38. This "never extinguished resonance" also seems to be of Merleau-Pontean provenance.

39. Castoriadis, "The Discovery of the Imagination," 215–16.

40. Heidegger, "Die Zeit des Weltbildes" (1938), in *Holzwege* (Frankfurt-am-Main: Vittorio Klosterman, 1977), 106.

41. "Only a God Can Save Us" is the 1976 title of the posthumously published interview *Der Spiegel* conducted with Heidegger a decade earlier.

42. In fact, Augoyard's characterization of the imaginary's "industrious *circulation*" provides us with the key dynamic phrase for following these otherwise paradoxical movements of redundancy and repetition. The best work on this question is that of the Italian philosopher Fabio Ciaramelli; see my translation: "The Self-Presupposition of the Origin: Homage to Cornelius Castoriadis," in *Thesis Eleven* 49 (May 1997): 45–67. I thank Ciaramelli for pointing me to Heidegger's "The Age of the World Picture" and helping me to orient myself in relation to that text.

43. Cornelius Castoriadis, "The 'End of Philosophy'?" in *Philosophy, Politics, Autonomy,* ed. David Ames Curtis (New York: Oxford University Press, 1991), 15.

44. Let it be noted that *Arlequin,* the name of this housing project, is French for "Harlequin": the traditional comic character of pantomime theater. Augoyard's book is not without its own humor. And the hexagon form of the Arlequin's basic architectural design recalls France's general hexagonal shape.

(France is often referred to as "the Hexagon.") In many ways, *Step by Step* is a lively and witty critique of an entire French way of thinking about building, housing, and residing.

45. In the time of the polis, political terms and cosmological terms creatively intertwined and interpenetrated within ancient Greek philosophy. See Jean-Pierre Vernant's 1962 book *The Origins of Greek Thought* (Ithaca, N.Y.: Cornell University Press, 1982). To account for cosmogenesis as well as anthropogenesis, philosophers, historians, and poets created cosmogonies and anthropogonies. On the latter, see Castoriadis's "Aeschylean Anthropogony and Sophoclean Self-Creation of Man" (1991), in *Figures of the Thinkable (Including Passion and Knowledge)*, available online starting at: http://notbored.org/FTPK.html.

46. In light of the originary redundancy of representation, it might be worthwhile to examine more closely a phrase from Freud. Despite his scientistic leanings as a medical man and a nineteenth-century offspring of the Enlightenment, Dr. Freud managed not only to integrate the imagination (via phantasy) into his psychoanalysis but also to place it, at least implicitly, at the center of his concerns. When he writes of the *Vorstellungsrepräsentanz des Triebes*—representation's representative of the drive—he is providing a useful justification, in metapsychological terms, not only for representations and for representing as *Vorstellungen* and *Vorstellen* but also for representation as re-presentation in representation of an a-representational drive. (In "Logic, Imagination, Reflection" [1991], now in *World in Fragments,* Castoriadis provides the references in Freud as follows: *Gesammelte Werke*, 10:285 = *Standard Edition*, 14:186. Although Castoriadis knowingly described this phrase as "limpid," I do not believe that he ever explicitly explored the significance of its startling redundancy.)

47. Here and elsewhere I have heightened the point by translating *savoir* as "scientific knowledge" in order to contrast it with familiar knowledge (*connaissance*). In French, after all, a *savant* is a "scientist."

48. Augoyard is himself an accomplished musician, his wife a former dancer. He is the editor of *La qualité sonore des espaces habités/Sound Quality in the Living Environment* (bilingual acts of a March 1991 colloquium; Grenoble: CRESSON, 1992), and the coauthor, with Henry Torgue, of *À l'Écoute de l'environnement. Répertoire des effets sonores* (Marseille: Éditions Parenthèses, 1995). Today, he directs the "Ambiances, ambiance" series at Éditions à la croisée. His volume *Sonic Experience: A Guide to Everyday Sounds,* also edited along with Henry Torgue, with a Preface by R. Murray Schafer and translated by Andra McCartney and David Paquette, was just published by McGill-Queen's University Press in 2006.

49. Augoyard offered the example of a student of his who spent months studying how people actually go into and out of a commercial center's revolving

and fixed doors, noting how such practices differ from the designer's theoretical anticipations thereof.

50. When I raised this issue with Augoyard near the end of my tour of the Arlequin complex, he readily admitted that there was a point to what I was saying but it was not possible to analyze these narratives from all perspectives—a point he had already rightly made in general in his book, and that is in fact a basic principle of his "step-by-step" approach that makes no pretense to offering a general overview.

51. We find at http://crisis.vianet.on.ca/march.htm the following excerpt from a "Take Back the Night" statement: "Women are often told to be extra careful and take precautions when going out at night. In some parts of the world, even today, women are not allowed out at night. So when women struggle for freedom, we must start at the beginning by fighting for freedom of movement, which we have not had and do not now have. We must recognize that freedom of movement is a precondition for anything else. It comes before freedom of speech in importance because without it freedom of speech cannot in fact exist." Given that this *statement* is itself an instance of speech, the hierarchization between freedom in movement and freedom in speech seems implausible. Yet we should remain attentive to the salutary emphasis on the importance of unencumbered and unthreatened pedestrian *movement* that this statement articulates.

52. Rocard, it may nevertheless be noted, made this astute comment in April 1974, just as he was preparing to leave the *autogestion* (self-management)-inspired PSU, with its legacy of post–May '68 politics, so as to lead a minority of its members to join the regrouped French Socialist Party.

53. Similarly, in a 1974 interview summarizing the work of the postwar French revolutionary group Socialisme ou Barbarie (1948–67), Castoriadis declares apropos of workers' gestures: "The history of modern industry, however, is not only the history of great pitched union battles; it is also and especially the history that unfolds eight hours a day, sixty minutes per hour, sixty seconds per minute in production and apropos of production; during each of these seconds, each gesture of the worker has two sides to it, one that conforms to the imposed production norms, the other combating those norms. Effective output is the result of the struggle that unfolds upon this terrain. Labor power, therefore, has no definite use value that one might grasp independent of this struggle and its effects" ("'The Only Way to Find Out if You Can Swim Is to Get into the Water': An Introductory Interview," in *The Castoriadis Reader,* ed. David Ames Curtis [Malden, Mass., and Oxford: Basil Blackwell, 1997], 18). A decade earlier, in the third point of his programmatic text "Recommencing the Revolution," Castoriadis had already articulated such gesture analysis in terms of everydayness: "Certainly, society today still remains profoundly divided. It

functions against the immense majority of working people. In their everyday lives, these people express their opposition to this society with half of each one of their gestures. The present crisis of humanity will be able to be resolved only through a socialist revolution. But these ideas run the risk of remaining empty abstractions, pretexts for sermons or for a blind and spasmodic activism, if we do not strive to understand how society's divisions are concretely being realized at the present hour, how this society functions, what forms of reaction and struggle laboring people adopt against the ruling strata and their system, what new kinds of revolutionary activity related to people's concrete existence and struggle in society and to a coherent and lucid view of the world are possible under these conditions" (ibid., 107).

54. In *Step by Step*'s quotation from *One-Dimensional Man,* Marcuse explains that this "new conformism" is "new because it is rational to an unprecedented degree," instead of examining (through people's involved everyday struggles against it) the *irrationality* inherent in modern bureaucratic-capitalist *rationalization* processes.

55. See Grace Lee Boggs, *Living for Change: An Autobiography* (Minneapolis: University of Minnesota Press, 1998).

56. Hastings-King, "Fordism and the Marxist Revolutionary Project," 176.

57. These oral and written narratives that Augoyard obtained are not at all to be confused with detached and isolated individual responses to the usual "scientific survey" questions.

58. This is one of Hastings-King's critical conclusions about the limitations on Socialisme ou Barbarie's use of workers' narratives: in neither Lefort's 1952 programmatic text advocating phenomenological analysis of such narratives (via eidetic variation) nor in subsequent efforts by the group to solicit, publish, and employ such texts did it succeed in controlling for these texts' rhetorical origins. In later life, Lefort published a collection of essays whose aim was to come to terms with the political aspects of literary texts and the literary aspects of political texts; translated into English by me as *Writing: The Political Test* (Durham, N.C., and London: Duke University Press, 2000), this book strangely makes no explicit reference to his earlier efforts in "L'Expérience prolétarienne."

59. See Brown's insightful review, "Henri Lefebvre's *The Production of Space,*" *Not Bored!* 30 (February 1999): 65–76, also available at http://www.notbored.org/space.html.

60. In a 1957 Socialisme ou Barbarie text that forms the second part of a three-part series "On the Content of Socialism," Castoriadis had already articulated this more positive understanding of the everyday: "Socialism aims at giving a meaning to people's life and work; at enabling their freedom, their cre-

ativity, and the most positive aspects of their personality to flourish; at creating organic links between the individual and those around him, and between the group and society; at reconciling people with themselves and with nature. It thereby rejoins the most basic goals of the working class in its daily struggles against capitalist alienation. These are not aspirations about some hazy and distant future, but rather the content of tendencies existing and manifesting themselves today, both in revolutionary struggles and in everyday life. To understand this is to understand that, *for the worker, the ultimate problem of history is an everyday problem.* To grasp this is also to perceive that socialism is not 'nationalization' or 'planning' or even an 'increase in the standard of living.' It is to understand that the real crisis of capitalism is not due to 'the anarchy of the market' or to 'overproduction' or to 'the falling rate of profit.' Indeed, it is to see the tasks of revolutionary theory and the function of the revolutionary organization in an entirely new way. Pushed to their ultimate consequences, grasped in their full strength, these ideas transform our vision of society and the world. They modify our conception of theory as well as of revolutionary practice" (*The Castoriadis Reader,* 51; emphasis in the original). As a member of Socialisme ou Barbarie for a brief period during 1960–61, Situationist International founder Guy Debord was certainly familiar with the contents of this key programmatic text, which accords a positive centrality to everyday life and struggle.

61. A translation (by John Fullerton and Paul Sieveking) of this celebrated text, the counterpart to Debord's *The Society of the Spectacle* (also from 1967), is now available online, for example, at http://www.scenewash.org/lobbies/chainthinker/situationist/vaneigem/rel/roel.html, which is where I found this and the following Vaneigem quotations.

62. The following Vaneigem quotation from *The Revolution of Everyday Life* allows us to gauge the full distance between that book and Augoyard's *Step by Step: Everyday Walks in a French Urban Housing Project*: "The revolution of everyday life will blot out ideas of justice, punishment and torture, which are notions dependent on exchange and fragmentation. We don't want to be judges, but, by destroying slavery, masters without slaves recovering a new innocence and gracefulness in living. We have to destroy the enemy, not judge him. Whenever Durruti's column freed a village, they would assemble the peasants, ask which were the Fascists and shoot them on the spot. The next revolution will do the same. With perfect composure. We know there'll be no-one to judge us, nor will there ever be judges again, because we will have gobbled them up." Here we see what can result when someone else's "everyday lived experience" is fetishized into an excuse for not thinking on one's own and for not exercising responsible judgment.

63. A point Augoyard reiterated to me several times.

Bibliography

Anaximander fragments. In G. S. Kirk, J. E. Raven, and M. Schofield, *The Presocratic Philosophers: A Critical History with a Selection of Texts,* 2d ed. Cambridge: Cambridge University Press, 1983.

Arlequin (journal de l'). *Le Manteau de l'Arlequin* (from December 1973 to May 1974) and *L'Arlequin démasqué* (starting May 2, 1974). Grenoble: Médiathèque du quartier de l'Arlequin.

Ascher, François. "Contribution à la critique de l'économie urbaine: Essai d'analyse économique de la production d'un élément urbain: le cadre bâti" (thesis). Grenoble: Unité d'Études et de Recherche "Urbanisation-Aménagement," 1972.

Augoyard, Jean-François. "Des opérationnels autour de l'Arlequin." In Jean-François Augoyard, Christian Bousset, Alain Medam, Alain Pessin, and Henry-Skoff Torgue, *L'Urbain de l'action, l'Urbain du savoir à Grenoble.* Genoble: Unité d'Études et de Recherche "Urbanisation-Aménagement," 1975.

———. "Imagination et Nature chez Giordano Bruno." Master's thesis. Lyon: Université des Sciences Sociales, 1964.

———. "Le Pas: Étude de la vie quotidienne dans un habitat collectif à travers la pratique des cheminements." Grenoble: Unité d'Études et de Recherche "Urbanisation-Aménagement," 1976.

Augoyard, Jean-François, and Alain Medam. *Situations d'habitat et façons d'habiter.* Paris: Unité de Recherches Appliquées de l'École spéciale d'architecture, 1976.

Barthes, Roland. "Introduction to the Structural Analysis of Narratives" (1966). Trans. Stephen Heath. In *A Barthes Reader,* ed. and intro. Susan Sontag. New York: Hill and Wang, 1982.

Baudrillard, Jean. "The Precession of Simulacra" (1978). In *Simulacra and Simulation,* trans. Sheila Faria Glaser. Ann Arbor: University of Michigan Press, 1994.

Beckett, Samuel. "The Expelled." Trans. from the French in collaboration with the author. In *Collected Shorter Prose 1945–1980.* London: John Calder, 1985.

———. *Molloy* (1950). In *Molloy. Malone Dies. The Unnameable.* London, Montreuil, and New York: Calder Publications, 1959.

Bergson, Henri. *L'Énergie spirituelle* (1919). Paris: Presses Universitaires de France, 1967.

———. *Matter and Memory* (1896). Trans. Nancy Margaret Paul and W. Scott Palmer. New York: Zone Books, 1988.

Binswanger, Ludwig. "Dream and Existence" (1930). In Ludwig Binswanger and Michel Foucault, *Dream and Existence,* ed. Keith Hoeller. Atlantic Highlands, N.J.: Humanities Press, 1985.

Borges, Jorge Luis. "The Aleph." In *The Aleph and Other Stories, 1933–1969,* ed. and trans. Norman Thomas di Giovanni in collaboration with the author. New York: E. P. Dutton, 1970.

Braque, Georges. *Cahiers.* Paris: Fondation Maeght, 1950.

———. *Illustrated Notebooks, 1917–1955.* Trans. Stanley Appelbaum. New York: Dover, 1971.

Bruno, Giordano. "La Cena de le Ceneri." In *Dialoghi italiani.* Florence: Sansoni, 1958.

———. *De imaginum signorum et idearum compositione.* Naples and Florence: Tocco-Vitelli, 1879–91.

Castells, Manuel. *La Question urbaine.* Paris: Maspero, 1972.

Char, René. "La Route par les sentiers." *Au-dessus du vent.* Paris: Seghers, 1961.

Choay, Françoise. Interview. *Metropolis* 6 (May 1974): 65–69.

———. *L'Urbanisme, utopies et réalités: une anthologie.* Paris: Éditions du Seuil, 1965.

Chomsky, Noam. *Syntactic Structures.* The Hague: Mouton, 1971.

Claustre, Henri. *L'Enfant ou la quatrième dimension: Le projet pédagogique de la Villeneuve de Grenoble.* Grenoble: Centre de recherche et de rénovation pédagogique, Université des Sciences Sociales, 1975.

CRESAL (Centre de recherche et d'études sociologiques appliquées de la Loire). *Les Équipements socio-culturels et la ville.* Saint-Étienne: CRESAL, 1972.

———. *Le Fonctionnement de la mobilité résidentielle intra-urbaine.* Saint-Étienne: CRESAL, 1974.

———. *Les Nouvelles Formes du refus de la ville.* Saint-Étienne: CRESAL, 1976.

———. *Les Processus d'évolution des grands ensembles.* Saint-Étienne: CRESAL, 1974.

————. *Production de l'espace urbain et idéologique.* Saint-Étienne: CRESAL, 1972.

Debord, Guy. *The Society of the Spectacle* (1967). Detroit: Black & Red, 1983.

Deleuze, Gilles. *Expressionism in Philosophy: Spinoza* (1968). Trans. Martin Joughin. New York: Zone Books, 1990.

Derrida, Jacques. *On Grammatology* (1967). Trans. Gayatri Chakravorty Spivak. Baltimore and London: Johns Hopkins University Press, 1976.

Desfontaines, Pierre. *L'Homme et sa maison.* Paris: Gallimard, 1972.

Durand, Gilbert. *Science de l'homme et tradition: Le Nouvel Esprit anthropologique.* Paris: Tête de feuilles-Sirac, 1975.

————. *Les Structures anthropologiques de l'imaginaire: Introduction à l'archétypologie générale.* Paris: Bordas, 1969.

Fauque, Richard. "Pour une nouvelle approche sémiologique de la ville." *Espaces et Sociétés* 9 (July 1973): 15–27.

Garin, Eugenio. *Dal Medioevo al Rinascimento: Due saggi.* Florence: Sansoni, 1950.

Goldstein, Kurt. *The Organism: A Holistic Approach to Biology Derived from Pathological Data in Man* (1934). New York: Zone Books, 1995.

Hegel, G. W. F. *The Phenomenology of Mind* (1807). Trans. J. B. Baillie. New York and Evanston, Ill.: Harper & Row, 1967.

Heidegger, Martin. *Being and Time* (1928). Trans. John Marcquarrie and Edward Robinson. New York and Evanston, Ill.: Harper & Row, 1962.

Husserl, Edmund. *Ideas: General Introduction to Pure Phenomenology* (1913). Trans. W. R. Boyce Gibson. London: Collier-Macmillan, 1962.

Jakobson, Roman. "Closing Statement: Linguistics and Poetics." In *Style in Language,* ed. Thomas A. Sebeok. Cambridge: MIT Press, 1960, 350–77.

————. "Two Aspects of Language and Two Types of Aphasic Disturbances." In Roman Jakobson and Morris Halle, *Fundamentals of Language.* The Hague: Mouton, 1956.

Janet, Pierre. *L'évolution de la mémoire et de la notion du temps.* Paris: Chabine, 1928.

Kandinsky, Wassily. *Concerning the Spiritual in Art and Painting in Particular* (1912). New York: Wittenborn, Schultz, 1947.

Kant, Immanuel. *Critique of Judgment, Including the First Introduction.* Trans. Werner S. Pluhar. Indianapolis: Hackett Publishing Company, 1987.

————. *Critique of Pure Reason.* Trans. F. Max Müller. Garden City, N.Y.: Anchor, 1966.

Klee, Paul. *The Thinking Eye: The Notebooks of Paul Klee* (1956). 2d rev. ed, ed. Jürg Spiller. Trans. Ralph Manheim with the assistance of Dr. Charlotte Weidler and Joyce Wittenborn. New York: George Wittenborn, 1964.

Klein, Robert, and André Chastel. *L'Europe de la Renaissance*. Paris: Éditions des Deux Mondes, 1913.

Lalande, André. "Symbole." In *Vocabulaire technique et critique de la philosophie*. Paris: Presses Universitaires de France, 1968.

Ledrut, Raymond. *L'Espace social et la ville*. Paris: Anthropos, 1968.

―――. *Les Images de la ville*. Paris: Anthropos, 1973.

―――. "Parole et silence de la ville." *Espaces et Sociétés* 9 (July 1973): 3–14.

Lefebvre, Henri. *Critique of Everyday Life* (1947, 1962). Trans. John Moore. 2 vols. London and New York: Verso, 1991.

―――. *The Production of Space* (1974). Trans. Donald Nicholson-Smith. Oxford and Cambridge, Mass.: Blackwell, 1991.

"Longinus." *On the Sublime (Peri upsous)*. Trans. W. Rhys Roberts. Cambridge: Cambridge University Press, 1899.

Lugassy, Françoise. With Jacqueline Palmade and Françoise Couchard. *Contribution à une psychologie de l'espace urban: La Dialectique du logement et de son environnement. Étude exploratoire*. Paris: Publications de recherches urbaines, 1970.

―――. *Le Discours idéologique des architectes et urbanistes*. Paris: Documentation Action concertée des recherches urbaines, 1972.

Lupasco, Stéphane. *Logique et contradiction*. Paris: Presses Universitaires de France, 1947.

―――. *Les Trois Matières*. Paris: Herman, 1969.

Marcuse, Herbert. *One-Dimensional Man*. London: Routledge & Kegan Paul, 1964.

Martinet, André. *Éléments de linguistique générale*. Paris: Colin, 1967.

Medam, Alain. *Conscience de la ville*. Paris: Anthropos, 1977.

―――. *La Ville-Censure*. Paris: Anthropos, 1971.

―――. *La Ville, l'imaginaire* (research paper). Paris: Unité de Recherches Appliquées de l'École spéciale d'architecture, 1975.

Merleau-Ponty, Maurice. *Phenomenology of Perception* (1945). Trans. Colin Smith. New York: Humanities Press and London: Routledge & Kegan Paul, 1962.

Parent, Jean-François. *Villeneuve de Grenoble-Echirolles: Objectifs et réalisations*. Genoble: Société d'Aménagement du département de l'Isère (SADI), 1961–73.

Pessin, Alain, and Henry-Skoff Torgue. "Villes imaginaires: Introduction à l'imaginaire urbain" (thesis). Genoble: Unité d'Études et de Recherche "Urbanisation-Aménagement," 1976. Paris: Éditions du Champ Urbain, 1980.

Peytard, Jean, and Émile Genouvrier. *Linguistique et enseignement du français*. Paris: Larousse, 1970.

Ponge, Francis. *La promenade dans nos serres*. Paris: Gallimard, 1967.

Rocard, Michel. "La France en quête d'un avenir." *Le Monde*, April 19, 1974.

Rossi, Paolo. *Clavis universalis: Arti mnemoniche e logica combinatoria da Lullo à Leibniz*. Milan: Riccardi, 1969.

Sansot, Pierre. *Poétique de la ville*. Paris: Klincksieck, 1971.

Saussure, Ferdinand de. *Course in General Linguistics* (1916). Ed. Charles Bally and Albert Sechehaye with the collaboration of Albert Riedlinger. Trans. Roy Harris. London: Duckworth, 1983.

Segaud, Marion. "Anthropologie de l'espace: catalogue ou projet?" *Espaces et Sociétés* 9 (July 1973): 29–38.

Simondon, Gilbert. *Du mode d'existence des objets techniques*. Paris: Aubier, 1958.

Spinoza. *Ethics*. In *Complete Works,* trans. Samuel Shirley, ed. Michael L. Morgan. Indianapolis: Hackett Publishing Company, 2002.

Straus, Erwin. *Vom Sinn der Sinne*. Berlin: Springer Verlag, 1935.

Verdillon, Claude, et al. *Habitat spectaculaire et misère de la vie quotidienne* (thesis). Grenoble: Unité d'Études et de Recherche "Urbanisation-Aménagement, 1973.

Worringer, Wilhelm. *Abstraction and Empathy: A Contribution to the Psychology of Style* (1908). New York: International Universities Press, 1967.

Index

abandonment, 17, 28, 153; and
    abstention, 151
absence, 16–17, 28, 62, 70–73,
    128–34, 142–43, 156, 166, 182,
    184; of conjunction, 72, 74,
    128; of connections, 67–70, 72,
    161; figured, 129; -in-abeyance,
    132; and the present, 59, 113,
    128–29, 131–34, 137–39, 156,
    161; prolonged, 102; pure, 28;
    "really," 117; symbolic, 35; of
    symmetry, 61; transitory, 131
abstractness, 19–20, 23, 66, 80,
    127, 132–34, 161, 166–67,
    169, 172–75, 183, 185, 187;
    originary, 109
abstract observer/subject, 21, 23
accidents, 7, 34–35, 41, 45, 54, 59,
    70, 118, 135, 143–44, 146–48,
    153–55, 166, 172
acted: and felt, 131; and suffered,
    71, 113–14, 117, 122, 125, 138,
    156, 158, 161
activity, 3, 17, 19–20, 23, 25, 34,
    57, 82, 124–25, 127, 133,
    147; daytime, 142; feverish,
    54; fragmented, 7; impromptu,
    19; and passion, 155; social,
    151; sociocultural, 190;

spatiotemporal, 26, 57; and
    submission, 25
activity areas, 56, 82, 87, 91
activity coordinators, 89, 151
actors, 88, 172; expressive, 27
adolescents. *See* young people
adults, 29, 35, 52, 54, 61, 86, 89,
    100, 144
"advocacy planning," 10
aesthetics, 123, 154, 173; Bauhaus,
    234n2
affectivity/the affective, 21, 120, 133,
    147, 156
afternoon, 49, 69, 72, 96, 226n12
age group, 52, 68, 87, 99
aggregates, 89, 92, 99, 102, 111,
    166; collective, 90; social, 100–
    101, 110, 145
Agora, 86–87
air, 119–20, 142, 150, 228n8. *See
    also* wind
"Aleph," the, 128, 230n26, 230n28
Algerians, 91, 104, 145. *See also*
    North Africans
alien, 94–96, 109, 118, 126, 131,
    139, 145–47, 153, 169, 182–83
alternation(s), 27, 29, 58, 141–42;
    symmetrical, 72
ambiance, 116, 120, 133

81, 102, 112, 165, 233n20.
See also social practice; spatial
practices
preconception, 4, 126, 165, 168,
170, 176–77, 183
pregnancy, 107, 109, 111, 115–16,
124, 147, 160, 186; of archaic
space, 12, 176; of atmospheres,
116–17, 184; climatic, 116–17,
159; of the imaginable, 157
premonition, 125, 131, 145, 150
preoccupations, 17, 72, 142;
ordinary, 135
presence, 21, 48, 75, 115, 122–23,
128–29, 131–34, 147; collective,
117, 121; immediate, 151; lived,
118
present, the, 20, 59, 71, 113, 126,
129, 131–32, 134, 137–39,
146–51, 152, 156, 161; and the
eventual, 148; lived, 126, 128,
134, 139–40, 146, 148, 153,
159; ordinary, 146; and the past,
146; and the possible, 136–37,
139, 145, 147–51, 153, 157,
161, 232n10; "really," 137
presentiment, 17, 102, 108, 131, 143
present tense, 28, 151
private, the, 19, 89–91, 132, 186–87
produced, the: and the reproduced,
25, 78
produced space, 121, 183
production, 10, 12, 14, 163, 170,
183, 187; artistic, 128; of the
built world/edified space, 8, 168,
176–78; of cities, 23; economic,
13–14; of habitat, 10, 134,
231n38; of high-density housing
complexes, 22; of images, 137;

planned, 154; of planned space,
5, 166, 168; relations of, 173;
of space, 112, 128, 134, 164,
168, 172, 179, 187; technical,
154; urban, 10–11, 165;
urbanistic, 171; of urban space,
7–8, 174. *See also* conception-
production; modes of production;
productivity
productivity, 176, 235n9
projectation, 170
projected, the, 17
projects, 9–10, 71, 80, 85, 96–97,
134, 141, 153, 178, 183, 185;
architectural, 9, 170; deferred,
148; of inhabiting, 152–53;
initial, 9; of our action, 133;
social, 176, 187
properties, 51, 94, 102
property, 9, 89–90, 93
proprioception, 117
prose, 26, 73–74, 114, 158, 163
protention, 20, 130, 133, 184
psychoanalysis, 11, 225n1
psycholinguists, 144
psychology, 12–13, 75, 116, 168;
depth, 78; "of faculties," 123,
137, 154; perceptual, 229n20
psychosociology, 12–13; applied,
222n9
public, the, 9; and the private, 19,
132, 186–87
public life, 69
public services, 18
public spaces, 90, 167
public sphere, 17, 95
public transport, 8
public use, 104
pursuit, 24, 121

remainders, 6, 14, 168

Renaissance, the, 138–39, 162, 225n1, 227–28n5, 233–34n28

renting, 44, 168

repair work, 29, 35, 127

repetition, 4, 5, 7, 25–26, 31, 48, 51–52, 55–56, 58, 60, 68–69, 71, 77–79, 116, 121, 130, 146–48, 152, 170, 183, 185; amplified, 51; collective, 29; in difference, 184; excessive, 148; logic of, 8; rules of, 59; spatial, 105; varied, 34, 54

re-presentable, 183

representational space, 234n28

representations, 4–5, 10–11, 17, 23, 28, 34, 67, 85, 101–2, 135–37, 164, 168, 170–71, 173, 179, 182, 186–87; abstract, 19–20, 185; cartographic, 40; causal, 187; of constructing-housing, 179; dominant, 11, 23, 110; of everyday life, 118; and everyday lived experience, 25, 34, 51, 153–54, 166; general, 179; geometric, 15; graphic, 15, 71; of homogeneity, 183; housing, 170, 174; ideal, 164; of neighborhood design plan, 85; of neighborhood practice, 23; of poses and positions, 185; pure, 91; social, 120; of social space, 112–13; of space, 107, 185, 233–34n28; of the spatial totality, 156; spatio-geometric, 109; streams of, 157; stroboscopic, 185; synchronic, 16, 63; systematic, 111; theoretical, 161; of time, 156; of a totality, 166–67; totalizing, 14; of a trip, 67; of the whole, 98

reproduction, 4, 11, 25, 78, 81, 90, 102, 126–27, 138, 179, 187; symbolic, 56. *See also* social reproduction

repulsion, 29, 39, 55; and fascination, 39, 66

res extensa, 234n28

resistance, 56, 58, 110, 153

resonances, 120, 186; affective, 133; eventful, 113; imaginary, 157; qualitative, 121

retention, 20, 40, 130, 133, 184; of the other as other in the same, 105

return. *See* coming and going/ returning

reversals, 106, 139, 144, 148–49, 156–57, 159–60, 170

rhetoric, 6, 26, 28, 33, 37, 50, 52, 57, 60, 67, 74–75, 77, 110–14, 122, 126, 128, 132, 134, 166, 175, 225n1; ambulatory, 158; art of, 77; classical, 27; electoral, 225n1; everyday, 158; goal of, 77; modern, 75; of one's walks, 26, 67, 72–75, 98, 100, 111, 114, 133, 152, 159, 189; "savage," 225n1. *See also* inhabitant rhetoric

rhetors, 226n2

rhythm, 3, 17, 34, 61, 73, 108, 113–14, 129–32, 158, 165, 178; ambulatory, 141; bodily, 132; change in/of, 33, 130; of everyday life, 133, 182; variations in, 61

right. *See* left and right

rubbish. *See* garbage

rules, 79, 110, 135; of the code of appropriation, 90, 94, 97, 101,

Jean-François Augoyard is professor of philosophy and musicology, and doctor of urban studies, at the Center for Research on Sonorous Space and the Urban Environment, School of Architecture, Grenoble, France.

Françoise Choay is professor emeritus of history and theory of urbanism and architecture at the University of Paris VIII and Paris I.

David Ames Curtis is a translator, editor, writer, and citizen activist. His translations and writings have appeared in American, European, and Australian journals, books, and art catalogs.

Lightning Source UK Ltd.
Milton Keynes UK
UKHW042350081118
332040UK00001B/138/P